Playing with Time

TRADITIONAL ARTS OF AFRICA

Editors
Paula Girshick, Roy Sieber, Robert Farris Thompson

Mary Jo Arnoldi

Playing with Time ART AND PERFORMANCE IN CENTRAL MALI

Indiana University Press

BLOOMINGTON AND INDIANAPOLIS

Library of Congress Cataloging-in-Publication Data

Arnoldi, Mary Jo.
    Playing with time : art and performance in central Mali / Mary Jo
Arnoldi.
        p.   cm. — (Traditional arts of Africa)
    Includes bibliographical references (p.   ) and index.
    ISBN 0-253-30900-X (acid-free paper)
    1. Bambara (African people)—Rites and ceremonies.   2. Bambara
(African people)—Folklore.   3. Bambara (African people)—Social life
and customs.   4. Puppet theater—Mali—Ségou (Region)
5. Puppet theater—Mali—Kirango.   6. Folklore—Mali—Performance.
7. Time—Social aspects—Mali.   8. Ségou (Mali : Region)—Social
life and customs.   9. Kirango (Mali)—Social life and customs.
I. Title.   II. Series.
DT551.45.B35A76   1995
791.5'3'0899634—dc20   94-38744

    1   2   3   4   5   00   99   98   97   96   95

Contents

List of Illustrations   vi
Preface: Playing with Time: Art, Puppetry, and Performance   ix
Acknowledgments   xvii
Note on Orthography   xxi

One   A Bamana Tonko Festival, Kirango, June 1979   1

Two   The Definition and History of the
Segou Puppet Masquerade Theatre   18

Three The Sogo bò's Expressive Forms   58

Four   Time, Timing, and the Performance Process   107

Five   Bringing the Past into the Present
in Masquerade Theatre   131

Six   The Production of Meaning and the Play
of Interpretations   149

Conclusion   Kuma man nyi; Kumabaliya fana man nyi   186

Notes   191
Glossary   205
Masquerade List 209
Bibliography 213
Index   221

Pref.1. Mali Kònò, the Bird of Mali color
Pref.2. Ntilen, the Giraffe x
Pref.3. Puppets of a farmer and a *balafon* musician xi
Pref.4. Yayoroba, the Beautiful Woman color
1.1. Preparing a masquerade armature 2
1.2. Misi, the Cow 3
1.3. Testing Jarawara, the Wildcat 3
1.4. Gòn, the Baboon, leading the New Year's procession 4
1.5. Young boys playing at masquerading 5
1.6. The senior drum team performing 6
1.7. A toddler dancing on the sidelines 7
1.8. Youth performing circle dances color
1.9. Young men performing the *Bònjalan* color
1.10. Gòn, the Baboon 8
1.11. Suruku Nama, the Hyena 9
1.12. Sumusonin, the Sorceress 10
1.13. The Ntomo masquerade 11
1.14. The theatrical reenactment of a Kòmò processional 12
1.15. A hunter stalks Waraba, the Lion 13
1.16. Jobali maskers 14
1.17. Mali Kònò, the Bird of Mali 15
1.18. Taasi Dòoni, Reflect a Little 16
1.19. Waraba Caco, the Striped Wildcat 16
1.20. The Madame Sarata masquerade 17
2.1. The Sòmonò masquerade Soden Mali la, Malian Horsemen color
2.2. The Boso singer Budagari Coulibaly 27
2.3. The sculptor Siriman Fane and his son Adama 31
2.4. Karankaw, People of Karan, by Siriman Fane color
2.5. The sculptor Bafing Kane 32
2.6. Bafing Kane's grandson holding a children's mask 33

2.7. The sculptor Numu Jon Diarra with the puppet Dajè, the Roan Antelope 34
2.8. The sculptor Youssouf Diarra with the puppet Tubabu, the European 36
2.9. Njona, the Wildcat 37
2.10. A genie masquerade 38
2.11. An airplane masquerade 39
2.12. Mei Diarra and Nanyan Coulibaly, lead singers 39
2.13. Nama, the Hyena 44
2.14. Falakani, a generic bush animal 44
2.15. Bilanjan, a generic bush animal 45
2.16. Bala, the Porcupine 45
2.17. Suruku Malobali, the Shameless Hyena 49
2.18. Taasi Dòoni, Reflect a Little, appears as an antelope 50
2.19. Sigi, the Buffalo, by Siriman Fane 50
2.20. Mali Kònò, the Bird of Mali, by Siriman Fane 51
2.21. Mali Kònò, the Bird of Mali, by Manyan Kumare color
2.22. Sogoni Kelen, an Antelope, by Manyan Kumare 52
2.23. Saga, the Sheep, by Mamary Fane 54
2.24. Dajè, the Roan Antelope 54
2.25. Dajè, the Roan Antelope 54
2.26. Dasiri Sogo, the Dasiri Antelope 55
2.27. Sigi, the Buffalo 56
2.28. Jarawara, the Wildcat 56
2.29. Jarawara, the Wildcat 57
3.1. Ciwara crest mask 59
3.2. Kòmò helmet mask 60
3.3. Baninkònò, the Stork 61
3.4. Kònò Meguetan, a bird masquerade 62
3.5. Sinè, the Gazelle 64
3.6. Sanfè Sa, the Tree Snake 65

3.7. Gòn, the Baboon 66

3.8. Wòkulò, the Bush Genie 66

3.9. Nyò-susu-musow, Women Pounding Millet 67

3.10. Sotigi, the Horseman 67

3.11. Sama, the Elephant 69

3.12. Cèkòròba, the Elder 71

3.13. Yan Ka Di, This Place Is Good 72

3.14. Kamalen Sogo, the Young Man's Antelope 73

3.15. Kuruntigi, the Boso Boatman 74

3.16. Tubabu Muso, a European Woman 74

3.17. Tubabu Muso, a European Woman 74

3.18. Bama, the Crocodile 76

3.19. Dajè, the Roan Antelope 76

3.20. Kalakadane, the Antelope 78

3.21. Koon, the Roan Antelope 79

3.22. Mali, the Hippo 79

3.23. Ntilen, the Giraffe 80

3.24. Duguma Sa, the Ground Snake 80

3.25. Saalen, the Nile Perch 81

3.26. Sigimuso, the female Buffalo 81

3.27. Bilisi, a genie 83

3.28. Jinè-Faro, a female water genie 83

3.29. Jinèjan, the Tall Genie 84

3.30. Wòkulò, the Bush Genie 84

3.31. An antelope puppet with a hunter and a bird 85

3.32. Sotigi, the Horseman 86

3.33. Mali Bonyè, Celebrate Mali 87

3.34. Pari, the Credit Association color

3.35. Two Ciwara masquerades 88

3.36. Ntomo masker 88

3.37. An antelope puppet by Numu Jon Diarra color

3.38. Waraba, the Lion color

4.1. A drawing of Bilanjan, the Bush Animal 119

4.2. Drawings of Waraba Caco, the Striped Wildcat, and Misi, the Cow 120

4.3. Baisu Diarra with his toy masquerade of Dajè, the Roan Antelope 121

4.4. Nama, the Hyena 127

4.5. Nama, the Hyena 127

5.1. Wagadu Sa, the Snake of Wagadu 143

5.2. Baninkònò, the Stork color

5.3. Vadama Traore, a Boso singer 145

5.4. Soden Mali la, the Malian Horsemen 147

6.1. Sigicè, the male Buffalo 165

6.2. Cèw-ye-kelen-ye, All Men Are Equal 169

6.3. Sigicè, the male Buffalo 182

6.4. Sigi, the Buffalo color

Color plates follow page 104

Tables

2.1 Kirango Masquerade Repertoire 1896–1987 47

2.2 Kirango Bamana Masquerade Repertoire 1978–1980 53

2.3 Kirango Bamana Terminology for Masquerade Theatre 63

3.2 Segou Masquerade Characters, Forms, and Costumes 75–88

The heightening of sensory perceptions through the massing of forms, colors, sounds, movements, and smells. The physical sensation of a rhythmic ebb and flow of time. The palpable energy and anticipation of the crowd. The laughter, the tumult, the confusion, the enthusiasm, the disengagement, the reengagement, the awe, the surprise, the shrieks of encouragement and excitement. These are the vivid and compelling images and impressions and my most enduring memories of youth association puppet masquerade performances in the Segou region in Mali. This masquerade theatre—like storytelling, the performance of epic poetry, dance events, songfests, and other masked and non-masked theatres—is a masterful and wholly vital form of artistic activity which enlivens Malian community life in the late twentieth century [Figure Pref.1].

Throughout Segou, the youth association puppet masquerade stands out among the region's performances. Troupes invest enormous creative and monetary resources in the production of these theatres and communities eagerly anticipate the annual performances. The masquerade represents, for many individuals, the region's mode of entertainment par excellence. Troupes continually make and remake the theatre. Each individual performance is fashioned through the endeavors of actors and audiences, who cast a knowing, creative, and often reflexive eye upon their shared and individual contemporary experiences and upon their collective historical memories.

Segou puppet masquerades are multidimensional, multivocal, and multifocal, and they have enormous affective power. As a specialized form of performance they exhibit all of the distinguishing features of what anthropologists and folklorists designate as cultural performances. These masquerades are one of the most prominent performance forms in Segou communities. The performances are clearly set apart from daily life: they have a limited time span and a defined place and occasion of performance. They are public, exhibit an elaborate program of activity, and involve a designated set of performers and an audience (Bauman 1977, 11).

My first encounter with the Segou puppet theatre had been outside Mali through the medium of sculpture and specifically through a group of theatrical rod puppets, body puppets, and articulated masks in an American private collection. While articulated masks are well known especially in West Africa, rod puppets have been documented for fewer than forty African societies (Proschan 1980; Darkowska-Nidzgorska 1980).

Malian rod puppets representing the heads of various animals range in height from just under two feet to five or six feet [Figure Pref.2]. Generally, the sculptor hollows out a cavity on the underside of the puppet head. He then inserts a thick wooden rod, often

Pref. 2. A rod puppet head of Ntilen, the Giraffe. 1978. Bamana quarter, Kirango, Mali. *Photograph by Lynn Forsdale.*

several feet in length, into the cavity and secures it with nails and cord or wire. Many of these puppet heads have articulated jaws or ears carved as separate pieces and attached to the core form. A few puppet heads also have secondary figures attached to their crown or horns. The puppeteer either sets these secondary figures into motion through the movement of the larger puppet head itself, or he activates them separately by means of additional string mechanisms. Complementing these animal heads are smaller individual rod puppets portraying a full range of human characters, animals, and spirits [Figure Pref.3]. These small figures range in height from just under a foot to several feet. A third puppet type takes the form of a carved figurative bust with separately carved arms. This type is generally over three or four feet tall [Figure Pref.4].

I was initially struck by both the similarities and the differences that this single collection of articulated masks and puppets exhibited formally and stylistically with the large body of Malian sculptures featured in museum collections and documented in the art literature. These latter sculptures are variously labeled Bamana (Bambara), Boso (Bozo), and Maraka. Unlike most other Malian sculpture the masks and puppets I examined in this private collection were all brightly painted. Most were cleverly articulated by various rod and string mechanisms. What also greatly impressed me was the range of different characters represented in this one assemblage. This collection's medley of characters went far beyond those already documented for other performance traditions in Mali and adjacent countries. Such a diversity of forms and characters raised a serious challenge to the still frequent pronouncements about "traditional" African arts as static

Pref. 3. Small rod and string puppets of a farmer and a balafon musician. 1978. Bamana quarter, Kirango, Mali. *Photograph by Lynn Forsdale.*

and conservative, dead or dying. These masks and puppets also raised a number of compelling questions about their history, their production, and the meanings assigned to them. Such questions could never be answered by examining the masks and puppets solely in their recontextualization as individual Fine Art objects.

While these theatrical masks and puppets represented a significantly large group of objects, a thorough search of the literature revealed that surprisingly little notice had been taken of them as sculptures, and even less had been written about their performances (Arnoldi 1977). This lack of any serious attention paid to a corpus of objects that had regularly found their way into Western museums and private collections from at least the 1930s was curious indeed. It was what initially led me to Mali and to the study of these sculptures in performance.

Although my interest in the puppet masquerade was originally piqued by a group of what I have come to think of now as disembodied heads, it was clear even from the outset that these masks and puppets were intended as but one artistic element in a multimedia theatrical assemblage that also included costume, dance, music, and song. It is only through studying the interrelationship of these sculptures with other expressive forms in performance that their aesthetic effect and the multiplicity of meanings assigned to them can begin to be understood.

Every puppet masquerade performance I documented exhibited several common features, and many communities shared masquerade characters. These shared features of the performances made the theatre recognizable as a regional genre. Yet, the variations across villages in terms of presentational style and dramatic content defy a homogenized description of the masquerade's history and its contemporary manifestations. While the shared theatrical conventions and structures do provide troupes with precedents, conventions, and guidelines for constructing their individual performances, each troupe also saw its own community's theatre as original (Bauman 1986, 4). People's sense of the originality of their theatre is grounded in their own community's memories of its theatrical history. In hopes of capturing some sense of the variability and fluidity that characterize theatres in local settings, I have chosen to center this study of the Segou puppet masquerades in the contemporary performances of the Bamana quarter in Kirango.

Kirango is a large community of over six thousand residents that sits on the right bank of the Niger River about 40 kilometers northeast of Segou city.[1] Kirango is administratively in the cercle of Segou and within the arrondissement of Markala. Kirango families are farmers or fishermen although a number of adult men from these families work full time for government services in neighboring Markala.[2] Kirango has six residential quarters or neighborhoods. Bamanakin, Thierola, Konela, Danbelela, and Diakakin are the five oldest quarters and all border the Niger River. The Quartier de Service is a more recent neighborhood and sits behind the older quarters. The five oldest quarters are organized roughly along ethnic and occupational lines. Most residents in the Bamanakin identify themselves as Bamana and most are farmers. Thierola, Konela, and Danbelela residents identify themselves as Sòmonò and they are fishermen. People living in Diakakin identify themselves as either Boso or Sòmonò, although the quarter is known as a Boso residential neighborhood. They are also fishermen. The Quartier de

Service houses many different families. Some of these families came to this area during the colonial and postcolonial period to work in various capacities for government services. The Quartier also houses the overflow from families in the five original quarters. For these latter compounds, the nexus of social relations remains firmly embedded in households located in the five original quarters.

There are three active *kamalen tonw*, youth associations, in Kirango. One kamalen ton is in the Bamana quarter; another is located in the Boso quarter; and there is a third association whose members come from the three Sòmonò quarters. Both men and women belong to these associations. Young men from the age of about fourteen until around age forty-two are active members. Young women from the age of about fourteen until they marry in their late teens or early twenties also participate as members. In all of the discussions of the Kirango events, I will draw comparisons with other troupes in Segou in order to move between regional and local settings. These comparisons will illuminate how this theatre produces peoples' sense of differences and affinities with the lives and experiences of other communities, locally, regionally, nationally, and, to some extent, internationally.

I arrived in Kirango in December of 1978. Because Kirango's puppet masquerade theatres are performed only twice annually, it was only after nearly seven months of living in this community that I saw my first performance in the Boso quarter in May of 1979. I can vividly recall, even today, my impressions during and after that performance. I found myself both awestruck and bewildered. I remember the rising feeling of panic that first afternoon. How would I take it all in? Where should I focus? How would I make sense of it at all? The descriptions and commentary about the theatre that I had gathered in the months leading up to that performance were elliptical. People based their responses to my questions on the mistaken assumption that I shared with them the same experience of the theatre appropriate to any other socially competent adult in the community. Their discussions of the theatre remained for me a body of often seemingly unrelated comments that made little sense in the abstract.

In a peculiar way my first experience of a puppet masquerade performance resonated with the powerful sensory and emotional memories of my first childhood experience of the circus. Like the circus, the convergence of visual, aural, and olfactory stimuli of the masquerade theatre is immediate and saturating. This immediacy and the artistry of the music, song, dance, and masquerade remain the most difficult qualities of the theatre to capture in a text. Yet all participants experience and respond to these qualities. It was this shared sensory experience of the theatre that served as a point of departure in subsequent conversations about the organization and interpretation of the theatre with people in Kirango and throughout the region and beyond.

Over that first performance season and during the two performance seasons the next year, I began to discover and become conversant with the ways in which theatrical and dramatic conventions and plans were invoked and negotiated in performance. My continued participation in performances over the past decade has been primarily from the vantage point of non-actor. As an adult woman living in Kirango, I eventually mastered a few women's dances. I learned several masquerade songs and could join in, if somewhat hesitantly, during the performances as part of the women's chorus. In many respects my position was always much more akin to that of preadolescent children in the audience. These children are on the verge of "becoming" performers and are in the process of learning the expressive skills that will guide their future participation as youth association performers. Yet, neither myself nor the local children came to these performances as tabulae rasae. Young boys and girls brought to the performance cultural and social knowledge garnered through lived experience and a budding mastery of essential performance skills that they acquire from infancy on (Ottenberg 1975, 1989; Jackson 1983). As toddlers, children begin to master musical rhythms and learn dances and songs. They also become conversant with the stories, legends, and tales that give meaning to the expressive forms and the dramatic content of the masquerade theatre. During their tenure as performers in puppet masquerade they build upon this basic knowledge and early training.

For my part, I brought to the performance my understanding of theatricality gained through participation and attendance at my own cultural performances and those I attended as a Peace Corps volunteer in Senegal.[3] Many of the same performance dynamics and processes—the shifting tempo within events, the gendered styles of expressive forms, the give and take between performers—that I experienced in the various Senegalese events are also fundamental features of Segou's youth association puppet masquerade. I spent the first seven months in the community researching the organization and history of the Bamana quarter's kamalen ton, the youth association. I also participated in a variety of work and entertainment activities in this quarter that provided me with an initial introduction to the social organization and everyday practices of the village. Insights drawn from these other activities would become increasingly more germane as the research on the theatre progressed.

My analysis of the puppet masquerade theatre in Mali has been profoundly shaped by the recent convergence of ideas and perspectives about practice and performance within the humanities and social sciences. These approaches have refocused attention away from the isolated object or text to one which locates these forms, objects, and their structural features in performance. This shift to process foregrounds time, change, and human agency in the constitution of the masquerade as both an aesthetic and a social practice. These practice- or performance-centered perspectives have developed in parallel or in conjunction with one another in drama studies (Schechner 1977, 1985; Drewal 1989, 1991, 1992) and in anthropology, folklore, sociolinguistics, and sociology (Bateson 1972; Bauman 1977, 1986; Bourdieu 1977; Fabian 1983, 1990; Giddens 1979; Goffman 1974; Turner 1969, 1974, 1986). Several recent studies of Mande peoples have also taken a practice- or performance-centered approach (Brink 1978, 1980, 1981, 1982a, 1982b; Grosz-Ngate 1986; Hardin 1987, 1988, 1993; Hoffman 1989, 1990). Each of these excellent studies has shaped in significant ways my own analysis of Segou puppet masquerade theatre. The problem at the heart of this book is to describe and understand the theatre as an arena of artistic action and a site for the production of knowledge.

The title *Playing with Time: Art and Performance in Central Mali* was chosen to highlight several interrelated issues. The concept of play and playing is central to people's own definition of their puppet masquerade performances. The play frame defines youth theatre and it allows young men and women to create an imaginary universe. Within these performances participants can explore and comment upon their lives through the arts. These arts have the potential and power to evoke strong feelings and emotional responses (Bateson 1972, 1973; Bauman 1977; Beidleman 1986; Brink 1978, 1980, 1981; Handelman 1977; Hardin 1988, 1993; Huizinga 1938; Jackson 1982). Although actors frame the masquerade theatre as play, the performances continually move from the ludic and celebratory to a seriousness of mood, tone, and intention.

In Kirango, and elsewhere in Mali, time is always linked to practice. The masquerade performances provide a context where multiple notions of time converge in the production of the events. Within the performance and in discussions about performance, people invoke many different temporal templates, performative, diurnal, cyclical, developmental, and generational. Each template constitutes a way of knowing, organizing, contextualizing, and commenting upon the theatre that encapsulates local definitions of history. Performance duration and periodicity are central to a community's definition of the event, as is theatrical timing and tempo. These templates shape people's production, interpretation, and evaluation of the event.

Understanding the contemporary masquerades demands an attention to the history of the theatre, which is embedded in the larger framework of regional and local community pasts. Throughout this last century, puppet masquerade has demonstrated a remarkable receptivity to change and innovation. When one becomes conversant with the drama's history, the changes and innovations in the theatre are revealed. The oral record of these innovations constitutes a commentary on the specific historical conditions and contradictions of people's lives in these communities throughout the past century.

Both actors and audiences participate in a shared artistic and social project to create and give meaning to the imaginary world produced in theatre. Within these events the values of the community are thrown into high relief. Ancestral time and contemporary time are pulled into alignment (Jackson 1982, 271). Schechner suggested that the world within the theatre is created through a "doubling of time and place." It is this double presence that consists of the "there and then" and the "here and now" that is critical to understanding the theatrical process (Schechner 1985, 37–40). The definition of performative behavior as "restored" or "twice behaved behavior" that is played out in the subjunctive mood of possibility is especially useful for understanding the symbolic and reflexive nature of artistic experience in Mali (Schechner 1985, 36).

Simultaneity, as defined by Mikhail Bakhtin, also emerges as a significant dimension of the theatrical experience and is important for understanding the interpretations people hold of these events. Bakhtin has persuasively argued that within any single event, and moreover within any single act or utterance, what he calls "official and unofficial ideologies" can be conveyed. It is through expository means, whether verbal, musical, gestural, or material, that a variety of messages, both complementary and competing, can be produced simultaneously (Bakhtin 1981, 1984; Drewal 1992; Karp 1987). Using this concept of multivocality, this present study of Segou masquerade examines the ways in which attitudes and beliefs about social roles, gender, and age inform the production and content of these performances and find expression in the masquerade's artistic forms and performance practices. The multiple voices in the theatre carried by song, masquerade, dance, and drumming contribute to the production of divergent and sometimes competing interpretations of the dramatic action. It is the interplay of these multiple voices that energizes these performances.

I have divided the analysis of the theatre into two parts. The first three chapters concentrate on the puppet masquerade as an artistic event and a performance process. In the first chapter I examine the local definitions of the puppet masquerade and explore the theatre's relationships to other performance forms within the Segou region both historically and today. The second chapter focuses on the categories of expressive forms used in the theatre. It documents the flow of forms across different performance contexts and examines the ideology of aesthetic expression as it shapes the evaluation of these expressive forms and the performance event. Chapter three explores how different notions of time emerge in practice and how they shape the performance process. My concerns in this chapter revolve around understanding cultural notions of artistry and theatricality and the strategies and plans that performers use to move these events forward in time. The temporal structuring of the masquerade performance and its internal timing and tempo are important aesthetic dimensions of these performances. Timing and tempo are critical elements in a troupe's performance strategies and they contribute in significant ways to the evaluations of performance artistry.

The last two chapters shift the discussion to the production of meaning in the theatre. Chapter four examines how, through the selective use of artistic forms, troupes use the past as a potent cultural resource for creating their contemporary group identities. Chapter five explores the beliefs, values, capacities, and attitudes that shape social relationships in these communities and the specific ways this moral universe emerges in the organization of the theatre and in its dramatic content.

Participants define Segou puppet masquerade performances as special moments, outside the flow of everyday life. The "specialness" they accord to these events carries with it a heightened sense of the masquerade's moral force. It is this sense of morality that underlies the creation and interpretation of expressive forms and dramatic characters and that is the basis for people's evaluations of the theatre. Much of my understanding about the Segou drama came through sharing observations about this theatre with men and women of different ages who had, to varying degrees, invested themselves in the masquerades. Through these exchanges I began to learn the range of different ways people in Kirango and throughout Segou see, know, speak about, interpret, and evaluate these masquerades. I hope to elucidate in the following chapters some of the ways that people organize their knowledge and the experience of these events as they engage in creating anew their moral, artistic, and social universe.

ACKNOWLEDGMENTS

In late September 1978 I arrived in Mali. Following several months of discussions with interested Malian colleagues in the Ministry of Culture, Cheik Omar Mara introduced me to people in Kirango in the Segou region. Kirango enjoyed a certain regional celebrity for its puppet masquerade theatre and happily for this study it had three active troupes, a Bamana, a Sòmonò, and a Boso troupe. After several days of discussions about the project with local residents, the Bamana quarter graciously agreed to allow me and my colleague Lynn Forsdale to live in their community. We settled into Mr. Ousmane Diarra's household in early December.

I have based this analysis of the Segou masquerade theatre on my participation in over fifteen performances since 1979 and upon ongoing discussions with men and women in Kirango and in other communities within the Segou region and in adjacent regions. Some of these discussions transpired informally and these conversations were recorded as notes. I also taped over sixty hours of formal interviews and these recordings have been transcribed by Sekou Ba Camara. In 1979 and 1980 I videotaped several performances and used these tapes in playback interviews with performers in several communities. These interviews provided me with many valuable insights into the performance process and about the criteria people use to evaluate their arts.

A number of the men living in the Diarra household, including the head of the household, Ousmane Diarra (recently deceased), were formerly or are active in the theatre. During his youth, Ousmane Diarra had been a drummer and he was the impresario for two masquerades that he introduced into the repertoire in the 1950s. Several of his younger brothers, especially Adama Diarra, who also lives in the household, remain active in the theatre. Adama involves himself in many aspects of the theatrical production. Throughout my two years living with the family and again in 1987, 1989, and 1992 Adama and his age-mates entertained with grace my many questions about these performances.

Until their marriages in the late 1980s, Ousmane's daughters were members of the Bamana youth association. Many leisure hours in the Diarra compound were spent with Ousmane's wives and these young women teaching the youngest members of the family the songs, music, and dances associated with the masquerade. Observing this play and the ways through which toddlers first learn the rudiments of expressive forms provided me with important insights into the ways artistry becomes embodied and how it comes to be evaluated. Several of Ousmane's preadolescent sons also aspired to the theatrical celebrity of their father and his brothers and they were keen observers and budding practitioners of the masquerade art. They and other groups of children throughout the quarter occasionally played at putting on performances, and their games were quite revealing.

Bakary Traore, my official host, was in the senior age-set of the youth association from 1978 to 1980. He and his age-mates and friends greatly facilitated my access to the performances in Kirango and in neighboring communities. He gained us access to behind-the-scenes preparations, and through his sponsorship we were accepted as members of the Bamana youth association. Bakary also introduced me to elder men in the village, former youth association leaders and blacksmiths, who shared their memories of past theatres with me. These individuals were knowledgeable about the history of the village and the history and development of the youth association theatre in the Bamana quarter. Bakary also initiated my first contacts with several farming villages in the immediate area who also had active puppet theatres. They in turn graciously introduced me to other communities.

Women were also important participants in this research. Mei Diarra is a lead singer for the puppet masquerade in the Bamana quarter and Maimuna Thiero is the lead singer in the Boso quarter. Through conversations with them and with many other women, including Khadia Diarra, Assita Tarawele, and Khadia Coulibaly, I learned about the history of the quarter's singers and the performative roles which women take in the masquerade. Throughout this past decade we have also often discussed women's interpretations of the theatre's dramatic content, which occasionally differs from the commentary offered by men.

Because I was living in the Bamana quarter and working closely with its youth association, local rivalries limited my relationships with the fishermen's associations. Although I attended all the fishermen's performances and interviewed people in these quarters, my working relationships with these associations were less relaxed and always more formal and reserved. I conducted interviews in four other fishermen's communities in the general area. I also extensively discussed the theatre with two Sòmonò/Boso male singers, Budagari Coulibaly and Vadama Traore. Both men lived in neighboring villages but both occasionally sang for the Kirango fishermen's performances. During the first year of the project I worked with Dr. Khalilou Tera, who was a linguist at the Ministry of Education. Together we did a survey of the puppet theatre in the eastern Segou region. Dr. Tera's interest in Mande culture and his generosity and enthusiasm provided me with important insights into the histories and current relationships among these eastern communities. As a result of this survey, I became aware of the intraregional differences in the terminology, history, and practices of the puppet theatre. These different histories from east to west and among communities in each zone have played a significant part in shaping the variation in style and dramatic content observable in the current performances.

In 1980 and again in 1987 and 1989, I continued research with my colleague Mr. Adama Mara, both in Kirango and in neighboring communities. We also revisited the eastern Segou area. Together we met and discussed the theatre with sculptors, singers, elders, and current members of performing troupes in a variety of different communities. In 1987 I also worked for several weeks in the Bamako region around Koulikoro with Mr.

Assimi Bengaly, Chef du Section de Musèe, Sites et Monuments in Koulikoro, and with Mr. Yaya Coulibaly from the National Museum in Mali. Our discussions in communities around Koulikoro confirmed the local theatre's historical links to the Segou region. They also provided important information on the historical, political, and social networks between Koulikoro and Segou and on the different periods when fishermen and farmers in this area began to play the puppet masquerade.

I am grateful to many Malian colleagues who have participated in this research project, but especially to Adama Mara, who is an exceptional and sensitive researcher. His reflections and insights on the culture, history, and social practices of the area helped to shape the directions which I pursued as this study progressed. I would also like to recognize Mr. Sekou Ba Camara and thank him for his careful transcriptions and supplementary notations on the taped interviews. A very special thanks is due to my friend and colleague Lynn Forsdale Denny, for her dedication, her professionalism, and her humor during the initial two years of this study. Her vibrant photographs of the puppet masquerades from this period document and bring this study to life.

Many colleagues have encouraged me in this study. Throughout the last decade they have generously shared their observations about Mande culture, history, and art with me. All of them have a deep and abiding respect for Malian peoples, their histories and their cultures. Many of their own excellent studies are liberally cited throughout this book. I would especially like to mention Claude Ardouin, Assimi Bengaly, Charles Bird, James Brink, Barbara Cashion, Gerald Cashion, Katherine Dettwyler, Kate Ezra, Barbara Frank, Bernhard Gardi, Kathryn Green, Maria Grosz-Ngate, Kris Hardin, Barbara Hoffman, John Johnson, Mamadou Kante, Martha Kendall, Martin Klein, Alpha Oumar Konare, Kassim Kone, Cheik Omar Mara, Patrick McNaughton, George Meurillon, Richard Roberts, Klene Sonogo, Khalilou Tera, Adama Timbo, Peter Weil, and Bonnie Wright. I would also like to thank Ambassador Robert Pringle for sharing his photographs of masquerade performances with me.

I am deeply grateful for the continued intellectual support of both Ivan Karp and Roy Sieber, who guided me through the initial phases of this study. More recently colleagues in the Department of Anthropology and in the Museum of African Art at the Smithsonian have encouraged me and offered helpful criticism on this manuscript. I would like to thank Adrienne Kaeppler for her advice on the analysis of musical and dance forms. I would also like to express my appreciation to Christraud Geary, Christine Mullen Kreamer, Robert Leopold, William Merrill, and Janet Stanley. The first period of research in Mali, 1978-80, was funded by a Fulbright-Hays Doctoral Fellowship and by the American Council of Learned Societies/Social Science Research Council Doctoral Fellowship. The Smithsonian Institution funded subsequent research in Mali, in 1987, 1989, and 1992. It also provided additional funds for the preparation of the photographs for this publication.

I would like to express my heartfelt thanks to my family and to my husband, Craig Subler, for their continued support of this research over the past decade and for their encouragement during the preparation of this manuscript. I reserve my deepest gratitude for the people of Kirango. These men and women shared with me their lives, their experiences of theatre, and their thoughts about art and performance. I would especially like to mention the Traore, Diarra, Diabate, Diakhite, and Doumbia families in Kirango and the former and current members of the kamalen ton. Finally, to all of Segou's artists and performers, past, present, and to come, I dedicate this book.

NOTE ON ORTHOGRAPHY

I am following the spelling of Bamana words in Père Charles Bailleul's *Petit Diction-naire Bambara-Français, Français-Bambara*, which was published in 1981, except for proper names, whose spelling may vary according to the individual's personal preference. Plurals of nouns in Bamana are indicated by adding the letter "w" to the end of the word. In this text I use singular and plural forms of nouns according to the grammatical context.

Official Bamana orthography has undergone minor changes since the dictionary was published; however, the dictionary remains one of the most complete published sources for current spelling of Bamana words. The reader who needs a more phonetic transcription of the Bamana words used in the text can consult Bailleul's dictionary for tone marks.

Playing with Time

CHAPTER ONE

A Bamana Tonko Festival, Kirango, June 1979

In 1979 in the village of Kirango, the Bamana quarter held its annual *Tonko* festival from June 9 to June 11. The festival celebrates the new year, *san yèlèma*, or, literally, "the year turns over." San yèlèma falls just before the first rains, which begin in late May or early June. Since many of the quarter residents now work in urban areas as far afield as Segou, Mopti, and Bamako, the *kamalen ton*, the youth association, wanted to choose dates for the 1979 festival that would correspond with both the period of the full moon and a weekend. The period of the full moon is the customary timing for many festivals within the village. Holding the festival on the weekend would also allow those absent members living and working elsewhere to return to the village to participate in the event. In discussing and choosing the date, some of the young men expressed concern over the wisdom of delaying the festival until the second weekend in June. They feared that the rains would have already begun and the performance would be thwarted. Indeed, during the morning of the first day of the festival there was a rainstorm, but the skies cleared by noon and the festival proceeded as scheduled.

In the weeks before the festival, the association met nearly every evening to plan the event. Members debated the roster of characters to be played and they brought the chosen masks and puppets out of storage in order to repair, refurbish, or repaint them. The leaders assigned the construction of groups of masquerades to various teams of young men. Each team was responsible for building the costume armatures and for constructing and costuming the masquerade. The young men cajoled their mothers, wives, sisters, and female friends into lending them textiles to create the temporary costumes for their masquerades. Several experienced senior members headed up each team and younger men acted as their apprentices. The youngest members energetically ran the countless errands that ensued, injecting the preparations with a sense of intense urgency. Older men, who were no longer members of the youth association, served as consultants in the construction of especially complex masquerades such as Mali Kònò, the Bird of Mali, and Yayoroba, the Beautiful Woman, two quarter favorites.

Several days before the festival the officers distributed grain to the wives of association members, who had agreed to brew the *dòlò*, millet beer. Although the quarter is now almost entirely Moslem, the consumption of home-brewed millet beer during the festival remains an important part of this event. Young men sent messages to kin and friends in neighboring villages inviting them to attend the performances. The association also arranged for the festival to be announced on Radio Mali, which broadcasts throughout the country.

At dawn on June 9, the young men gathered at the association meetinghouse and under the supervision of their leaders they slaughtered goats for the festival meal. Teams of young men brought in firewood from the bush and divided it into several equal portions. The firewood, measures of millet, and the goat meat were then taken to compounds in the quarter where young women from the association had gathered to cook the festival meal. Earlier that morning the young women had purchased the condiments for the sauce and were already busy preparing *lenburuji*, a nonalcoholic lemon and ginger beverage, which, along with the millet beer, is served to honored guests and association members during the performance. Throughout the morning the cooking compounds were bustling with activity. Between various phases in the food preparation, young women tressed each other's hair, gossiped, and joked and an atmosphere of high spirits and anticipation prevailed throughout the quarter.

Simultaneously in several compounds on the periphery of the quarter, men from the association were feverishly preparing the masquerades. Women, children, and strangers were banned from these areas and all morning a continual stream of men could be seen entering and exiting these houses. The teams first constructed the masquerade armatures, which were made by lashing together sturdy but flexible tree branches [Figures 1.1, 1.2]. Once the armatures were prepared and rigorously tested for strength and durability, the young men began creating the costumes by sewing grass skirting and textiles over the wooden armatures. When each costume was complete, the appropriate puppet head was inserted and one of the young men crawled underneath the costume and began to dance the masquerade. As he danced, other members carefully examined and evaluated the costume construction, adjusted the fit of the grass skirting and textiles, and tightened any lashings which showed signs of working loose

1.1. Preparing a masquerade armature for the Bamana Sogo bò. 1979. Kirango, Mali. *Photograph by Lynn Forsdale.*

[Figure 1.3]. When the young men had finished their adjustments, they carefully set the masquerades aside and sprinkled water on those with grass skirting to freshen them. The festival masquerades now stood ready for a final inspection by the kamalen ton's senior officers.

While the teams worked furiously behind the scenes, others began to prepare the *fèrè*, the open plaza in front of the association meeting-house on the upper bank of the Niger River. At one end of this clearing they constructed a large shelter for dignitaries and invited guests. From its roof they hung red, green, and yellow cloth bunting, the colors of the Malian flag. Around the dance ground they set up wooden benches and chairs borrowed from every household in the quarter. From the stately old shade trees they strung electric lights and they installed the public address system. Lights and the

1.2. The masquerade Misi, the Cow, being prepared for the Bamana Sogo bò. 1979. Kirango, Mali. *Photograph by Lynn Forsdale.*

1.3. Testing the durability of Jarawara, the Wildcat, prior to the start of the Bamana performance. 1979. Kirango, Mali. *Photograph by Lynn Forsdale.*

1.4. Gòn, the Baboon, leading the New Year's procession through the Bamana residential quarter. 1979. Kirango, Mali. *Photograph by Mary Jo Arnoldi.*

microphone were powered by a gasoline generator, which the troupe had borrowed from the neighboring government office. Throughout the morning, the association leaders made the rounds of these work areas checking on each group's progress, instilling a sense of urgency into the preparations and giving their approval to the completed tasks.

Around 11:00 A.M. all the members gathered at the association meetinghouse. Many of the youth were already dressed in their festival finery. The masquerade Gòn, the Baboon, accompanied by its attendants and the association drum team, led the revelers through the quarter. As the youth sang and danced exuberantly, the Baboon masquerade dashed madly from one street to the next. Periodically the masker was reined in by his attendants in order for the youth to pay their respects to elders in each household [Figure 1.4]. As the youth sang out their New Year greetings to each household, Gòn dropped down on one knee in a traditional salute of respect. After all the households had been greeted, the young men and women dispersed. Young girls returned to the cooking compounds to put the final touches on the festival meal. Shortly after midday, the association began distributing bowls of steamed millet and goat-meat sauce to each household in the quarter. After delivering all of the festival meals, the young men and women gathered together in various households to share their portion of the annual feast.

About midafternoon a series of short, rapid bursts from the *buru*, an animal-horn trumpet, could be heard throughout the quarter. The youth moved to reconvene at the meetinghouse while the general populace was served notice that the festival performance was imminent. Activity on the dance ground began slowly. Young children, always the first to heed the trumpet call, arrived almost immediately and in high spirits. A few boys ran to pick up the drums which were lying near the meetinghouse, while their mates danced and sang. Several boys wrapped themselves in remnants of grass skirting salvaged from the morning's masquerade construction and began to imitate Gòn, the Baboon [Figure 1.5]. The boys dashed around the circle and lunged at each other. Children scattered and tumbled over one another in mock terror.

During the ensuing hour, the adult drum team arrived and reclaimed their instruments from the boys [Figure 1.6]. They began to warm up and adults, who were attracted

1.5. Young Bamana boys playing at masquerading prior to the actual Sogo bò event. 1979. Kirango, Mali. *Photograph by Lynn Forsdale.*

to the music, gradually began to trickle into the plaza. In a holiday mood and dressed in their finery, people greeted their neighbors and good naturedly jockeyed for the best seats on the circle. By custom women sat in a group to the left of the covered shelter. The two principal women singers, Nanyan Coulibaly and Mei Diarra, settled front and center within this group. With great courtesy young men showed elder men and distinguished guests to seats under the covered shelter. Children found places in the front row of every section. They dashed back and forth across the circle and as the performance hour neared they received rebukes and an occasional thrashing from young men assigned to crowd control. Many of these young children were dressed in festival costumes identical to those worn by the junior age-sets of the youth association. On the sidelines, minicircles quickly formed and reformed and some of these young children were thrust forward to dance, encouraged by the clapping and singing of their peers, sisters, and mothers [Figure 1.7]. The din of the crowd, the drumming and clapping, and the crackling public address system acted like a magnet, drawing more and more people to the river. The crowd swelled.

As the audience steadily grew, young men and women in the kamalen ton filed into the meetinghouse. The leaders seated themselves in a group against one wall of the house, while the general membership crammed together on the other side of the room. The drummers entered, the young girls began to sing, and the ceremony called the Dònkan, literally, knowledgeable talk, began. The Dònkan reenacts a precolonial ceremony that

1.6. The senior drum team performing during the Bamana Sogo bò. 1979. Kirango, Mali. *Photograph by Mary Jo Arnoldi.*

took place just prior to battle. As the Dònkan progressed several groups of elder men entered the meetinghouse and offered their advice to the kamalen ton leaders. Finally a small group of old women arrived and spoke words of encouragement and gave their blessings to the assembled young people. The whole time, the drums reverberated within the meetinghouse and the members sang lustily of the exploits of the great warrior heroes of precolonial Segou.

After the ceremony was complete the drummers led the youth out of the house and onto the adjacent dance ground. Young women formed an inner circle while the young men took their positions behind them, forming an outer dance circle [Figure 1.8]. Both the men and women were organized by age-set, from eldest to youngest, and each age-set wore a different costume to distinguish itself from the others. The oldest girls wore brilliant yellow wrappers, blouses, and headties. The next group wore wrappers and blouses of *bògòlan fini*, handpainted mudcloth. They were followed by girls wearing white tops and light blue wrappers with a horizontal strip of handwoven blue and white checked cloth in the guinea fowl pattern. The youngest girls wore matching wrappers and blouses made from bright green and yellow industrial cloth.

The senior men wore long white robes made from handwoven cotton strips over blouson pants and sleeveless vests of the same material. On their heads they sported round white caps. The second group wore bark-dyed handspun cotton robes over blouson pants and vests of the same material. They wore the traditional *bamada* hats, bonnet type caps with two points worn to the front and back of the head. The younger age-sets

1.7. A toddler dancing on the sidelines during a Bamana performance. 1979. Kirango, Mali. *Photograph by Lynn Forsdale.*

sported knee-length dark blue blouson pants and sleeveless vests of handwoven white cotton. A woven strip of the guinea fowl patterned cloth was sewn down the center of the vest in the front and back.

When the drummers began playing, the dancers quickly moved into a choreographic unity. The tempo of the dance gradually increased until it reached such a pitch that the dancers could no longer keep up. As the circle broke, the dancers rushed about, laughing, shouting, and collapsing on the sidelines. Within a few moments the dancers revived themselves, and they once again took up their positions on the plaza and the dance began anew. The singers accompanied the dancers and sang songs extolling unity and cooperation in the community.

After about an hour, the action shifted and the *Bònjalan*, a men's acrobatic dance competition, began [Figure 1.9]. The competition was first launched between two young men from the same age-set. As the young men stepped forward their male friends showed their support by giving them both verbal and gestural encouragement. The young dancer's age-mates pulled on his arms and raised them high into the air in a sign of camaraderie, strength, and victory. The young men demonstrated their acrobatic skill and prowess within the tempos and rhythms defined by the drummers. In unison the two dancers danced around the ring, leaping high into the air and executing backflips and somersaults. Immediately after each team's performance, young girls rushed into the ring to praise their favorites by bestowing colorful headties on them. The young men tied their trophies around their waists, foreheads, and biceps and strutted in a triumphant display

1.10. Gòn, the Baboon, opening the afternoon masquerade segment of the Bamana Sogo bò. 1979. Kirango, Mali. *Photograph by Lynn Forsdale.*

before the crowd. Throughout the competitions, the women sang about heroes and chided young men who did not have the courage to compete. As the afternoon progressed, several dance teams from different age-sets began competing in the ring simultaneously. Between these sets of acrobatic displays other dancers performed. Occasionally both men and women performed together; at other times young men performed bawdy and comic dances to the delight of the crowd.

The Bònjalan continued well into the third hour of the afternoon. Suddenly, Gòn, the Baboon, dashed into the ring, darting from one side of the circle to the other [Figure 1.10]. As the crowd strained to see the masquerade, the singers immediately switched to Gòn's signature song. The masquerade mimed the movements and the often lewd gestures of baboons. It pranced around the ring and occasionally vaulted through the air. Young men rushed in to form a line behind the Baboon and they began dancing with the masker. Gòn soon quit the dance line and began cavorting between and behind the dancers. He then darted into the center of the circle, performed solo for several minutes, and finally dashed out of the arena altogether. As he disappeared the action quickly shifted back to the circle dances, which were again followed by men's dance competitions. By this time the sun was setting and the afternoon performance was brought to a close. People returned to their houses to relax, gather up their energies, eat supper, and say evening prayers.

Around 8:00 P.M., the audience slowly began to reassemble for the *su fè sogo*, the evening masquerade event. Suruku Nama, the Hyena, officially opened the event. This puppet head was painted black with white accents that gleamed in the semidarkness. The masquerader wore a costume of black cloth over grass skirting that hid his feet [Figure 1.11]. The hyena moved quickly into the arena, flapping its jaw and exposing its formidable teeth. Suddenly it stood bolt upright. It then dropped back down again on all fours and began to twirl and swish around the circle as the women sang its praises. When the masquerade exited, its attendants led it from the circle, dancing and shouting in appreciation of its performance.

Suddenly, without advance warning, Suruku Malobali, the Shameless Hyena, dashed into the circle. It rushed at the audience, flapping its oversized mouth. Startled, the crowd

1.11. Suruku Nama, the Hyena, opening the evening masquerades during the Bamana Sogo bò. 1979. Kirango, Mali. *Photograph by Lynn Forsdale.*

rose to its feet. Never one to stay long, however, the Hyena quickly bolted from the plaza. As the crowd settled back into their seats, the chorus began a musical interlude.

After about ten minutes a male and a female version of Dajè, the Roan Antelope, entered the ring. These two antelope puppets were crowned with long, delicately carved horns that formed graceful concave arches over their backs. Their costumes were a combination of somber textiles and grass skirting. They moved gracefully, but quickly around the arena. As the puppets danced the women sang a lament for the antelope's great beauty and of the feelings of loss that its death evokes in humanity. The female antelope, more diminutive in size, exited first, and the male stayed behind to perform a short acrobatic solo. When it was finally led from the arena, a mass of young men from the association rushed from the sidelines into the circle and danced enthusiastically, raising great clouds of dust.

1.12. Sumusonin, the Sorceress, performing in a Bamana theatre. 1979. Kirango, Mali. *Photograph by Lynn Forsdale.*

Once the circle was cleared of dancers, Jado Nama appeared. No ordinary beast, this hyena puppet was constructed of layers of silvery material that picked up the light and sparked and flashed as it danced. It entered the ring slowly, then soon moved into an energetic dance display, twirling and dropping to the ground, raising and lowering its head and turning it completely around. A few elder women and some of the young men entered the ring to sing the masquerade's praises. The singers sang of the healer Nama from the village of Minjado, who had saved the celebrated singer Ba from poisoning.

As Jado Nama exited, the lights were suddenly cut and two versions of Sumusonin, the Little Sorceress, stole into the ring [Figure 1.12]. The two grass masquerades were just barely visible in the moonlight. They swished around the circle and whirled, changing their shapes. The singers asked of the audience, "Who has called the sorceress into the village?" As the masquerades left the arena, the lights were reilluminated and Sigi, the Buffalo, lumbered majestically into the ring. This masquerade stood well over six feet high and the puppet head was crowned with great curving horns. This lone buffalo moved slowly around the arena, stopping periodically to break into a more energetic

1.13. The Ntomo masquerade performing in the Bamana Sogo bò. 1979. Kirango, Mali. *Photograph by Lynn Forsdale.*

dance, dipping its head and body and twirling around. The audience registered its wholehearted approval by rising to its feet and shouting the animal's praises.

As the night wore on, the tempo of the performance began to accelerate and Sigi was soon followed by Sinè, the Gazelle. In contrast to the slow and ponderous movements of the Buffalo, the Gazelle leapt and cavorted around the circle, bringing the audience to its feet. The puppeteer, hidden under its grass costume, raised the masquerade's head several feet into the air, then abruptly lowered it flush with its shoulders, as he twirled and dipped.

As the performance moved into its final hour, Bakòrò, the Ram, entered and lunged and twirled as he completed his circuit. He was followed by Misicè, the Bull and Misimuso, the Cow, who abruptly slowed the pace [Figure 1.2]. These masquerades were followed in quick succession by two different wildcat characters, Jarawara [Figure 1.3] and then Njona.[1] Both of these masquerades gave lively performances, suddenly leaping in one direction and then the other and frequently running headlong into the crowd, scattering the gleefully frightened children in every direction.

Finally at about 2:00 A.M., Ntilen, the Giraffe, with its head towering above the crowd, entered. His appearance signaled the end of the night's drama. The audience, exhausted, but satisfied, soon dispersed. As the adults and children slowly headed home, the kamalen ton members remained behind and moved into the meetinghouse, where they kept an all-night vigil, singing and drumming until dawn.

1.14. The reenactment of a Kòmò processional performed during the Bamana Sogo bò. 1979. Kirango, Mali. *Photograph by Lynn Forsdale.*

The next morning, as the village awoke, there was a feeling of anticipation in the air. In the late afternoon the horn again called the quarter to the dance grounds. This day's drama began with a brief performance by Gòn, the Baboon. Gòn was followed by the character Ntomo. This mask, with its human features and seven horned projections, was formerly performed during boys' initiation in the village. The masked dancer moved once around the ring, leading a line of boys and girls from the junior age-sets in the association. [Figure 1.13]. These young dancers moved to the center of the arena and seated themselves in a semicircle. Then Ntomo began to dance in front of them. Toward the end of his performance, all rose and accompanied him from the arena.

The more senior men's age-sets then entered in a dignified and solemn procession. The performance alluded to the ceremonies of the Kòmò men's association, which until the 1950s had been active in Kirango. Drummers played the Kòmò rhythms and the procession was led by a musician playing a harp lute and by a man with a tethered goat [Figure 1.14]. However, no Kòmò masquerade appeared. The procession inched its way around the arena. Midway around the circle, the performance was short-circuited by the entrance of the puppet Yayoroba, the Beautiful Woman. As she entered the ring, the Kòmò dancers moved to the sidelines and Yayoroba took center stage [Figure Pref.4].

Over ten feet tall, Yayoroba wore yards of deep blue and green patterned velvet. Her skin was painted a brilliant pink and she wore an elaborately carved coiffure. The puppeteer moved gracefully into the ring, first stopping and bowing respectfully to the honored guests under the shelter and then moving to greet the assembled women's chorus. The

1.15. A Bamana hunter stalks the masquerade Waraba, the Lion. 1979. Kirango, Mali. *Photograph by Lynn Forsdale.*

masquerade then saluted the general audience and moved slowly and gracefully around the circle, guided only by the sound of a bell rung by its escort. Yayoroba was greeted with murmurs of admiration from the crowd. She was clearly a village favorite. As she exited, a number of married women from the quarter entered the circle and danced together, moving counterclockwise around the arena. After five minutes the women were forced to the sidelines by the reentry of the Kòmò procession. However, after only a few minutes, they too were displaced by the entry of a male and a female Waraba, the Lion. Each lion mask was covered with animal skins, and its eyes, made of brown glass, glinted in the sunlight. With feline grace the two lions prowled around the circle. Suddenly a hunter emerged from the sidelines carrying his rifle, and he began to stalk his prey. The male lion lunged at the hunter, who first retreated into the crowd and then reemerged to take up the hunt. Suddenly the hunter dropped to one knee and fired [Figure 1.15]. The sound reverberated off the nearby compound walls and startled the crowd. The male lion fell, as if

1.16. Jobali maskers representing Boso women perform during a Bamana Sogo bò. 1979. Kirango, Mali. *Photograph by Lynn Forsdale.*

mortally wounded. In classic dramatic style the masquerader went through the exaggerated agony of the death throes. The hunter then jumped up and broke into a triumphant dance, and men in the audience rushed into the circle to sing and dance his praises.

As the men moved the lions out of the arena, the Kòmò procession again took up its position in the circle. The Kòmò processional made one complete circuit around the arena and then brought the performance to its climax by miming the sacrifice of a goat. As the Kòmò procession exited the dance arena two Jobali maskers made their entrance.

Jobali represents a Boso woman, and each masker wore a woman's wrapper and blouse and carried a strip of headtie cloth in his hand. The faces of the masks were painted white and were topped with elaborately carved hairstyles [Figure 1.16]. First one masker, then the other, performed a graceful but physically exacting dance. Each dancer used the unfurled strip of headtie cloth to accentuate his undulating hand movements. Finally the maskers began to dance together and two daring young women from the kamalen ton en-

1.17. A performance of Mali Kònò, the Bird of Mali. 1979. Kirango, Mali. *Photograph by Mary Jo Arnoldi.*

tered the circle to dance alongside the maskers, much to the audience's delight.

Jobali was soon followed by Mali Kònò, the Bird of Mali [Figure 1.17]. Celebrating Mali's independence from French colonial rule, Mali Kònò's entry elicited an audible outburst of approval from the audience. The masquerade stood well over seven feet tall. Its beak measured over a yard in length, and its wing span was several yards. Its head was painted in bright stripes and chevron patterns and its body was costumed in yards of printed and striped material. It moved majestically into the ring and glided, seemingly effortlessly, around the circle as if in flight. Periodically it raised its great wings and lowered its beak to the ground as if it were fishing, then lifted its head high into the air to swallow its catch.[2] During a number of interludes, Mali Kònò broke into an energetic dance,

1.18. Taasi Dòoni, Reflect a Little, appearing as a female masquerade character. 1979. Kirango, Mali. *Photograph by Lynn Forsdale.*

twirling and flapping its wings and quickly raising and lowering its head. In response to this crowd-pleaser, people rushed into the circle to praise this symbol of their new nation.

At sunset, Taasi Dòoni, Reflect a Little, entered the ring [Figure 1.18]. The masquerade appeared as a woman with well-padded bust and an exaggerated derriere. Her entrance brought a roar from the audience, as she sashayed around the arena. Bent slightly at the waist, the masker punctuated the dance with undulating hip movements whose effect threw Taasi Dòoni's male escorts to the ground in mock ecstasy. The young men in the crowd catcalled and laughed uproariously. In contrast to Taasi Dòoni's bawdy performance, the women's chorus invoked a more somber mood as they sang of the merits of reflection before action.

As the evening began to grow darker, the generator was engaged and lights illuminated the circle. Waraba Caco, the Striped Wildcat, lumbered forward [Figure 1.19]. The masquerade was well over five feet high and six feet long. Out of its large mouth silver foil covered teeth flashed in the light. At several points Waraba Caco stopped, squatted on the ground and the puppeteer animated its head, bobbing it from left to right and up and down. It then slowly rose again and lumbered around the circle. As Waraba Caco exited, the drumming and singing faded and the day's performance was brought to a close.

On Monday, in the late afternoon, only a small crowd gathered on the plaza. The audience consisted mainly of women, children, and young people from the quarter. Many visitors had already departed and many adult residents had gone to work in Markala or gone to their fields. The dancing started and continued for about an hour. Then the ka-

1.19. Waraba Caco, the Striped Wildcat, waiting to perform. 1979. Kirango, Mali. *Photograph by Lynn Forsdale.*

malen ton introduced a new masquerade, Madame Sarata [Figure 1.20]. Two identical versions of Madame Sarata appeared and the two maskers danced and flirted with the crowd. After their performance the drama unceremoniously ended, thus bringing the festival to a close. The performers, although exhausted and spent from their three-day efforts, were ebullient and, in the days and weeks that followed, they judged the festival to have been a rousing success.

The 1979 Kirango spring festival was only one of many puppet masquerade festivals in the Segou region that year. While it is true that each masquerade performance is unique to a specific time and place, it is equally true that masquerade troupes throughout the region draw upon similar notions of art and performance and a shared constellation of dramatic characters to create these festivals. The following chapter will examine the local definitions of this masquerade theatre and its history within the Segou region.

1.20. The Madame Sarata masquerade awaits her entrance cue during the Bamana Sogo bò. 1979. Kirango, Mali. *Photograph by Lynn Forsdale.*

CHAPTER TWO

The Definition and History of the Segou Puppet Masquerade Theatre

There exists an extensive body of literature devoted to the history of precolonial states in Mali and no dearth of ethnographic studies of Malian social and cultural institutions, religion, myths, and ritual practices. Despite this extensive literature, there has been until quite recently a conspicuous lack of attention devoted specifically to the examination of Malian entertainment traditions like that of the youth association puppet masquerade theatre. We do know from oral traditions and published accounts that this masquerade genre is a precolonial tradition. Indeed, there have been regular if only cursory published notices of the masquerade in Europe since 1886. Most of these accounts have focused almost entirely on one or two individual masquerade characters that appeared in the theatre and we learn very little about how the performances themselves unfold.

The widely divergent interpretations in the published literature on this masquerade theatre are reminiscent of the well-known Indian fable of the blind men examining an elephant. Early observers described the genre as popular entertainment (Soleillet 1886, 170; Labouret and Travélé 1928, 95–96). Later accounts discussed these masquerades as rituals or panegyric performances (Dieterlen 1957, 136; Ligers 1964, I: 134–135; B. N'Diaye 1970, 438) or characterized the current theatre as the contemporary secularization of once sacred rites (Pageard 1962, 17–18). While each of these interpretations does contain some element of truth, each remains only a partial view. None is wholly consistent with local definitions of the masquerade nor with people's recounting of its history and development since the precolonial period.

Paul Soleillet, an amateur geographer, wrote an early journal account of the masquerade in 1878–79. While traveling up the Niger River in late September, he came upon a puppet performance. He wrote in his journal:

> About three forty-five in the afternoon, I passed by the bambara village of Mognogo . . . and I stopped there. . . . Why . . . to see Guignol! A square tent of white and blue striped fabric is installed in a boat with two paddlers, an ostrich head fixed upon a long neck extends from the front, it draws itself up, grows taller, drops, shrinks, turns to the right, turns to the left with an

air of curious and anxious expectation; then two marionettes appear suddenly out of the middle of the tent, one clothed in red, the other in blue, and they abandon themselves to some grotesque pantomimes. The drums, placed in a second boat, accompany the spectacle with deafening music. Among the bambara they call this game "kounou-doukili." (Soleillet 1886, 170; my translation)

Soleillet described the manner in which the men brought the puppet to the village in boats. They then took it from the canoes and paraded the masquerade into a large clearing in the village, where the performance continued. This feature of the event is consistent with theatrical practices carried out in the late twentieth century by fishermen living in communities along the Niger River [Figure 2.1]. Soleillet described only one bird masquerade being performed that day, and it is not clear if any other masquerades appeared. However, he did note that the villagers were enthusiastic about his presence at the event. Their openness to his participation does seem to suggest that even in the precolonial period people defined the theatre as a public event and not restricted to particular groups or segments within the community.

Fifty years later, in 1928, Labouret and Travélé corroborated Soleillet's account of the puppet masquerade theatre. They, too, described it as a public entertainment, but identified the form specifically with the Islamized Sòmonò fishermen living along the Niger River (Labouret and Travélé 1928, 95–96). Oral traditions relating to the theatre indicate that by 1928 not only fishermen, but farmers in the Segou region were regularly performing the theatre. What is noteworthy for the study of African art history and supports Bravmann's findings in the northern Ivory Coast and Ghana is that Islam as it was practiced in this zone during the early twentieth century was not rigidly iconoclastic (Bravmann 1973). Perhaps the local definition of these youth association masquerades as public entertainment, rather than as sacred rite, accounts in part for the theatre's continued popularity throughout this century in many Muslim communities in Segou.

Since 1886, brief written notices and field photographs of performances, as well as photographs of Malian puppets in European museums and private collections, have regularly appeared in newspapers, journals, art catalogues, and books (Courrier colonial 1933, supplement to October 15; Leiris 1934, 50; Labouret 1941, 270, plate XV; Chenais 1947, 223; Lem 1949, plates 13 and 16). Despite these periodic published photographs of the masquerades, this theatre was never the subject of any in-depth field study.

Part of this neglect might stem from the fact that most early ethnographic research in Mali was directed toward precolonial state histories, the origins of various ethnic groups, and the study of myths and rituals.[1] Later studies of masquerades focused attention primarily on events associated with powerful men's initiation societies (Dieterlen and Cisse 1972; McNaughton 1979, 1988; Zahan, 1960, 1980). In the few instances when ethnographers mentioned the youth association theatre, they used its masquerades to illuminate other Malian beliefs and practices. For example, in 1964 Ligers published a three-volume ethnography on the Boso [Sorko] fishermen. In this study, Ligers mentions these masquerades in the section on hunting and he associated them with post-hunting celebrations.

The performance that Ligers described took place on the evening following a successful hunt in the Boso quarter of Banankoro, a village located near Segou city. The festivities opened with a dramatic reenactment of the successful hunt and included three characters: the hunter, his boatman, and a masquerader representing the hippo. Ligers described the play as part panegyric and part comedy. Establishing the scene required only a minimum of props. The hunter carried a harpoon and the boatmen used several sticks to suggest their canoe. The performance opened with the hunter and the masquerader processing around the circle. A bard accompanied them and sang the praises of the hunter. This segment was followed by the drama of the hunt (Ligers 1964, I: 134–135). Ligers's account focuses solely on the hunting drama and he notes only as an aside that it was but one performance in a much larger masquerade event which included lion, python, antelopes, cattle, and porcupine masquerades.

While Ligers described the event as taking place following an actual hunt, his description closely resembles similar hunting scenarios that people remembered being regularly played during the annual youth association festivals in both farming and fishing villages in this area [Figure 1.15]. The performance of the hunting scene in two different events underscores the dynamic cross-fertilizations among performance traditions that have occurred regularly for at least a century.[2]

In 1957 in an article devoted to the Mande creation myth, Dieterlen included a brief mention of masked performances in Segou. She interpreted these performances as reenactments of the Mande creation myth (Dieterlen 1957, 136). Based on the timing of these performances at the onset of the dry season in late October, and the fact that more than one ethnic group performed them, I would surmise that she was describing performances of the youth association puppet masquerade theatre. Youth puppet masquerade theatre is the only masquerade tradition that people in Segou report being shared by both fishermen and farmers. In contrast to this youth theatre, most men's association masquerades generally did not cross ethnic lines. Different masquerades were performed by men's associations in farming and in fishing communities in Segou. For example, everyone associates the Kòmò men's association and its distinctive masquerade with farmers, while they define the Jara men's association and its repertoire of masquerades as the property of fishermen. Dieterlen's interpretation of the puppet masquerades as a "more or less complete representation of the creation myth" is an awkward fit at best. Certainly by the time that Dieterlen was doing research in the 1940s and 1950s the dramatic content of the youth association masquerade was already quite diverse. By this period the theatre included an array of characters from bush animals to automobiles and from depictions of mythic personages to those of colonials. This diversity of characters, drawn not only from the past but also from the contemporary scene, does not lend itself to any coherent narrative of the Mande creation myth as she has suggested.

Pageard's account of these performances, written only a few years later than Dieterlen's, suggested an alternate interpretation for these events. He described a series of performances he attended in and around Segou city in 1958–59. In the opening paragraphs of his article he remarks:

> In these spectacles elements borrowed from animist religious ceremonies are mixed with realistic elements pulled from daily life, sometimes the most modern (a reproduction of an automobile for

example) . . . these spectacles constitute important factual evidence in the passage of the geron-tocratic society, founded upon secret instruction of the age grades and professional castes, to an egalitarian society, founded upon the rational knowledge divulged by Europeans and accessible to everyone. We are witnessing here a process of vulgarization and degradation of traditional re-ligious beliefs, which constitutes perhaps the route through which beliefs will settle in the Negro-African culture of tomorrow. (Pageard 1962, 17–18)

If we examine the history and social role of these youth associations, Pageard's state-ment that the theatre represents evidence that these societies were moving from a gerontocratic to an egalitarian society based on European influence does not ring true. First, people always said that the village youth associations and their masquerades were precolonial institutions, and not colonial introductions. While internally these associa-tions promote a sense of egalitarianism among young men, their role within the larger community contributes to the reproduction of the gerontocratic system.

Pageard claims that the theatre constitutes a process of secularization of traditional religious beliefs. This is a misreading of the essential nature of these events.[3] All of the different masquerade events once extant in these Segou communities have their own par-ticular traditions of origin and people never saw them as having ever been historically related to each other. They do not believe that the youth association masquerade theatre evolved out of masquerade ceremonies owned by the powerful men's associations. They do recognize, however, that these different masquerade traditions occasionally share a few of the same expressive forms. People see no contradiction or degradation of their tra-ditional beliefs and values in the selective juxtaposition of images and expressive forms drawn from the sacred and the mundane, the past and the present. The youth associa-tion theatre has existed alongside the different men's association rites since the precolonial period. By its very definition, and borne out by its history, discussed in detail below, puppet theatre is inherently inclusionary, pulling its ideas and forms from every domain of people's experience. The puppet masquerade is timely, open to invention, to change and modification. Every generation strives to respond to its own contemporary issues and concerns. These performances remain important public artistic contexts for the produc-tion of knowledge and meaning in many Segou communities today.[4] It seems imperative, then, to turn to the local definition of youth association masquerade theatre as the frame-work within which to examine and interpret these performances.

Local Definitions of Youth Association Masquerade Theatre

Throughout Segou people define the youth association puppet masquerade theatre as a nyènajè, an entertainment or amusement that is part of the larger category of tulon, play. Nyènajè as a particular subset of play implies both sociability and group participation (Grosz-Ngate 1986, 127–128). It includes formal events such as youth association puppet masquerades, dance events, Kotèba theatre, and performances by itinerant musicians and singers. However, it also includes the daily informal gatherings among small groups of people to tell stories and to exchange news and gossip.

The definition of the puppet theatre as entertainment establishes a metacommunicative frame for the theatre that instructs the participants to interpret the messages contained within these events as play (Bateson 1972, 184). Play is a reflexive activity, and, as most everyone would agree, what is communicated through play, while defined as an amusement, can be quite serious indeed. In the youth theatre, actors use masquerade, dance, music, and song to comment upon moral values, the conditions of existence, and the ambiguity and indeterminacies that arise in social relationships in the everyday world of experience. While the sentiments and flavor of the theatrical experience may extend into people's daily lives following the event, the theatre, unlike marriage and initiation rituals, does not permanently effect a transformation in the status and social identity of its participants (Handleman 1977; Brink 1980).

People's definitions of youth association masquerades and men's initiation associations' masquerades do involve discussions of the relative potency and instrumentality of these different events and their artistic forms. It was in the comparisons that people drew between the youth association and men's associations that they most clearly articulated their definition of the youth theatre as play. In Segou, people regularly distinguish between youth association masquerades and the performances of certain men's association masquerades, such as Kòmò, Kònò, and Nama. They classify the former as an entertainment and amusement, and the latter as a rite that revolves around the use and manipulation of *boli*, a power object.[5] Power objects refer to a whole range of items, including masks, sculptures, flutes, whisks, amulets, etc. that are infused with potent *dalilu*. McNaughton defines these daliluw as

> concise, goal-oriented clusters of information and instruction, recipes for the successful completion of an endless array of activities. Simultaneously they are the power behind human acts, the right to perform them and their cause. (McNaughton 1988, 42–43)

While some power objects may be readily seen by the public, McNaughton emphasizes that both a boli and the daliluw that activate it are defined as secrets. An object constituted as a boli is always considered powerful and dangerous. In general, people shied away from any public discussion of these power objects. People considered such discussions to be inappropriate and potentially dangerous for the participants (McNaughton 1988, 59).[6] Only the person(s) who owns the specific dalilu that renders a power object potent can control it.

In contrast to power objects, youth association masks and puppets are not infused with daliluw, nor do they carry the same prohibitions and precautions regarding their handling and use. While dancers, singers, or drummers may own an individual dalilu to enhance their performances in the youth theatre, people never classified a youth theatre mask or puppet as a boli. People define any youth association mask or puppet as a *tulonko fèn*, a plaything. They always spoke of these performances as entertainments. Interested parties were usually not reluctant to join in casual discussions of sculpture or other expressive forms used in these events. They did not hesitate to discuss the drama's history or changes in the repertoire or in theatrical practices.

In his research on Kotèba drama in the Beledougou region, Brink described the contrasts that people regularly drew between performances involving power objects and those they defined as play and amusement.

Teatri is also said to be *nyenanje* which is open to the public (*jama*), in contrast to private performance (*nyene-fe* or *nyan-fe*, "before the fetish"). Private performance is conducted to honor a fetish and to recognize the assembled body of initiates who know or are learning its secrets and who fall under its protective cloak of spiritual powers. It occurs in the bush, usually in sacred areas specified by the cult societies, and is attended by persons who are formally initiated. Public performance, on the other hand, takes place in public areas, normally in the village on the public square (*fere*), crossroads, or in the street before the compound of the family sponsoring or being honored by the performance. Anyone may attend, regardless of personal circumstance, age, ethnic or religious persuasion. (Brink 1980, 95)

Like their Beledougou neighbors, people in Segou also invoke nearly the same set of oppositions—private/public, restricted/open attendance, bush/village, power object/plaything—to characterize what they understand to be the critical differences between Kòmò, Kònò, and Nama masquerades and those used by the youth association. People emphatically stated that these men's associations' performances and the youth theatre are unrelated and have historically formed two separate categories of performance events in their communities. They consider any men's association's masquerade performance involving the use of a boli to be a powerful and serious affair.

Kòmò, Kònò, and Nama masquerades are intrinsically different from the performances of the youth association masquerade theatre. While young men own and produce puppet masquerade theatre, elder men control the ceremonies and performances that utilize power objects. Attendance at ceremonies involving a boli is generally restricted to the initiated, while participation in puppet theatre is open to every member of the community. Men, women, and children living in the village and strangers from outside the community can and do regularly attend the puppet theatre. Many villages today even announce the date of their puppet masquerades on Radio Mali to maximize attendance at these events. People also said that today, as well as in the past, both the nyene [nyan] fe and the nyènajè performances have existed and sometimes still exist parallel to one another in a single community. Even in those villages where men's initiation associations' masquerade performances have not been held for some time, people still invoke the conceptual opposition between the two categories of performances to define the contemporary youth puppet theatre as play in these communities.

What has caused some confusion in the literature on Malian masquerades is the fact that a boli sometimes appears within larger events defined as entertainments. As McNaughton noted, not every power object is hidden from public view. I found that it was not unheard of for a local boli's performance to be inserted into the larger youth association masquerade event. When a power object did appear during the annual youth association festival, its performance was carefully constructed and orchestrated. In the instances that were recounted to me, it was the carefully managed physical separation between the power object and the audience that distinguished this type of performance from the performances of the youth association masquerades. For example, in the Bamana quarter of Kirango people said that until quite recently there existed a power masquerade known as Manyan which was owned by a group of elders in the quarter.[7] The elders brought out Manyan only once every seven years, but it always appeared during the youth association festival. Its performance was strictly managed by the elders and not by the members of the youth association. When discussing Manyan, people repeatedly made the point that both this power object and its performance were qualitatively different from the youth association masquerades. The instrumentality associated with Manyan was encapsulated in the belief that it had the capacity to kill. Everyone said that any unauthorized contact between the masquerade and a person not initiated into its secrets was extremely dangerous. Thus, the elders maintained a clear and careful separation between the masquerade and the uninitiated audience. This shift in the performance frame between sequences defined as play and the performance of Manyan defined as powerful seemed to cause little confusion for the participants.

Performance etiquette clearly precludes women and children from handling the youth association masks and puppets in public or assisting in their preparation. Yet people did not consider these sculptures to be inherently dangerous. Unlike their discussions of Manyan and other power objects, they expressed no anxiety about these puppets or masks inadvertently coming into contact with ordinary people. That the definition of youth association masks and puppets as playthings was widely shared was borne out on one occasion in the household where I lived. During a discussion of the theatre with several boys about the age of seven or eight, one boy dashed into a storage shed and proudly brought out a youth association rod puppet. After his initial enthusiasm, I realized that he was becoming increasingly nervous. Finally he asked me not to tell the older men in the family that he had shown me the roan antelope puppet head. His trepidation stemmed not from the fact that he thought the puppet was a boli—even he would not have been so foolhardy—but from the fact that he was not yet a member of the youth association. He knew that he faced certain castigation from his father for having taken such liberty with youth association property.

While the inclusion of a power masquerade within the larger youth association event was not commonplace, it was not unique to Kirango. In several other farming and fishing communities in this area, people indicated that they too occasionally performed power masquerades within their annual youth puppet theatre.[8] However, it is essential to be aware that a particular object or mask which is a boli in one village is not necessarily a power object in another community. No mask or masquerade is inherently powerful; it must be constituted as a boli through the use of a specific set of daliluw. In the case of the Manyan masquerade, and of another power masquerade which appeared as a bird puppet in a nearby village, I found that identical masks and masquerades, called by identical names, were being used in youth theatre in other neighboring villages. In these other villages neither Manyan nor the bird puppet was a power object. They had always been considered tulonko fènw, playthings, and part of the repertoire of the youth association masquerades. Whether a sculpture or masquerade is a power object or a plaything requires knowing who owns and controls the masquerade, as well as discovering its particular performance history within specific communities.

Segou Puppet Theatre—The Late Nineteenth Century to the Present

Segou's puppet masquerade theatre has a long and dynamic history in Mali, and performances like those in Kirango are still widespread in the late twentieth century. The history of this theatre extends in time and space from the precolonial era to the present and from within the Segou region to communities in adjacent regions in Mali and beyond. Within Segou, people's sense of the masquerade's unique identity is built upon their perceptions of its origins in their region, its close identification with the local ka-malen ton, its pan-ethnic endorsement, and its incorporation of an extensive and varied repertoire of expressive forms. Any discussion of the contemporary theatre must take into account the masquerade's history because today's performances are always played against the background of the theatre's distant and recent past.

The complexity of the puppet masquerade's history over the last century is clearly reflected in the three local terms, *Sogo bò, Do bò,* and *Cèko,* currently used for the theatre in the Segou region. The name that any group or village gives to the theatre can signal its investment in a particular group identity. It can mark the history of local relationships among villages, or it can indicate a community's particular location within the region.

Boso and Sòmonò fishing groups in the region, who today all speak Bamana, gen-erally use the Bamana term Do bò, the secret comes forth or is revealed, for their theatre. Many of these fishermen explained that the term *do* is a contraction of the Bamana word *gundo,* secret. In puppet theatre, troupes do surround the preparations of the masquer-ades with a certain secrecy. In several fishing villages along the Niger River, troupes regularly prepared their masquerades outside the village and only brought them into the community on the day of the performance.[9] The construction of particular masquerades and the operation of the mechanisms that are used to articulate the puppets are the se-crets of the theatre. People never described this secrecy as of the same order or as having the same instrumentality and potency as that associated with a boli.[10]

In the Bamana quarter of Kirango and among most farmers living inland from the rivers, people use the Bamana term Sogo bò, the animal comes forth or is revealed, for the youth association masquerade theatre. In Kirango the farmers unequivocally state that their ancestors borrowed the theatre from the fishermen. Their choice of the term Sogo bò, rather than Do bò, reflects one of several ways that these farmers have remade the theatre over into their own ethnic performance tradition.

Most farming communities in the eastern portion of the region use the term Cèko for the youth association masquerades. Since Independence in 1960 a few troupes employ an alternative term, *Sogo nyènajè,* the animal masquerade entertainment.[11] Cèko, which literally translates as the affairs of men, has radically different meanings in eastern and western communities within Segou. In the east Cèko is the proper name for the youth as-sociation puppet masquerade. Cèko as a proper name for youth association masquerades distinguishes these performances, whose masquerades are owned by the young men, from activities and associations owned and controlled by women. In the western portion of the region, the term cèko, however, is reserved solely for discussions of men's initiation as-sociations, such as Kòmò, Kònò, and the like, and conversely it is never used as a term for the youth association puppet theatre. In these western Segou communities, youth as-sociation activities including puppet masquerades are not cèko, affairs of men, but are tonko, affairs of the kamalen ton. In the western zone youth theatre is always called Do bò or Sogo bò and neither fishermen nor farmers ever refer to the youth masquerade the-atre as Cèko. In these western communities when people invoke the terms cèko and tonko to discuss masquerade ownership, they are foregrounding categories of relative age (elders and youth). In eastern communities gender distinctions (men and women) rather than categories of relative age are implied in explanations about the meaning of the term Cèko and its application to the youth association masquerade theatre.

Most people in the region seem to agree about a general outline for the history of the theatre. This masquerade had its origins with the fishermen (and in some quarters specifically with the Boso fishermen). It spread first through fishermen's riverain networks within Segou and beyond. Later it was adopted by farmers in and around Shianro and by the late nineteenth century it was embraced by farming communities in western Segou. Throughout this century many farming and fishing villages have adopted the theatre. Today it continues to take hold in communities within and outside of the Segou region. The flow of ideas and objects seemed to have been initially between fishing villages and then between fishing and farming communities and between various farming communities from east to west. Already in the first decades of this century new sculptural forms and dramatic innovations were passing among all groups and in every direction. However, this masquerade theatre was never unilaterally adopted by every group or community in the Segou region. Villages even in the same locale did not always embrace the theatre at the same time.

In many villages the masquerade theatre is said to date to the precolonial era. We know from Soleillet's journal that indeed it was already well established along the Niger River by the 1870s. Yet, in discussions with fishing communities on the Niger, only a few Boso villages retain any specific myth of origin for the theatre. Farmers who lived in close proximity to these fishermen, and farmers in the eastern area of Shianro, where there were once substantial communities of fishermen, readily acknowledge that the fishermen were the first practitioners of the theatre. These farmers claim no knowledge of the theatre's origins. Other farming communities who have no close historical ties to fishing groups remember only that they borrowed the theatre from other farmers during the early colonial period.

Among those Segou communities who embraced the theatre during the precolonial era, people use quite different temporal criteria for establishing when they first began to play the masquerades. Some Boso communities date the drama's emergence to a mythical ancestral past. Some communities tie it to specific precolonial states, whether to Mali or Segou. Several communities with no collective investment in state histories use the period before their conversion to Islam as the benchmark for their adoption of the theatre. Others simply invoke a generational template when discussing its rise in their communities.

I recorded one Boso origin myth for the theatre in 1979 from Budagari Coulibaly, a Boso singer [Figure 2.2]. According to his account it was the culture hero Toboji Centa who first introduced the masquerade to the fishermen. Sometime in the distant past the *wòkulòw*, bush spirits, took Toboji Centa into their domain and taught him how to play the puppet masquerade. When he returned to his village of Gomitogo on the Niger River in the province of Shianro, he taught his community how to perform these masquerades (Budagari Coulibaly, Banankoro, 1980). This account of the origins of the masquerade performance with the bush spirits is consistent with many origin myths for other artistic forms in Mali. In Brink's research on Kotèba theatre among Bamana communities in the Beledougou region, for example, people also stated that the bush spirits had taught the theatre to the human progenitor of Kotèba (Brink 1981).

The Toboji Centa myth, however, has a limited distribution within the Segou region. People in fishing communities along the Niger River from just south of Segou north to Mopti, where Budagari Coulibaly regularly performed, knew the myth. However, most of the farmers, as well as many communities of Sòmonò fishermen, recalled only that fishermen were the original owners of the masquerade theatre. According to Budagari Coulibaly and other Boso elders, the masquerade theatre's distribution was historically limited to those Boso communities located south of Dia along the Niger and Bani rivers. These men claimed that puppetry was never played by Jibala Boso or Bosofin, fishermen living along the Niger and its tributaries from Mopti north to Lake Debo.[12]

Cheik Omar Mara collected a different tradition of origin for the theatre from Sòmonò fishermen living around Segou city. This tradition links the introduction of puppetry to the rise of the Segou state in the eighteenth century.

2.2. The Boso singer Budagari Coulibaly from Banankoro, Mali. 1980. *Photograph by Lynn Forsdale.*

These Sòmonò drew a direct relationship between the origin of the puppet masquerade and the formation of the precolonial Segou state. As Mara notes:

> It was explained to us that the performance of the Bozo [Boso] bird in Segou dates from the origins of the great 17th century Bamana empire [18th century], when Biton Coulibaly, founder of the empire, agreed to let the Bozo live in peace within his kingdom. In return for this assurance, the Bozo gave the king control over river traffic. The performance of the mask before the rulers of Segou thus recapitulates this agreement in which the Bozo recognize the political autonomy of the Bamana in the Segou region. (Arnoldi 1977 [10])[13]

Throughout the colonial period communities regularly performed masquerades during official celebrations for French holidays such as Bastille Day (Leiris 1934, 50). The Segou Sòmonò tradition, which relates the story of their ancestors' playing the masquerades before the ruler of Segou, suggests that this common colonial practice may well have had its roots in the precolonial period.

While Segou city Sòmonò link the origin of the masquerade theatre to the precolonial Segou state, most other fishermen who live along the Niger River make no such claims. However, what these fishermen do share with the Segou city Sòmonò are the historical memories of the longstanding economic and political domination of fishermen by the precolonial Segou state. The historical condition of fishermen is well documented, not only in their own accounts but in Segou state epics, as well as in a variety of local village histories. One version of the history of Segou, which was published by Monteil in 1924, chronicles how Da Monzon Diarra (1808–1827) resettled fishermen along the Niger to serve the interests of the state (Monteil 1976 [1924]).[14] In Banankoro local Boso histories claim that fishermen were forced to resettle into Segou from the area around Dia, an area north of Segou, by order of the precolonial Segou state. The recounting of the historical power relations between fishermen and the Segou state encoded in the Sòmonò tradition that links puppetry to the state is relevant for understanding contemporary political relations between Bamana farmers and Sòmonò and Boso fishermen in most communities along the Niger River today. In these communities farmers, not fishermen, hold the office of village chief.

Most everyone agrees that the theatre predated the introduction of Islam into Segou. Fixing a date for the origins of the theatre in terms of Islamic conversion, however, is nearly impossible. There is no one date for the adoption of Islam in Segou. Although there are references to Islamic advisors in the courts of the precolonial states of Mali and Segou, the widespread acceptance of Islam outside of major commercial towns or political centers has been an ongoing process spanning centuries and is by no means complete in the Segou region even today. Maraka farmers and Sòmonò and Boso fishermen claim to be early adherents to Islam, and many family genealogies among these ethnic groups include imams among their ancestors. However, away from administrative and commercial centers, the acceptance of Islam among Bamana farmers seems to have gained momentum in the late nineteenth century with conversions continuing into the present. Many farming communities in the Shianro area, for example, date their conversion to Islam to the period of El Hadj Oumar Tall's conquest of Segou in the second half of the nineteenth century. Yet, as late as 1940, French colonial statistics on religious affiliation in the Segou region listed forty-four percent of the region's inhabitants as "animists."[15]

What does emerge from these different accounts is a sense that at least some farming communities in Shianro must have adopted the theatre from their fishing neighbors by the mid to late nineteenth century. Throughout Segou, people call the Shianro area the *sogo jamani*, the country of the masquerades. They credit many early developments in the theatre's sculptural repertoire to the *cikènumuw*, blacksmiths attached to farming communities, in this area.

In several villages in Shianro, people used neither state histories nor the conversion to Islam to date their acceptance of the theatre. Rather they invoked a generational template when discussing the history of their theatre. Elders in several villages stated emphatically that the generation that preceded their grandfathers' was the first to adopt the masquerades. A conventional genealogical reckoning would place the adoption of the theatre in these communities at sometime in the latter half of the nineteenth century or later. However, these elders' statements might also be intended to indicate some arbitrary point in the ancestral past, thereby emphasizing that the theatre is now an important and authentic part of their cultural patrimony.

Those Bamana communities living in the core area of the precolonial Segou state, who like the Bamana of Kirango claim descent from the Diarra ruling dynasty, are by their own accounts latecomers to the puppet theatre. Kirango elders in the Bamana quarter said that it was only after the French defeat of Ahamadou Tall in 1890 that they began to play these masquerades as a village entertainment. They do acknowledge, however, that before this period fishermen in Kirango were already performing the masquerades.

During the first decades of this century, the theatre even spread to farming communities outside the Segou region, although Sòmonò fishermen living on the Niger River south of Segou were by their own accounts already performing these masquerades before French occupation (Arnoldi 1989). In general, the theatre's adoption by communities outside Segou seems to have remained concentrated in villages located along the Niger River and its tributaries. Oral histories of this puppetry tradition in the Guinea highlands relate it back to the Segou region in Mali (el Dabh 1979, 56).

The distribution of the theatre within the region over the past century reads as a complex network that highlights various intervillage relationships in and through time. I found that frequently clusters of communities in close physical proximity to one another and related through networks of *balima siraw*, kin roads, or *furu siraw*, marriage roads, adopted the masquerade during the same historical time period. In some of these villages, troupes said that they often lent each other masks and puppets for these performances. It is also true that villages close to one another, but who are involved in different social networks, adopted the theatre earlier or later than their neighbors or never demonstrated any interest at all in performing it.[16]

The development of the youth masquerade throughout the last century involved the active participation of three principal groups: blacksmiths, young men, and women. Blacksmiths, as professional sculptors, have supplied local theatres with the carved wooden masks and rod puppets that are the hallmark of the contemporary theatre. While smiths carve the theatre's puppets and masks, young men in the youth association are the owners of these masquerades and are the theatre's active promoters, puppeteers, and musicians. Women, who are the singers for the theatre, are equally important in the theatre because they are the masquerades' voices. Each of these three groups has contributed in distinctive ways to the flow of ideas and expressive forms within the region during this century.

Blacksmiths and the Development of the Youth Masquerade Theatre

For centuries Segou blacksmiths have engaged in the production of a wide range of diverse goods. They regularly made agricultural tools and household wares in iron and wood and guns for hunting and warfare. Some blacksmiths also carved sculptures and masks for use in various ritual contexts. By at least the late nineteenth century in the Shianro area, some smiths began producing wooden puppets and masks for the youth association theatre. Individual blacksmiths' biographies provide one fruitful avenue for exploring regional professional networks that contributed to the development and dissemination of the theatre in this century.

While the Boso are considered to have inaugurated the theatre, people always credit the Shianro blacksmiths with creating the theatre's first carved wooden masks and puppets. In Shianro people cited several villages which were historically important centers for the production and development of these sculptures. Blacksmiths from these centers were generally itinerant and regularly traveled to other villages to complete their commissions. Many farming villages who today claim to have adopted the theatre in the precolonial era either had resident blacksmith families or had longstanding links with smiths from these Shianro centers.

In interviews, elder Shianro smiths often said that the original Boso masquerades were grass constructions. They emphasized that it was their grandfathers who had carved the first puppets and masks in wood for the theatre. Most of the elder men I interviewed in Shianro would have been young men in the mid 1920s. While they could not recall the specifics of their fathers' generations' production, they were quite willing to cite villages for which they themselves had personally carved puppets. They also regularly identified the specific masks they had carved for particular communities. In addition it was clear from their accounts that it was not unusual for them to have accepted commissions for masks and puppets from local fishing communities.

By the late nineteenth century Shianro smiths were already carving wooden puppets and masks for their local theatres. However, it seems that at that time most fishermen in the western zones still used grass and cloth masquerades for their performances. In those farming communities like Kirango, who adopted the theatre from local fishing communities at the turn of the century, the first characters that were performed were grass and cloth masquerades. The introduction of carved wooden masks and puppets into the theatrical repertoire did not occur much before the end of the first decade of this century. In Kirango and elsewhere, this introduction is often credited to a Shianro smith. Shianro smiths played a critical role as catalysts in the development of the masquerade's material repertoire throughout the Segou region. They are occasionally still remembered by name in local oral histories of village theatre. However, by the 1920s blacksmiths in western Segou villages who had traveled and worked in Shianro, or who copied the early models introduced into the area by Shianro smiths, soon took over much of the local production of theatrical sculptures for both farming and fishing villages. In a few western farming villages, people remembered a non-blacksmith carving an occasional mask, but this was clearly exceptional and never became a common practice. Throughout Segou, wood carving is still generally considered the exclusive domain of smiths.

Many smiths I interviewed in the Segou region said that they had carved a few masks or puppet heads for their local theatre, especially when they were members of the youth association. Yet the majority of smiths described their primary vocation as providing the range of necessary agricultural and domestic items that supported life in these farming communities. Only a few smiths considered carving theatrical puppets and masks to be central to their life's work. This smaller group of smiths gained a certain local and regional celebrity as sculptors and their masks and puppets were sought after by many villages. For example, Siriman Fane of Koke, who died in the mid 1980s, was a celebrated puppet sculptor in the area around Kirango [Figure 2.3]. According to his own account, which I recorded between 1978 and 1980, he began carving theatrical sculpture around 1925 during his apprenticeship with a Shianro smith. He listed the first village for which he carved a puppet as Siela in the Shianro area.[17] Siriman recalled many villages within and outside the Segou region, from Siela in the east to Kirango

2.3. The blacksmith sculptor Siriman Fane (l) and his son Adama (r). 1980. *Photograph by Lynn Forsdale.*

in the west and to Koulikoro south of Segou in the Bamako region, where he had carved masks and puppets for the youth theatre during his long and prodigious career. Like most smiths he began his career by making the full range of agricultural tools. As his celebrity as a sculptor grew, he devoted more of his creative energies to the carving of puppets and masks for youth theatre. During much of his career he was semi-itinerant and would travel to various villages to carry out requested commissions for sculptures and other items. He also noted that during the colonial period he had accepted commissions from Europeans, including several for Ciwara antelope crest masks.

Siriman sculpted many masks and puppets still extant in his own quarter's theatre, and he regularly carved for neighboring villages. Many of his puppets and masks dating from the late 1950s and early 1960s are still being performed in these villages. In one of these villages, Siriman's eldest sister married into a local blacksmith family and Siriman's own second wife came from this village. These marriage paths between the two blacksmith families established a strong link between the two villages. Later in the 1960s this link greatly facilitated the youth association's negotiations for Siriman's artistic services. In Kirango, Siriman's sister married into the Kumare family. His sister's son, Manyan Kumare, served as Siriman's apprentice when Siriman worked in Kirango in 1959 and 1960. In addition to the link between the blacksmith families in Koke and Kirango, several *hòròn*, freeman, lineages in these two communities claim a common descent from Ngolo Diarra, the founder of the Diarra dynasty, who ruled Segou from 1766 to 1787 (Konare and Konare 1983, 231). According to Siriman's family traditions, Siriman's own father had fashioned guns for the Diarra rulers of the precolonial Segou state. His family has enjoyed a longstanding patron-client relationship with the Diarra and their descendants in Segou.

Siriman said that when he carved puppets for his own quarter's theatre he did so in exchange for young men's labor in his fields. When he traveled to other villages, payment generally included his board and additional gifts of grain or other suitable gifts. Compensation for commissions by Europeans were regularly negotiated as cash payments. In 1980, when I spoke with him, he was probably in his mid to late seventies, but he was still relatively vigorous and still accepted commissions. One of my visits to see him in 1980 coincided with a delegation who had traveled to Koke to negotiate for a set of his theatrical sculptures. At that time his son Adama was working with him on these commissions. Since Siriman's death, his son has taken over the production of puppet sculpture for this quarter in Koke.

Siriman was a well-known sculptor and many people in this general area readily recognized his carving style. In 1980 people associated him with a specific repertoire of characters. He developed some of these characters in the 1950s and he created another group a decade later. His sculptures from this period included, among others, Mali Kònò, a rod puppet representing a large fishing bird, Sigi, a rod puppet of a buffalo, Yayoroba, a large sculpture representing a young woman, and various small rod and string puppets. These small puppets included farmers, women pounding millet, fishermen in their boats, and colonial officers, among others [Figure Pref.3]. In 1968 Siriman developed a set of rod and string puppets that he identified as President Moussa Traore and his honor guard [Figure 2.4].[18]

Several of Siriman's elder brother's sons, including Moussa, Saliya, and Bafing, his own son, Adama, and his sister's son, Manyan Kumare, initially carved under his tutelage.[19] Moussa, Manyan, and Bafing said that they also carved for local residents and occasionally made a piece for colonial officials.[20] Bafing Kane (Fane), the son of Siriman's eldest brother, is the most prodigious carver of his generation [Figure 2.5]. Now in his mid to late sixties, he remains active today. As a young man he was apprenticed to Siriman and he carves in a style that is almost identical to Siriman's.

As the senior carver in the lineage, Siriman was always credited with any sculptural innovations even though the actual inspiration for a character or the actual carving of a piece may have been done by one of the junior black-smiths in the family. In an interview in 1989, Moussa recounted that although all of the surrounding villages credit the invention of the puppet character Yayoroba to Siriman, it was actually Moussa who carved the first Yayoroba for Koke in the 1950s. He also suggested that Saliya and Bafing had invented various new characters and carved many pieces that are credited to Siriman today. The attribution of these sculptures to Siriman follows the accepted

2.5. The blacksmith sculptor Bafing Kane at his atelier. 1987. Segou region. *Photograph by Mary Jo Arnoldi.*

practice of attributing pieces to the owner of the forge. As the senior carver, Siriman was the recognized *tigi*, owner, of this atelier.

In discussions with Bafing in 1987 he recalled a number of blacksmiths outside his immediate family who were also apprenticed to Siriman during Bafing's own youth. Of the group he named, he said that he was the only one currently carving for the theatre. Bafing's career mirrors that of Siriman's and of many other blacksmiths in this region. As a young smith, Bafing frequently traveled to other villages. He often took up temporary residence in these communities, sometimes for several years, to complete commissions for agricultural tools, household items, and occasionally theatrical sculptures. When I talked with him in 1987 he said that he had carved theatrical sculptures for many of the same villages for which Siriman had once carved. Today, Bafing has settled permanently in a small village southeast of Koke. As in Siriman's later career, Bafing now forgoes traveling and he completes commissions for masks and puppets at his own atelier. He has no sons, but his daughter's son, who is about ten years old, lives with him. His grandson has already carved several small children's masks under Bafing's watchful eye [Figure 2.6].

2.6. Bafing Kane's grandson holding a children's mask he had carved. 1987. Segou region. *Photograph by Mary Jo Arnoldi.*

In May 1987 I accompanied Bafing to a neighboring village where one of his puppets was being inaugurated in the annual theatre. During our conversations that evening he recalled that Siriman had carved many masks and puppets that were once used in this village. When these pieces eventually fell into disrepair, the village commissioned Bafing to replace them. He later created a number of new characters for this village's repertoire. He pointed out to me the only sculpture by Siriman that was still being played that evening. It was a small rod and string puppet representing a mother breast-feeding her baby. It appeared with a group of small rod puppets out of the back of one of the larger masquerade constructions.

When Bafing's new puppet arrived on the dance arena, the lead singer began to sing his praises. Bafing jumped up and entered the ring and danced exuberantly alongside the masquerade. The public recognition of Bafing's artistry and the singing of his praises during the performance were not unique to either Bafing or to this performance. In many villages theatrical sculptures remain linked to their smith-creators, living or dead, through praise lines embedded in the masquerade songs. The public recognition of

2.7. The blacksmith sculptor Numu Jon Diarra with his version of Dajè, the Roan Antelope. 1980. Nienou, Mali. *Photograph by Lynn Forsdale.*

named sculptors during these performances is further evidence for refuting, at least for Mali, the still popular Western assumption that African artists remain anonymous within their own societies.

Another blacksmith, Numu Jon Diarra of Nienou in Shianro, is equally well-known throughout this area as an exceptional carver [Figure 2.7]. Nienou is one of several Shianro villages regularly identified as an early center for the production of theatrical sculpture. Interviews with Numu Jon and other elder blacksmiths in Nienou in 1980 and in 1987 established a list of seven blacksmiths from two of Nienou's residential quarters who had regularly carved Cèko masks and puppets since the late nineteenth century. According to these accounts, Marou Diarra was the first blacksmith from Nienou to carve for the youth association theatre. They estimated that Marou Diarra had died sometime in the late nineteenth century. The first Cèko puppet that they credited to him was the character Mèrèn.[21]

Numu Jon Diarra was born in 1935 and according to his own account he has been carving Cèko puppets and masks for well over thirty years. During our conversations he named over thirty villages besides Nienou for whom he has carved puppets. He also listed approximately ninety additional communities in the Shianro area and in adjacent provinces who now play or once performed the Cèko, but for whom he never carved masks or puppets. According to Numu Jon's own accounting then, he has carved for only thirty-five percent of the villages who play the theatre in this larger area. His statements corroborate others I recorded and they underscore the fact that a significant number of smiths from many different villages in the Shianro area were active in the production of theatrical sculpture throughout this past century. That Shianro is known as the sogo jamani, the country of the masquerades, is clearly no exaggeration. Among other smiths who are renowned in this area for their carving are those from Tiebala, Ngarababougou, Berta, and Nienemou.[22]

Segou blacksmiths who worked outside the region in various colonial services also played a part in the spread of the theatre southward into the present-day Bamako region. These smiths were often responsible for introducing theatrical sculptures into local communities. One smith, Bina Fatouma Coumare, migrated from Shianro to Koulikoro in 1914 to work for the colonial river navigation service. According to his son, who currently resides in Koulikoro, Bina Fatouma learned to carve puppets as a young blacksmith in the village of Ngarababougou.[23] While living in Koulikoro he introduced the theatre into the farming community of Kolebugu and regularly provided its youth association with carved masks and puppets. His son said that his father had also carved masks and puppets for the Sòmonò Do bò theatre in Koulikoro. Today, a number of smiths in Koulikoro and in surrounding villages carve masks and puppets for troupes in this area.

Although most of the literature on smiths' artistic production in this region implies that carving is a highly secret activity, I did not find this to be the case with Bafing, Siriman or most other sculptors engaged in the production of theatrical masks and puppets.[24] For example, during the 1987 dry season, I arrived at Bafing's home on several occasions without having previously announced my intention to visit. I found him engaged in carving at his open-air atelier located outside his compound next to a public path. There were always a number of men, who were not smiths, lounging about, chatting about village affairs and passing the time. Women often passed by his atelier on various errands. Most stopped to greet the assembled men, chatted and joked for a few moments, and then continued on their way. There seemed to be no attempt by women to avoid passing the atelier as they moved through the village, nor did Bafing demonstrate any discomfort at their or my presence. All the time, Bafing continued working and he did not seem at all concerned to hide his activities.

In Siriman's case, even though his atelier was inside his compound, once a person was inside the family courtyard Siriman's work area was not especially hidden from public view. Numu Jon Diarra's atelier is located inside his household compound directly across the courtyard from the family's living quarters and is clearly visible to any visitor. In discussing his art, Numu Jon once told me that he did not consider the actual carving of the Cèko sculpture to be secret. Rather, he jealously guarded the secrets of the different mechanisms that he had devised to animate certain puppets. These were the secrets of the Cèko. This was borne out graphically when in 1987 he agreed to let me photograph a group of his puppets which were then stored in his compound. In preparing the scene, he first set up a textile screen in front of a wall. He then carefully arranged the rod and string puppets behind this screen to mask their operating mechanisms.[25]

Clearly not all Nienou's puppet sculptures were so jealously guarded. In 1980 when I photographed a group of Numu Jon's and Youssouf Diarra's puppets, only two of Youssouf's puppets were set up behind a cloth screen. This group included a puppet of a colonial officer who takes up a real box of matches and lights and smokes a real cigarette, and a puppet representing a colonial soldier on horseback [Figure 2.8]. All of the large rod puppet heads that were operated by a simple rod or string mechanism were casually propped up against a wall and there were no restrictions against my photographing any of these uncostumed sculptures.

Young Men as Catalysts in Developing the Theatre

Young men who are members of the youth association are the second important group of catalysts in the development of the theatre. During the dry season, from about January to May, young unmarried men regularly travel along the various kin roads, taking up temporary residence in villages where they have relatives. These young men travel for adventure, to visit and strengthen ties with age-mates and relatives, to celebrate marriages,

2.8. The blacksmith sculptor Youssouf Diarra standing in front of his version of the Tubabu, the European. 1980. Nienou, Mali. *Photograph by Lynn Forsdale.*

and to meet young women. Hunters also travel extensively throughout the region during the dry season. They often lodge with fellow hunters, who as members of the hunter's association classify themselves metaphorically as kin. Throughout the colonial period, military conscription and labor recruitment for public projects, along with short-term migrations to other labor markets in Mali and beyond, contributed to a steady flow of young men to other areas. These migrations provided alternative avenues to established kin and marriage paths for the dissemination of theatrical ideas and forms. Even today, it is primarily through the agency of young men that interest in the drama continues to grow within the region and elsewhere.

Many innovations in a community's masquerade repertoire were attributed to an individual young man or to a group of young men in the same age-set. Although blacksmiths often talked about the specific characters they had invented for the theatre, they also said that occasionally they were asked to carve a new puppet or mask based on an idea proposed by a young man or group of young men. In Nienou, Youssouf Diarra, one of the elder blacksmiths, recalled several occasions in his career when he had been approached by young men with ideas for new masquerade characters. Youssouf explained that if he did not have a clear idea of what the young men actually wanted he would often question them to get clarification. Sometimes he made quick preliminary sketches in the sand until everyone could agree on what form the new mask or puppet should take.

A number of masquerades that are performed today are constructed only from cloth or grass skirting sewn over wooden armatures. These masquerades are formal descendants of the early fishermen's masquerades and are re-created anew for every performance. Young men in the troupe, not professional smiths, make these grass and cloth masquerades. Some of these masquerades, like the four grass masquerades which open the evening performance in the Bamana quarter of Kirango, have a long history in this quarter's theatre. Others enjoy a much shorter life span, some lasting for several decades while others endure for only one or two performance seasons. These grass and cloth masquerades can represent everything from bush animals and genies to contemporary objects such as automobiles and airplanes [Figures 2.9, 2.10, and 2.11]. When discussing the history of a theatrical repertoire, the youth association, rather than resident blacksmiths, generally provided a more complete list of masquerades that had been or are now played in their village. From their professional perspective, blacksmiths tended to dismiss the

2.9. A Bamana performance of Njona, the Wildcat. 1979. Segou region. *Photograph by Lynn Forsdale.*

ephemeral grass and cloth masquerades constructed by the young men, except for the earliest grass masquerades, as minor and unimportant.

Today, groups of young men still regularly attend their neighbors' performances, where they see new characters and bring back innovative ideas to be incorporated into their own village performances. They may "borrow" characters wholesale or modify another village's character by substituting a different sculpture, song, or drum rhythm for its performance in their own village. There is a certain amount of subterfuge and there can be an intense rivalry involved in this "borrowing." Some troupes openly stated that if they knew that representatives from a certain village would be in the audience they might choose not to perform one of their particularly spectacular masquerades. Even if they did perform the masquerade, they would instruct the dancer to shy away from the area where their rivals were seated, so the visitors could not get a good view of the character. Young men in Kirango and neighboring villages cited the names of various villages from which they "borrowed" particular characters. They also openly discussed what troupes in the area they judged to have the best examples of a particular masquerade.

Women's Roles in the Masquerade

Women in their roles as singers are the third important partner in the theatrical enterprise. Talented women singers will sometimes create songs for new puppet characters that are invented for theatre. Lead singers also regularly incorporate popular songs from a variety of other performance contexts into youth association theatre. They either link these

2.10. A Bamana performance of a genie masquerade. 1979. Segou region, Mali. *Photograph by Lynn Forsdale.*

songs to particular masquerades or insert them into the musical interludes between individual masquerade displays. Young women who have grown up participating in their own village's theatre and marry outside their natal village carry their knowledge of a body of songs and theatrical characters to their new homes. Many of these talented young women have become lead singers in their husbands' villages.

I found that the history of singers in the Kirango Bamana quarter was not kept as part of the youth association's official history of the theatre. These singers, however, were well remembered by women in the quarter. The first lead singer for the Kirango theatre recalled by name was Namaja Diakhite. She was born in Kirango and was probably singing by at least the mid to late 1930s. She was followed by Assista Coulibaly, who married into Kirango from a village around Yamina. Women remembered that Assista started performing as a young bride and that she continued singing for the masquerade performances until she was quite old. The next lead singer was Fatimata Boure, originally from a village near Dioro. Fatimata was later joined by Nanyan Coulibaly sometime in the early 1950s. Nanyan was born in Temou and married into the Bamana quarter in Kirango. Nanya was later joined by Mei Diarra, who was born in Kirango and married into a Kirango family [Figure 2.12]. Of the five singers remembered by local women, three married into the village from neighboring villages and two were born in the village and married men from this village. That over half of the quarter's lead singers married into the village from elsewhere underscores the role that women have traditionally played in the transmission of theatrical songs from one community to another in their movements along marriage roads.

The Electronic Media, Government Festivals, and the Dissemination of the Theatre

More recently, moving beyond the sphere of marriage paths, women singers from the region participate in ever widening networks of influence by performing on radio programs. Malian national radio airs a variety of programs featuring both professional bards and amateur performers from throughout the nation. Some

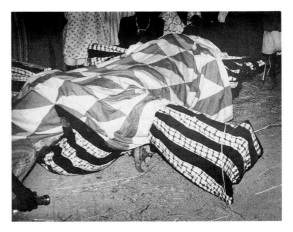

2.11. A Bamana performance of Avion, the Airplane. Its armature sits on wheels and attendants roll the masquerade around the arena. 1979. Segou region, Mali. *Photograph by Lynn Forsdale.*

2.12. Mei Diarra (l) and Nanyan Coulibaly (r), the lead singers for the Kirango Bamana troupe. 1987. Kirango, Mali. *Photograph by Mary Jo Arnoldi.*

of the women singers from Segou who have been featured on these programs have chosen to perform songs from the puppet masquerade theatre as part of their musical repertoire. These programs provide an important contemporary avenue for the dissemination of theatrical songs, both within the Segou region and nationally.

In several additional ways the national radio and more recently the national television have greatly contributed to people's growing awareness of the puppet theatre outside the Segou region. Segou troupes often announce their upcoming performances on Radio Mali. These announcements are meant to alert neighboring communities, and individuals from their own village who live and work outside the region, to the upcoming event, inviting visitors and encouraging former community members to return to the village for the theatre.

The national government's interest in the performing arts also played a significant role in rekindling many Segou communities' interest in the theatre. Puppet masquerades were performed in the regional and national arts festivals organized by the Ministry of Culture between 1962 and 1988. Their appearance in these festivals exposed the theatre to a diverse Malian audience.[26] As part of these events and as a by-product of the festivals, several celebrated puppet sculptors, including Bafing Kane and Numu Jon Diarra, were invited into the capital by the National Museum of Mali. The National Museum has systematically added documentary photographs of puppet masquerade performances to their photo archives. They have also videotaped various performances, including the 1979 performance in the Bamana quarter of Kirango. Within the last decade Malian and international filmmakers have made several documentary films and videos of village performances. In the last five years American art study tours have regularly attended puppet masquerade performances around Koulikoro.[27]

Locally in the last two decades cassette tape players have become increasingly available in rural communities and individuals frequently record performances and people listen to these tapes throughout the year. With the recent introduction of camcorders some video tapes taken by urban visitors to village performances are beginning to circulate informally in Bamako.[28] At the 1987 and 1992 performances that I attended in Kirango I noticed that there were several men from the community photographing the event, something which just a decade ago was rare indeed. The proliferation of cameras and electronic media to record the theatre and the celebrity bestowed on particular troupes or individual singers through their participation in regional and national festivals continue to stimulate interest in the drama in Mali and especially in those Segou communities whose investment in the theatre had waned during the last generation.

The Demise of Local Theatres

Throughout this century, at the same time that new communities were choosing to embrace the genre, other communities were abandoning the tradition. The decline in interest in the theatre in these latter communities is as much a part of the complex regional history of the theatre as is the tempo of its growth. Discussions in villages who formerly played the masquerade but who have since abandoned it elicited a variety of explanations for their decision. In a few communities people saw the theatre in potential conflict with their Islamic beliefs and practices. This explanation was given to me in several Boso and Sòmonò communities, who say they abandoned the theatre a generation ago. In other communities Islamic conversion was not given as the reason for the decline in the the-atre. People simply said that there was not enough interest among their young people in continuing it. While seasonal migrations of young men have a long history in this area and were often instrumental in the growth of the theatre, recent economic constraints fol-lowing a series of disastrous droughts beginning in the late 1970s have accelerated long-term migration of young men from rural communities to labor markets both within and outside Mali. Many young men are now staying away for longer periods of time and their absence has adversely affected many smaller communities' ability to stage the per-formances. In 1989 in the village where Bafing Kane now resides the youth association did not perform the theatre because too many young men were absent on labor migra-tion. This youth association had until quite recently a lively tradition of masquerade theatre. The older men in the village with whom I spoke expressed the sincere hope that by the 1988 rainy season enough young men would have returned to the village so that the theatre could be reprised. The regional history of the drama and its ebb and flow is encapsulated in the local histories of individual communities. It is through an examina-tion of the history of local village theatres that the range of competing impulses which have contributed to either the renaissance or the decline of puppet masquerade through-out this past century can be most fruitfully understood.

Kirango's Bamana Theatre: The 1890s through the 1980s

In Kirango there are three youth associations and all three of them performed the puppet masquerades between 1978 and 1980. The Bamana quarter performed their masquerade twice annually, once in early June and again in late October. The Boso quarter's perfor-mance took place in May, while the Sòmonò troupe performed in mid October. The Bamana quarter has been performing the puppet theatre for nearly a century and the fishing quarters in the village have played the masquerades even longer. In the late twentieth century the Kirango theatres enjoy a certain local, regional, and national repu-tation for their longevity and for the scale and artistic quality of their performances.

As in most communities in the Segou region, people in the Bamana quarter in Ki-rango have never considered the masquerade theatre to be a closed or finished form. Its history can best be described as a process that involved repeated transformations, ap-propriations, adjustments, and even dislocations in forms and theatrical practices through time. The theatre's vitality and relevance have always depended on each successive troupe's ability to exploit received forms and characters from the past while artfully em-bedding new forms and dramatic content into their performances. Performers cull a variety of sources to create innovative forms and content. They pull from their experi-ences in daily life. They appropriate ideas and expressive forms from neighbors' masquerade theatres and from a host of other performance traditions current in the region. Ideally each troupe hopes that its innovations will be favorably received and that their "new" forms and ideas will persist beyond their time to become part of the masquerade's historical legacy.

The quarter's oral traditions concerning the theatre are part of a larger discourse about the history of their community. The Bamana quarter clearly divides its past into two distinct periods and they locate the theatre in the second of these periods. Quarter historians said that though the ancestors of the Boso and Sòmonò in the village performed the puppet masquerades during the first period, their ancestors did not.

According to the Bamana, the first period which figures in their collective history might well be described from their perspective as Kirango's heroic age. It began with the rise of the Diarra dynasty in the eighteenth century and continued up through Segou's defeat by the forces of El Hadj Oumar Tall in the mid nineteenth century. In the Bamana quarter everyone agrees that during the Diarra dynasty (circa 1766 to 1861) the Bamana quarter's primary form of entertainment was not the Sogo bò, but was the *kèlèko nyènajè*, a warrior dance. Kirango was closely aligned with the Segou warrior state and was an important military and administrative center. According to oral traditions collected by Delafosse in the early colonial period, Ngolo Diarra placed one of his five sons in Kirango to administer and protect the canton (Delafosse 1972 [1912], 298). Quarter traditions recall that a significant number of military divisions, including both elite cavalry, *sofa*, and common foot soldiers, *jònba*, were garrisoned in the village. In 1843, the grandson of Ngolo Diarra, Kirango ben Diarra, assumed the position of *faama*, the head of the Segou state (Konare and Konare 1983, 231). People in the Bamana quarter identify themselves as Ngolosi, people of Ngolo Diarra.

Details of the period between Tall's defeat of Segou and the establishment of French forces in the region (1861–1890) did not figure prominently in the local history except to intimate that there were massive dislocations in the village following Segou's defeat. Elders in a few neighboring fishing villages in the area did recall that during this period Tall's administration attempted to repress their Do bò performances because they found them antithetical to Islamic beliefs. According to the oral history, it was only after the arrival of the French in the 1890s that the Bamana embraced this masquerade theatre. It was also during this period that many former residents returned to the village and that the Bamana quarter shifted its orientation from the production of warfare to that of agriculture. The current kamalen ton, young men's association, dates its emergence to this last decade of the nineteenth century. The present kamalen ton participates in the collective harvest of millet, provides labor for community public works projects, and organizes village-based entertainments, which include the puppet masquerade, various dances at member's weddings, and other theatres and dance events throughout the year. Its contemporary membership includes both young men and unmarried young women.

The history of the masquerade for the last century remains an important part of the oral traditions of the kamalen ton. Although the Bamana quarter always recognizes the fishermen's original ownership of the masquerade, the Bamana quarter's Sogo bò history contains few details of their neighbor's performances or of the larger regional history of the theatre before their own investment in the genre.

Since the 1930s and 1940s, when the Office du Niger established an agricultural irrigation scheme at Markala, men have become increasingly more involved in wage labor in Kirango than in many other villages at some distance from this government complex. Today, the Office du Niger operates a foundry, workshops, and garages to maintain these projects. In addition, Markala is the headquarters for the chef d'arrondissement and his staff and is the site of a military camp, a hospital, the post office, primary schools, and a high school. Many of the skilled and unskilled jobs which support this complex are filled by men from Kirango and Djamarabougou. While young men throughout the region are increasingly involved in long-distance labor migration inside and outside Mali, one or more men in most households in Kirango today enjoy steady employment in Markala. The availability of local wage labor opportunities ensures a regular influx of cash for Kirango households. While some percentage of each household's male labor force now works outside the village, the remaining men and women continue to actively engage in farming and fishing as full-time occupations. Kirango's proximity to the Markala government center and its current dual orientation to wage labor and to agricultural production have clearly affected the three village youth associations and their theatrical practices since at least the post–World War II period. Some of the changes in theatrical practices in the Bamana quarter are directly related to these larger patterns of change in the political, social, religious, and economic life within the community at large and which have intensified over the latter half of this century.

The Kirango Bamana Masquerades

In the Bamana quarter, discussions of the history of the theatre revolve primarily around the history of objects. I was continually struck by the emphasis that was placed on objects over the more ephemeral art forms even though people do consider all these arts to be essential to the production of the theatre. Unlike the association's detailed descriptions of changes over the past century in the material repertoire, their memory of innovations in dance, music, and song does not seem to survive beyond a generation or two.

The introduction of any new masquerade is always remembered in terms of the current leadership of the kamalen ton at the time it was brought into the theatre.[29] The way that the kamalen ton links the material well-being of the association to its individual leaders through a history of theatrical objects parallels the links that people regularly make between material well-being and histories of leadership in the community, in individual households, or in any number of other village associations (Grosz-Ngate 1986, 116). The official association account of the theatre, therefore, is simultaneously a history of objects and a history of generations of men.

Based on oral traditions and working backward from the present, I calculated that the Bamana quarter began performing the puppet theatre in about 1896. Association historians identified Boli Coulibaly as the kamalen ton's first leader and they credited him with

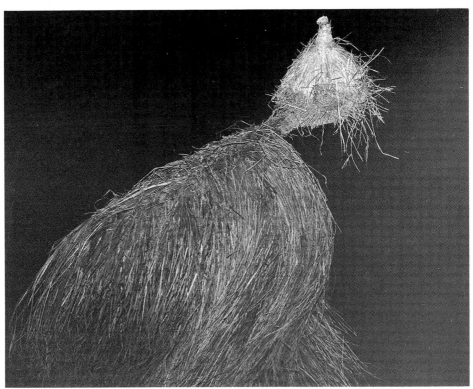

2.13. A Bamana performance of Nama, the Hyena. 1979. Kirango, Mali. *Photograph by Lynn Forsdale.*

2.14. Falakani, a generic bush animal, performing during the Sòmonò Do bò. 1979. Kirango, Mali. *Photograph by Lynn Forsdale.*

2.15. A Bamana performance of Bilanjan, a generic bush animal. 1979. Kirango, Mali. *Photograph by Mary Jo Arnoldi.*

2.16. A Bamana performance of Bala, the Porcupine. 1979. Segou region, Mali. *Photograph by Lynn Forsdale.*

the first masquerades. These first masquerades included Nama, the Hyena [Figure 2.13], Falakani, a generic bush animal [Figure 2.14], Bilanjan, a generic bush animal [Figure 2.15], Bala, the Porcupine [Figure 2.16], Minan, the Bushbuck, Sama, the Elephant, Sanfè Sa, the Tree Snake, Misi, the Cow, and Bakòrò, the Ram.[30] The early masquerades were all said to have been fashioned primarily from grasses and the characters were originally borrowed from the repertoire of the local fishermen's Do bò theatre. In the 1979 October performance, for example, four of the original grass masquerades—Nama, Falakani, Bala, and Bilanjan— were played and everyone considered them to be the quarter's most traditional masquerades. Although the Bamana say they originally borrowed the theatre and their first masquerade characters directly from the fishermen, they called their performance Sogo bò to separate it from the Do bò theatre. They also said that they subsequently created new songs for these masquerade characters and introduced a Bamana style of dancing and drumming into the performance to replace those of their neighbors.

There have been twenty association leaders since Boli Coulibaly. The oral history of the introduction of each new puppet masquerade, and in some cases the abandonment and later reprisal of certain characters, remains linked to particular ton leaders. Table 2.1 is a reconstruction of the quarter's theatre and the development of its repertoire based on interviews with former and current members of the ton in Kirango in 1978–80 and in 1987.

Since the theatre's adoption in the late nineteenth century, new characters have regularly been added to the Kirango repertoire. According to the oral history, there was relatively little change in the early decades of this century, but after 1936 characters were regularly added to the repertoire. This growth may well reflect Kirango's integration into the local wage labor complex. Access to wage labor provided Kirango with a certain amount of economic security, and the availability of cash provided young men in this immediate area with the means to expand their theatrical productions.[31] The period between 1936 and 1947 coincides with the building of the Markala Dam and the expansion of the Office du Niger's irrigation project. For over ten years a substantial number of men were brought into the area to work on this irrigation scheme (Magasa 1978). The influx of strangers from other areas within Segou and from elsewhere in Mali may also have been a catalyst in the creation and expansion of these local theatres. It was during this period that the Kalaka Sogo was first introduced into Kirango. This masquerade, which appeared as a large rectangular cloth-covered structure out of which small rod and string puppets emerged, was performed in a separate masquerade event as part of the spring festival. Kalaka Sogo was quite different from the bush animal masquerades that were then performed in the Sogo bò theatre. The small rod and string puppets on the Kalaka Sogo portrayed men and women engaged in everyday activities. In the mid 1950s the Kalaka Sogo masquerade was merged with the Sogo bò repertoire and this full complement of masquerades began to be played during both festivals.

The next period of marked expansion in the masquerade repertoire took place around Independence in 1960. The addition of eight new masquerades suggests that during this period Kirango was economically secure, with any setbacks in agricultural production offset by people's access to wage labor in Markala. Following Independence,

Table 2.1 Kirango Masquerade Repertoire 1896–1987

Dates (circa)	Tontigi	Masquerade Characters
1896–1902	Boli Coulibaly	Nama, Falakani, Bala, Bilanjan, Minan, Sama, Sanfè Sa, Misi, Bakòrò
1903–1922	Daka Coulibaly	Dankalankule (introduced and abandoned during this period), Mèrèn (spring performance), Duga, Gòn
1923–1934	Buba Tangara	Fali and Jarawara
1935	Toto Tangara	Duga abandoned
1936–1942	Sande Haidra	Kalaka Sogo (spring festival only), a second version of Kalaka Sogo, Duguma Sa, Waraba, and Kalakadane
1943–1947	Balla Diakhite	Dajè (two versions), third version of Kalaka Sogo
1948–1950	Kariba Tangara	Maisa, Jobali, a second version of Waraba
1951–1953	Benke Diakhite	Ntilen
1954–1956	Bamoussa Kone	none given
1957–1959	Bablunda Tangara	second version of Jobali, Suruku Malobali, and Sogoni Kelen
1960–1962	Moussa Coulibaly	Sigi, Karankaw, third version of Dajè, Yayoroba, Jinè-Faro, Mali Kònò, a third version of Waraba
1963–1965	Bajebile Togura	Waraba Caco and Bilisi
1966–1968	Kaouli Diakhite	none given
1969–1971	Boroma Traore	Jado Nama, Njona, second version of Mali Kònò
1972–1974	Zange Diakhite	Ntomo, Son-min-te-maa-na, Sumusonin, Taasi Dòoni, and a fourth version of Waraba
1975–1977	Bomissa Togura	none given
1978–1981	Bakary Diarra	Madame Sarata, Kònò Jolenjo
1981	Baba Togura	Saga, Kankari Kònò, and Nteke-dalen-be-Naje-kun
1982–1984	Jean Diarra	none given
1985–1987	Batinima Tangara	Ciwara, reprisal of Dankalankule, Moriba, Dasiri Sogo, Koon, Sotigi, fifth version of Waraba, and fourth version of Dajè

there was a much smaller but steady growth in the repertoire throughout the next two decades. This continued expansion coincides with the increasing local celebrity that the Bamana association's theatre enjoyed after they began staging performances twice a year. Men and women who were active in the association during this period recall that enormous numbers of people came from neighboring villages and from various towns to attend these performances. In 1975 Cheik Omar Mara conducted a survey of the Segou masquerade for the Ministry of Culture and it was his enthusiasm for the Kirango theatre and upon his recommendation that I settled into the village in 1978 to undertake this study.

When discussing developments in the repertoire over the last two generations, men outlined two different processes through which masquerades come into the theatre. Masks and puppets commissioned by the association, such as those commissioned from Siriman in the late 1950s, entered the repertoire as *ton sogow*, association-owned masquerades. These ton sogow are considered the communal property of the association and their introduction is linked in the association history to the ton leader then in office. However, an individual young man or a group of young men can also create a new masquerade. In this case these individuals must assume all the creative and financial responsibility for the construction. The first year they perform the new masquerade it is called a *kamalen sogo*, young man's masquerade. If the kamalen sogo is judged to be successful, the association will retain it as part of the masquerade repertoire. Ownership is then transferred to the association and the masquerade is transformed into a ton sogo. However, even after it becomes a ton sogo its original creator(s) has the right to dance alongside the masquerade during every public performance. In this way the masquerade remains associated with its creator in the public mind during the young man's tenure in the ton. I found that as a general rule the link between individual characters and named young men as their promoters or inventors survived in the collective memory no more than several decades. In Kirango it extended only back to the mid 1950s. The ton only remembers the older masquerades in terms of the *tontigi*, the leader of the association when the character was first introduced. Whether these masquerades entered the repertoire as ton sogow or kamalen sogow is clearly no longer critical in this official history.

Young men in the association today still recall the original promoters of characters introduced since the mid 1950s. In 1978 Suruku Malobali, the Shameless Hyena, was still associated with Ousmane Diarra, who "borrowed" the idea from the Djamarabougou theatre in the 1950s [Figure 2.17]. The link between the Diarras and this masquerade survives even today because Ousmane's younger brother, Adama, has taken over the responsibility for constructing the character. People remember many promoters of characters created in the last fifteen years because a number of these same young men are still active in the association and they regularly dance in attendance with their masquerades. In the 1970s Morbidane Coulibaly created the female character Taasi Dòoni [Figure 1.18]. His age-mates remembered the circumstances of its creation. They recalled that the popular recording of the song "Taasi Dòoni" by the orchestra Super Biton had inspired Morbidane to create the masquerade. The song is said to have been an old song in the region that gained renewed popularity with Super Biton's rendition, which was played

2.17. Suruku Malobali, the Shameless Hyena. 1987. Kirango, Mali. *Photograph by Mary Jo Arnoldi.*

2.18. Taasi Dòoni, Reflect a Little, appearing as an antelope masquerade. 1979. Segou region, Mali. *Photograph by Lynn Forsdale.*

2.19. Sigi, the Buffalo, carved circa 1959 by Siriman Fane for the Kirango Bamana. 1978. *Photograph by Lynn Forsdale.*

frequently on the radio. Morbidane conceived of Taasi Dòoni, Reflect a Little, as a female character and he commissioned a face mask from the Kirango smith, Mamary Fane. It is interesting that several neighboring villages also play this character, but in at least two of these villages it appears not as a female character but as a roan antelope puppet head [Figure 2.18].

Similarly, in 1979 Sebu Diakhite came up with the idea for another female character, which he named Madame Sarata [Figure 1.20]. He made a sketch of his idea for the masquerade and then asked a local smith to translate his sketch into a wooden puppet head. He also asked a local woman singer to compose a song for the character. I would hypothesize that over the next decade, when these young men begin to move out of the association, their original identification with these characters will dim. Eventually these two masquerade characters, if they survive in the repertoire, will be remembered only through the formal accounts that link each character to the particular ton leader in place when it was first introduced.

Interviews with blacksmiths in the Bamana quarter provided a second and parallel history of the masquerade repertoire that complemented the association's official accounts and individuals' personal recollections. Smiths were more interested in discussing the sculptures and masks produced by other professionals. Several resident smiths who were in their mid to late sixties in 1987 were quite knowledgeable about the history of sculptures. They were especially interested in the masks and puppets that had been produced during the period when they themselves were association members or when they had carved for the theatre. These men would have been active in the association from around the mid 1930s until the late 1960s. They were less knowledgeable about which smiths had carved during their fathers' generation in the decades prior to the 1930s and were markedly less interested in the masks and puppets recently carved by younger smiths in the village.[32] They also had very little information about those masquerade characters which were fashioned from grass and cloth by association members. In contrast to the association's accounts, smiths mostly dismissed any questions about these latter masquerades as irrelevant. They clearly did not consider it worthwhile to preserve any memory of them.

The association's oral histories state that an itinerant smith from Shianro introduced the first carved wooden puppets into the Bamana quarter. Elder smiths corroborated this account, but neither the ton nor the local smiths remembered the names of any of these early Shianro sculptors and their pieces are no longer extant in the village. The smiths did recall the name of Kari Ballo from Ngarababougou, who sculpted several puppets for Kirango. They credited him with the first Kalaka Sogo ensemble. This masquerade, according to the association history, was first played sometime in the mid 1930s. Ballo is also said to have carved a later version of this ensemble in the 1940s and the first version of Waraba, the Lion, during this same period. A third version of the Kalaka Sogo was credited to

2.20. A rod puppet of Mali Kònò carved by Siriman Fane. 1987. Segou region, Mali. *Photograph by Mary Jo Arnoldi.*

the smith Sungolo Traore and dated to the late 1940s. Several smaller figures of a balafon player and a colonial officer on horseback still survive although they were not performed in 1979 or 1980 [Figure Pref.3].

Elder smiths also mentioned two local smiths, Seri Kumare and Buwakoro Tarawele, whom they identified as being of their father's generation and who they remembered had carved versions of Gòn, the Baboon, for the theatre. Kumare and Tarawele also carved the Ntomo masks and Ciwara crest masks for the men's initiation associations in the Bamana quarter.

Smiths credited the original masks for Jobali, the Boso Woman, and the first wooden rod puppets of Misicè, the Bull, and Misimuso, the Cow, to Masana Ballo of Sanamadougou. According to association histories these sculptures probably date from the mid 1940s. One version of the rod puppet Suruku Nama, the Hyena, was credited to a smith from Pelengana, near Segou city, but they did not remember which of the various versions of this puppet he had carved. They attributed the first version of the rod puppet Ntilen, the Giraffe, in the early 1950s to Famassa Kumare from Kirango.

The largest group of puppets and masks performed today date from around Inde-

2.22. A rod puppet of Sogoni Kelen, an Antelope, carved by Manyan Kumare circa 1959 for the Kirango Bamana. 1979. *Photograph by Lynn Forsdale.*

pendence in 1960. Many of these were carved for the quarter by Siriman Fane of Koke. Siriman carved the puppets Sigi [Figure 2.19], Mali Kònò [Figure 2.20], Yayoroba [Figure Pref.4], a version of Ntilen [Figure Pref.2], Jinè-Faro, and Waraba [Figure 1.15]. He also carved smaller puppets for the masquerade Karankaw which replaced the older Kalaka Sogo.[33] Manyan Kumare, Siriman's nephew, worked with his uncle when Siriman carried out his commission for the village. Later, Manyan Kumare carved an occasional puppet for the association. Around 1968 he carved a replacement for Mali Kònò that was still being performed in 1987 [Figure 2.21]. Members of the kamalen ton said that the association had requested the new larger version because so many people now attended the theatre that Siriman's original puppet head was too small to be seen by the crowd. Manyan's version is in fact nearly double the size of Siriman's original model. Manyan Kumare also carved the

Table 2.2 Kirango Bamana Masquerade Repertoire between 1978 and 1980

Bakòrò †	Ram
Bala *	Porcupine
Bilanjan *	generic bush animal
Bilisi *	Bilisi, a genie
Cèkòròba †	Elder
Dajè †	Roan Antelope
Duguma Sa *	Ground Snake
Falakani *	generic bush animal
Fali †	Donkey
Gòn †	Baboon
Jado Nama †	Nama of Minjado (represented as a hyena)
Jarawara *	Wildcat (no ID)
Jinè-Faro †	Faro, a water genie
Jobali †	Boso Woman
Kalakadane *	Antelope (no ID)
Kankari Kònò †	Bird (no ID)
Karankaw †	Residents of Karan
Kònò Jolenjo †	Bird (no ID)
Kònònin †	Bird (no ID)
Madame Sarata †	Mrs. Sarata
Maisa †	Umu Assita, a woman (represented by an antelope)
Mali Kònò †	Bird of Mali
Misicè †	Bull
Misimuso †	Cow
Nama *	Hyena
Njona †	Wildcat (no ID)
Nteke-dalen-be Naje-kun †	Naje, a woman
Ntilen †	Giraffe
Ntomo †	Ntomo association mask
Saga †	Sheep
Sanfè Sa *	Tree Snake
Sigi †	Buffalo
Sinè †	Gazelle
Sogoni Kelen †	Antelope (no ID)
Son-min-te-maa-na †	The Character a Person Doesn't Have (represented by an antelope)
Sumusonin *	Sorceress
Suruku Malobali *	Shameless Hyena
Suruku Nama †	Hyena
Taasi Dòoni †	Reflect a Little (represented as a woman)
Tankon †	Hartebeest
Waraba †	Lion
Waraba Caco *	Striped Wildcat (no ID)
Yayoroba †	The Beautiful Woman

* = grass or cloth masquerade
† = rod puppet or mask

2.23. A rod puppet of Saga, the Sheep, carved by Mamary Fane circa 1975 for the Kirango Bamana. 1979. *Photograph by Lynn Forsdale.*

puppet Sogoni Kelen, an antelope puppet head [Figure 2.22], and a second version of the mask Jobali. He explained that he had not taken a more active role in the production of theatrical sculpture because his own father had discouraged his sons from carving sculptures. Manyan's father felt the only true vocation of a blacksmith was working iron. Although Manyan did carve a few puppets for the Bamana quarter and an occasional one for the fishermen's theatre in Kirango, he said that he had never carved theatrical sculptures for any other village's theatre.

2.24. A rod puppet of Dajè, the Roan Antelope, carved in the early 1960s for the Kirango Bamana. 1987. *Photograph by Mary Jo Arnoldi.*

2.25. A rod puppet of Dajè, the Roan Antelope, commissioned in 1987 by the Kirango Bamana to replace an older, damaged puppet. This new version appeared alongside the 1960s version of the Dajè puppet (see 2.24). 1987. Kirango, Mali. *Photograph by Mary Jo Arnoldi.*

Since the 1970s several theatrical sculptures have been carved by younger blacksmiths
from Kirango, while others continued to be
commissioned from smiths living outside the
village. Mamary Fane of Kirango carved Taasi
Dòoni, a female mask, in the 1970s [Figure
1.18]. During this decade he also carved Kan-
kari Kònò, a puppet head representing a bird,
and Saga, two rod puppets representing a ram
and a ewe [Figure 2.23]. He continues to sculpt
new and replacement puppets for the theatre on
demand. Saliya Kane from Koke, who is Siriman's elder brother's son, carved the puppet
Njona, a wildcat, and the mask Naje kun, a
female character, for the Kirango theatre in the

2.26. The character Dasiri Sogo, the Dasiri Antelope, was
added to the Kirango Bamana repertoire in the 1980s.
1987. *Photograph by Mary Jo Arnoldi.*

early 1970s. In 1987, a replacement Dajè, a roan antelope puppet, was commissioned from
a smith in a neighboring village [Figures 2.24, 2.25]. Most local smiths said they never
carved for any troupe outside the village and they do not enjoy the same regional celebrity
as the smiths from Koke or the smiths working in Nienou and other puppet centers in
Shianro.

While a number of older characters remain a critical part of the theatre's contemporary repertoire, others that figure in the official history obviously enjoyed a much
shorter life span and are no longer played today. Over the decade I have been attending
puppet performances I have seen some of the most popular characters of the late 1970s
such as Yayoroba, the Beautiful Woman, take a back seat to new characters in the 1987
and 1992 performances.

Table 2.2 lists the forty-three characters available to the Kirango troupe between
1978 and 1980. Several more have been added since 1980. Twelve of the characters (designated by an asterisk in Table 2.2) are grass or cloth masquerades and are constructed
by the association members themselves. Thirty-one are carved wooden masks or rod
puppets (designated by † in Table 2.2). Of this latter group of sculptures over seventy-
five percent are rod puppet heads.

Since 1981 several new characters, including Ciwara, the Ciwara men's association
mask, Moriba†, the Marabout, Dasiri Sogo†, an antelope (no species ID) [Figure 2.26],
and Sotigi*, a Horseman, as well as a reprisal of Dankalankule†, the Oryx, have been
added to the repertoire. New versions of well established characters, including Dajè†,
Ntilen, Suruku Nama, Jarawara*, and Sigi [Figure 2.27] have also been created.

New versions of older masquerades may involve having a new mask carved, altering
the costume, or even radically changing the presentation. For example, between 1979 and
1987 the troupe retained the rod puppet head of Jarawara, the Wildcat, but changed its
costume. In the 1979 version there was a half-moon design painted on the costume which
might have been loosely inspired by Islamic decorative motifs. However, in the 1987 version the Islamic star and crescent moon patterns were clearly the source for the decorative

2.27. A new version of Sigi, the Buffalo, appeared in the 1992 Bamana Sogo bò. Out of its back appeared several small puppets, including a balafon musician, a drummer, and Yayoroba, the Beautiful Woman. 1992. *Photograph by Mary Jo Arnoldi.*

2.28. The Bamana character Jarawara, the Wildcat. 1979. Kirango, Mali. *Photograph by Mary Jo Arnoldi.*

patterns on the costume [Figure 2.28 and 2.29]. In the case of Sigi, the Buffalo, the 1992 version involved a shift in presentation. In 1979 Sigi had been played as the lone buffalo character. For the 1992 version, a new rod puppet had been carved and this new Sigi carried on its back a group of small rod and string puppets representing musicians and dancers.

The history and transformations in Kirango's masquerade repertoire from an initial corpus of grass masquerades to over seventy percent rod puppet heads echo similar patterns of change within theatres that I documented widely dispersed throughout the Segou region. Currently within and outside the Segou region, the carved rod and rod and string puppets give this youth masquerade theatre its unique identity and separate it from all manner of other masquerade traditions in Mali today. This development of a distinct body of rod puppet sculptures for the theatre, which began to gain popularity throughout the region by the early colonial period, is closely tied to blacksmiths' ever increasing involvement in the production of theatrical sculpture. However, the actual composition of each village's individual repertoire and its history differ tremendously from village to village. While the blacksmith's role in the development of the material repertoire of the theatre is clearly significant in both regional and local histories of the genre, the specific changes,

2.29. A recent version of the Bamana character Jarawara, the Wildcat (see 2.28). The costume emphasizes the Islamic star and crescent moon motifs. 1987. Kirango, Mali. *Photograph by Mary Jo Arnoldi.*

additions, and deletions in the performance depend on each new generation of performers and their artistic investment in the theatre.

The reconstruction of the history of the theatre from both a regional and a local perspective laid out in the foregoing discussion reveals that while the masquerade is clearly a precolonial performance tradition, it has undergone significant modification and elaboration over this past century. Its inherent openness to change, experimentation, and innovation will be explored in more detail in the following chapter in the discussions of the different categories of expressive forms and their evaluations within the contemporary theatre.

CHAPTER THREE

The Sogo bò's Expressive Forms

Segou troupes exploit the full range of arts to create the illusory world of the youth association puppet masquerade, the Sogo bò. Wooden masks, puppets, and grass or cloth masquerades along with song, dance, and drumming are all skillfully woven together in these performances. This creative enterprise results in constellations of arts and dramatic characters that are considered to be unique to the youth theatre. This sense of the uniqueness of the Sogo bò arts does not deny that nearly identical masks, puppets, songs, dances, or drum rhythms can and often do have alternative performance histories outside the youth masquerade theatre. Rather, the invention of new forms or the selective borrowing of forms from other performance traditions seems to have been a continual and conscious strategy by performers. This strategy has contributed to a troupe's ability to generate new and innovative performances from season to season and from generation to generation. When a troupe plucks an expressive form from another performance tradition, the incorporation of the borrowed form into the Sogo bò creates a different set of artistic relationships. Although the troupe may intend to make a reference to the original context, these new artistic relationships are seen to be distinctive and wholly authentic to the youth theatre. After a borrowed form has been successfully inserted into a youth association performance, it becomes defined as the artistic property of the youth association. This makes it available for further exploitation in every subsequent performance. New constellations of expressive forms take on their own histories, opening up the play of potential interpretations. It is in this sense that people define Sogo bò arts as unique to the youth association masquerade performances.

Sculptural Forms: Puppets, Masks, and Masquerades

Throughout this century, the repertoires of most Segou youth association theatres featured masquerades fashioned entirely of grass and cloth, as well as carved wooden masks, rod puppet heads, and small rod and string puppets. These face, crest, and helmet masks are the very same mask types that appear in a variety of other performance contexts in the area. For example, nearly identical face and helmet masks representing lions, monkeys, and hyenas have been documented as part of the youth association masquerades and in Kòrè men's association performances (Henry 1910; Zahan 1960). Others, such as the face mask representing the character Gòn, the Baboon, appear in the early histories of masking repertoires. In some villages people remember this mask as part of the youth association theatre and in other communities they defined it as a boli, a power object. More recently troupes have begun to incorporate masks previously associated exclusively with the Ntomo and Ciwara associations into the youth association's repertoires [Figure 3.1].

While masks of every type are important in the repertoire, rod puppet heads and the rod and string puppets now dominate these performances. Throughout Mali these puppets are the signature sculptures in the contemporary Segou youth association theatre. These rod puppets separate youth association masquerades from other masquerade traditions and non-masked entertainments both within Segou and in adjacent regions.

3.1. A Bamana Ciwara crest mask used in annual ceremonies of the Ciwara men's association, Mali. Indiana University Art Museum, 60.10. *Photograph by Michael Cavanagh and Kevin Montague.*

While face, crest, and helmet masks appeared in different performance contexts in Segou, there is also some evidence in early ethnographies that historically rod puppets too might have been used in multiple performance contexts. Although most accounts describe Kòmò masks as horizontal helmet masks [Figure 3.2], Abbè Henry provided one brief description of an articulated Kòmò masquerade from the Segou region that was operated by means of a rod like the youth association rod puppet heads (Henry 1910, 148).

Henry's account of the Kòmò mask as a rod puppet parallels a description of Kòmò masquerades given to me in 1978 by an elder man living in a village near Kirango. During our conversations about different men's association masquerades, he described his impressions of the differences between the Kòmò and Nama masquerades. He stated simply that "Kòmò was tall and Nama was short." Further elaborating on his initial cryptic remark, he explained that in his experience when the Kòmò masquerade performed it shot into the air to a great height. From his description I surmised that it was operated by a rod inserted into the mask, in much the same way that the youth association puppet

3.2. A Bamana Kòmò helmet mask used in annual ceremonies of the Kòmò men's association, Mali. Indiana University Art Museum. 72.111. *Photograph by Michael Cavanagh and Kevin Montague.*

heads are manipulated by the masquerade dancers. The Nama's performance did not involve this type of formal manipulation and "it was short." His brief description suggests that the Nama mask was a horizontal helmet mask worn directly on the dancer's head.

Boso elders in fishing villages along the Niger River remarked that although rod puppets were an integral part of the public performances of the Do bò, they also appeared in the repertoire of the Jara men's association's performances. Although these associations shared many of the same mask and puppet forms, Do bò and Jara men's associations' performances are defined as historically different kinds of events. Only initiated men could attend the Jara events, while the Do bò masquerades were public performances.

The appearance of rod puppets in multiple performance contexts within Segou is not surprising considering the long history of masking throughout south central Mali and the fact that it was blacksmiths who generally carved all the sculptures used in these various events. Masking has a long history in south central Mali, extending back in time for at least six centuries. One of the first written accounts of masking appeared in the journals of Ibn Battuta, who visited the court of the ruler of the Mali empire, Mansa Souleyman, in 1352. Ibn Battuta described the following performance:

> On feast-days, after Dugha has finished his display, the poets come in. Each of them is inside a figure resembling a thrush, made of feathers, and provided with a wooden head with a red beak, to look like a thrush's head. They stand in front of the sultan in this ridiculous make-up and recite their poems. I was told that their poetry is a kind of sermonizing in which they say to the sultan: "This pempi which you occupy was that whereon sat this king and that king, and such and such

3.3. The Sòmonò in Kirango consider Baninkònò, the Stork, to be their *Do Mansa*, King of Puppets. 1979. Kirango, Mali. *Photograph by Lynn Forsdale.*

were this one's noble actions and such and such the other's. So do you too do good deeds whose memory will outlive you." . . . I was told that this practice is a very old custom amongst them, prior to the introduction of Islam, and that they have kept it up. (Ibn Battuta 1984, 329)

While Ibn Battuta's description of these court masquerades does not specifically indicate whether the bird masks were articulated, it does closely resemble descriptions of more contemporary rod puppet versions of bird heads. This type of articulated bird mask has been documented in multiple performance contexts within the last century throughout this zone. In the Segou region Soleillet described an articulated bird mask in 1878. This same type of bird mask has remained a central form in both fishermen's and farmers' youth theatres up to the present (Soleillet 1886, 170–171; B. N'Diaye 1970, 438; Arnoldi 1983, 251, 261) [Figures 3.3, 2.20, and 2.21]. An elder in Segou identified one village where a rod puppet bird was used as a boli in the mid 1920s. McNaughton documented the solo performances of a bird masquerade made and danced by the blacksmith Sidi Ballo. The bird head used in this masquerade was mounted on a long rod (McNaughton 1988, 47 plate 47). There is also a group of rod puppet bird heads performed to honor the descendants of the Diarra rulers of the nineteenth century Meguetan in Koulikoro [Figure 3.4]. The appearance of this bird rod puppet in multiple performance traditions suggests that rod puppet heads, like helmet, crest, and face masks, might have an equally long history within Mali and beyond.[1]

3.4. Kònò Meguetan masquerade. In Koulikoro this bird masquerade performs to honor the descendants of the Diarra rulers of the nineteenth century Meguetan. 1987. Koulikoro, Mali. *Photograph by Mary Jo Arnoldi.*

Local Taxonomies of Sogo bò Sculptures and Their Performances

People use the global term *yiri kun*, a wooden head, for all carved wooden masks and rod puppet heads, whether they appear in the youth theatre or in other performance traditions in the region. Everyone seems to be familiar with this term, yet they rarely invoke it when they discuss specific performance traditions or their constituent sculptures and masquerades. Even though similar types of mask and puppet sculptures are used across a variety of performance contexts, most people tend not to talk about these forms in the abstract. In my experience they always linked individual masks and puppets to the particular performance context within which they appear. Two recent notable exceptions that appeared within the last generation in the Kirango Bamana youth theatre are the distinctive Ntomo face mask and the Ciwara antelope crests. People still identify them as Ntomo and Ciwara masquerades, thus unambiguously preserving their link to the men's associations from which they were originally borrowed.

Within the youth theatre, the puppets, masks, and masquerades are differentiated according to terms that either highlight a particular formal feature of the masquerade or underscore distinctions made about certain performance practices. While many of Kirango's close neighbors use identical terms for theatrical sculptures and performances, I found that this terminology was not universal throughout Segou. Although there were equivalences among terms, the differences in terminology within the region clearly reflect local variations in the history and development of the youth theatre. Table 3.1 contains specific terms that people used when discussing the theatre in the Bamana quarter of Kirango. In several instances people used the same terms to define aspects of form, characterization, and performance practice. I have divided these terms in the table according to whether they describe form and character or performance history and practices.

The Bamana term sogo—literally, the antelope, and, by extension, the animal—includes all the masquerades used in the Kirango youth theatre. In Kirango it distinguishes the youth association masquerades from every other masquerade performed in the area. Sogo is also used to refer globally to all the dramatic characters in the theatre, whether they represent animals (antelopes and others) or portray human beings, spirits, concepts, or inanimate objects.

Table 3.1   Kirango Bamana Terminology for the Puppet Masquerade Theatre

Form and Character	Performance History and Practice
Sogo	*Sogo bò (Binsogo bò)*
binsogo and *finisogo*	*binsogo* and *finisogo*
binsogo and *finisogo*	*su fè sogo* and *tile fè sogo*
sogoba, sogokun, and *sogoden*	*sogoden*
sogoden and *maani*	*sogoden*

People use binsogo, the grass animal, and finisogo, the cloth animal, to describe the defining costume elements of these masquerades. In the contemporary theatre every masquerade falls into one of these two categories. Although historically Binsogo refers to masquerades made completely from grass skirting sewn over a wooden armature [Figures 2.13–16], it is now also used for those wooden masks and rod puppets whose primary costume element is grass skirting [Figure 3.5]. This type of grass masquerade was the original masquerade form played in the early theatre. In Kirango these grass masquerades were considered the signature masquerades for the Sogo bò theatre until rod puppets and wooden masks were introduced into the repertoire in the 1930s.

Finisogo refers to contemporary masquerades whose costumes are fashioned entirely from cloth [Figures 3.6 and 2.11]. This category also includes those masquerades with wooden masks and puppet heads whose costumes are fashioned from textiles [Figures Pref.1 and Pref.4]. Finisogo is also used in a historical sense when referring to old cloth masquerades, like Sanfè Sa, the Tree Snake.

Sogo bò, the animal comes forth, is the Kirango Bamana quarter's name for the performances. Performers will sometimes substitute the term Binsogo bò, the grass animal comes forth, for the term Sogo bò. However, Binsogo bò has a particular meaning when people discuss the early history of the theatre or the appropriate timing for performances.

The same two terms, binsogo and finisogo, are used to describe the history and organization of performances and to refer to a set of more contemporary performance practices that developed in the Kirango theatre during the mid 1950s. Before the 1950s, the Binsogo bò was performed only after sunset and only during *kawule*, the transitional period between the rainy and dry seasons beginning in October.

In the 1930s two cloth masquerades were introduced into a festival held during *samiyè da [daminè]*, the onset of the rainy season, which begins in late May or early June. The Mèrèn masquerade was a body puppet representing a woman, and Kalaka Sogo was a cloth-covered square stage out of whose top small rod puppets appeared during the performance. Unlike the Binsogo bò masquerades, these two cloth masquerades were played only during the late afternoon hours of the rainy season festival.

In the past, one way that people differentiated between the two masquerade festivals and their respective repertoires was to assign them definitions based on diurnal categories. The Binsogo bò grass masquerades became known as su fè sogow, evening masquerades, while Mèrèn and Kalaka Sogo, which were cloth masquerades, were called tile fè sogow, daytime masquerades.

In the mid 1950s the youth association merged these two festival repertoires and added a full-scale afternoon masquerade performance to the original Binsogo bò event. They also began playing an evening performance during the rainy season festival in May.[2]

3.5. A Bamana performance of Sinè, the Gazelle. 1979. Segou region, Mali. *Photograph by Lynn Forsdale.*

They did, however, retain the binsogo and finisogo distinctions for the types and timing of the different repertoires. The grass masquerades remained restricted to evening performances and most of the cloth masquerades are only performed in the afternoon segment. While this distinction still holds in the main, there are a few exceptions to this standard practice. The Kirango troupe regularly performs Gòn, the Baboon, a masquerade defined as a binsogo, in the afternoon segment whether the masker wears a bush costume or a cloth costume [Figure 3.7]. Because Gòn violates diurnal categories its appearance in the afternoon event is noteworthy, and it is made even more remarkable because the Baboon opens the afternoon masquerade event.

The troupe also now regularly performs a number of newly invented cloth masquerades, such as Waraba Caco, the Striped Wildcat [Figure 1.19], and Suruku Malobali, the Shameless Hyena, in the evening portion of the event [Figure 2.17]. Their appearance at night is little remarked upon because there is a precedent for cloth masquerades, which

3.6. A Bamana performance of Sanfè Sa, the Tree Snake. 1979. Segou region, Mali. *Photograph by Lynn Forsdale.*

represent bush animals, in the older Binsogo bò performances.[3]

A variety of terms are used to identify the elements which make up the masquerade form. Sogoba, the big animal, is the term used for the whole masquerade—the mask and/or puppets and the costumed armature. The carved wooden masks and rod puppet heads are called sogokunw, the animal heads. While there are no linguistic equivalents in Bamana for the English terms rod puppet, horizontal mask, crest mask, or face mask, people do regularly make clear formal distinctions among these sculptural types through similes drawn from the local masquerade repertoire. For example, the young men in Ki-rango described the formal variations among their sculptures in the following manner: Jobali is like Taasi Dòoni (helmet masks) [Figures 1.16 and 1.18]; Sigi is like Dajè (rod puppet heads) [Figures 2.19 and 2.24]; Yayoroba is like Madame Sarata (body puppets) [Figures Pref.4 and 1.20]; Gòn is like Wòkulò (face masks) [Figure 3.7 and 3.8]; Nyò-susu-muso is like Sotigi (small rod and string puppets) [Figures 3.9 and 3.10].

3.7. A Bamana performance of Gòn, the Baboon. 1979. Kirango, Mali. *Photograph by Lynn Forsdale.*

3.8. A Bamana performance of Wòkulò, the Bush Genie. 1979. Segou region, Mali. *Photograph by Lynn Forsdale.*

3.9. A Bamana *maani* of Nyò-susu-musow, Women Pounding Millet. 1978. Kirango, Mali. *Photograph by Lynn Forsdale.*

3.10. A Bamana *maani* of Sotigi, the Horseman. This version represents a colonial officer on horseback. 1978. Kirango, Mali. *Photograph by Lynn Forsdale.*

People refer to any small rod and string puppet or hand puppet which appears out of the back of the costumed stage/body or is attached to the core puppet or mask as a so-goden, a child of the animal. Sogoden also includes two subcategories relating to the puppets' characterization. Those small puppets that portray animals are also called sogodenw, children of the animal. Those that represent human beings or spirits in anthropomorphic form are maaniw, little persons.[4]

When discussing performances, the troupe called all the performers in the theatre sogodenw. This included not only the masqueraders, but the singers, dancers, and drummers. They also used this term in a more limited sense to refer specifically to the groups of young men who are responsible for constructing particular masquerades and who dance alongside them during their public performance.

Masquerade Characters and Sculptural Forms

The Kirango youth association draws its ideas for characters from almost every domain of life. Troupes today often perform over thirty masquerades in a single festival. Wild and domesticated animals, living or legendary persons, spirits, inanimate objects like automobiles and airplanes, and conceptual characters that speak to the human condition are all potential subjects for inclusion in the drama. This openness and the timeliness of the characters seem to have been longstanding features of this theatre. In 1989 Bafing Kane said that one of the current ideas he was mulling over for a new masquerade was a set of maaniw that showed young men engaged in playing the Sogo bò masquerade. If he realizes his invention, it will certainly be the most elegant sculptural statement of the inherent reflexivity of this theatrical tradition.

In all my conversations with the Kirango troupe they noted only one restriction in terms of exploiting themes for masquerade characters. They said that they would never incorporate a boli, in their case neither Manyan nor the Kòmò masquerade, into the dramatic repertoire. Today, the troupe never performs the Kòmò masquerade itself, although they do make direct and indirect references to this powerful association. In 1979 they performed a reenactment of a Kòmò processional, but minus the masquerade. They also regularly perform the Kòmò drum rhythms for several masquerades. This seems to confirm that, in these two cases at least, it was the mask as a boli, not the music or dance associated with Kòmò ceremonies, which was perceived to be powerful and dangerous and thus off-limits for the youth theatre.[5]

In contrast to the Kòmò mask among the Bamana, it was the sound of the Jara drum in the Boso Jara men's association masquerade performances that seems to have been the potent force. Boso elders said that the Jara performances always took place outside the village. During these performances the men produced the sound of Jara. This was accomplished by pulling a string back and forth through a drum head, causing a vibration that produced a deep, resonant roar. This was the *gundo*, the secret of Jara. While the Jara drum is never used in the youth association theatre, the Jarawara masquerade, once performed exclusively by this men's association, now regularly appears in youth theatres in both fishing and farming communities [Figure 2.28].

There does seem to be a general regional correlation between certain types of masquerades and the animals they represent. This correlation between form and characterization crosses several performance traditions and is not exclusive to the youth theatre. For example, face masks are generally chosen to represent baboons and monkeys. Lions and a variety of other wildcats generally appear as helmet masks in both the youth theatre and the men's associations like Kòrè. Rod puppet heads are the preferred sculptural form for a whole range of ruminants and birds. While the bird rod puppet cuts across a variety of performance contexts in farming and fishing communities, the only other documented use of antelope masquerades in Bamana communities in the

3.11. A Maraka performance of Sama, the Elephant. 1979. Segou region, Mali. *Photograph by Lynn Forsdale.*

Segou region is as part of the Ciwara association performances. However, in these performances the antelope-like character appears as a crest mask and not a rod puppet. Among the Boso the antelope rod puppets seem to have been a standard part of the repertoire of the Boso men's association performances, the post-hunting masquerade celebrations, as well as the annual youth association theatre.

The elephant, which appears in the youth theatre as a rod puppet, does not appear as a masquerade in men's association ceremonies in Segou [Figure 3.11]. Although the Kòmò Sama, the Kòmò Elephant, is part of Kòmò initiations, it is a carefully staged sound effect and not an actual object (Dieterlen and Cisse 1972, 52–55). In the Jo society in Bougouni, a carved wooden elephant mask, Sama, is used during initiation rituals. This mask is not performed, but is attached to a special house, the sama bugu, the elephant house, which is constructed especially for the initiation (Arnoldi and Ezra 1993, 108; Meurillon 1992).

A notable exception to the correlation between the animal character and its presentation in sculpture is the hyena. While the Kòrè men's association hyena masquerade has regularly been described as a face or helmet mask, the hyena in youth theatre can take the form of a grass masquerade, a rod puppet, or a cloth masquerade. For example in Kirango between 1978 and 1980, Nama, the Hyena, appeared as a grass masquerade [Figure 2.13] and Suruku Nama, the Hyena, took the form of a rod puppet masquerade [Figure 1.11]. Jado Nama, Nama of Minjado, also took the form of a rod puppet hyena masquerade. Suruku Malobali, the Shameless Hyena, was made entirely of cloth over a wooden armature [Figure 2.17].

As a rule villages close to one another and/or linked through kinship, marriage, or amicable historical relationships tend to play a similar repertoire of animal characters and to present them in identical forms. Blacksmiths also may have carved the same characters in identical forms for villages throughout the region and for a variety of different performance contexts. This also contributes to a certain statistical regularity between an animal representation and its material expression.

Compared with the animal characters, personages, whether humans or genies in anthropomorphic form, demonstrate more local variation between the character and its sculptural form. Genies may appear as face masks, body puppets, or small rod puppets. Unlike the bush animals that are widely distributed in youth theatre across the region, some of these characters appeared in a single community's theatre and often had a life span of only a few years or a single generation. There are, of course, several exceptions. A few characters representing personages from the early history of the theatre seemed to have enjoyed a regional popularity that persisted over a half-century. According to testimony from communities throughout the region, some of these characters, especially Mèrèn, appeared everywhere as body puppets.

Mèrèn, a late nineteenth century female character, was first invented for the Shianro Cèko, although it began to be performed within the context of the Sogo bò and Do bò and in other festivals in western Segou villages in the 1930s. While Mèrèn is still performed in a few villages in the region today, in many communities, including Kirango, she had fallen out of favor by the 1950s as other female characters came into vogue.[6] Yayoroba, the Beautiful Woman, another female body puppet, replaced Mèrèn in several western Segou villages [Figure Pref.4]. In Kirango, Koke, and elsewhere, especially where Siriman Fane or the other Koke smiths worked, Yayoroba regularly appears as a large body puppet. However, she has been documented as a small rod and string puppet (Imperato 1981, 21; Mara 1980), and I have occasionally seen Yayoroba performed as a face or helmet mask in villages around Kirango. Likewise the character Cèkòròba, the Elder, sometimes appears as a body puppet and sometimes as a small rod and string puppet [Figure 3.12].

Besides animals, persons, and genies there is a category of character called *k'a ye*, an imaginary being. These characters stand as metaphors for the whole range of human experience and behavior, both virtue and vice, strength and foible. They regularly appear in zoomorphic or anthropomorphic form. Of all the categories of masquerade characters, the form that a troupe gives these characters is the most arbitrary. Many of these characters, especially those that speak to issues like poverty and divorce, are contemporary inventions, although there are a few historical precedents for k'a ye in the early theatre. For example, around the early 1930s Shianro smiths said that one of their ancestors invented Yan Ka Di, This Place Is Good. It appeared as a carved wooden janus-faced female figure out of whose head projected a series of smaller carved female heads. Lem collected an example of Yan Ka Di in Siela in the 1930s (Lem 1949, 62 plate 16) [Figure 3.13]. When I showed elders in Shianro a photograph of this particular piece they commented that this elaborate female puppet was based on the original Mèrèn form. They based this relationship on Yan Ka Di's distinctive sagittal crest coiffure and her elongated features, which were indeed similar to other pieces they identified as Mèrèn. Like her elder sister Mèrèn, Yan Ka Di did enjoy a certain regional popularity during the colonial period, and in the late 1950s Pageard documented her appearance in a performance near Segou city (Pageard 1962, 19). Although I never saw Yan Ka Di being performed, people through-

3.12. A Bamana performance of Cèkòròba, the Elder. 1980. Segou region, Mali. *Photograph by Lynn Forsdale.*

out the region said that she had been a popular character in their theatres in the past, although she was no longer performed much today. Yan Ka Di puppets remain very popular in the tourist art market, however, and they can still be regularly found for sale in Bamako, Dakar, and elsewhere.

Today, most communities have created several new conceptual masquerades and, like the masquerades representing legendary and living persons, these conceptual characters have a relatively more limited spatial distribution. Their theatrical life span is also more limited than many animal characters or many puppets representing persons as conventional social types. In the 1970s in Banankoro the Bamana troupe created the character called the Kamalen Sogo, the Young Man's Antelope. It appears as a two-headed rod puppet antelope masquerade [Figure 3.14]. The Kamalen Sogo does not

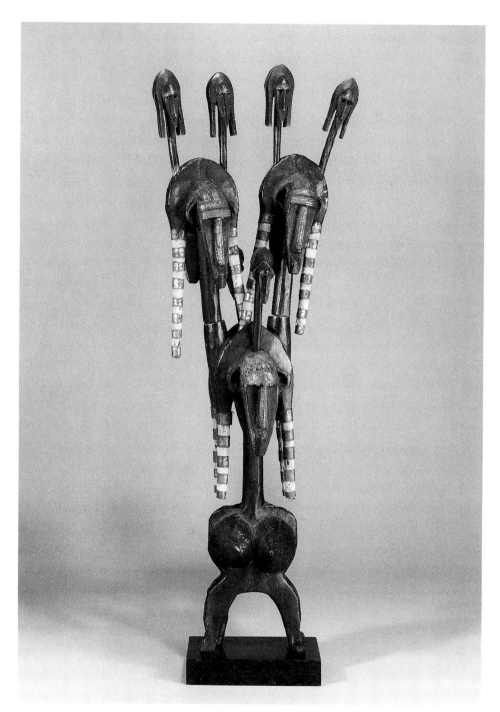

3.13. A Cèko puppet known as Yan Ka Di, This Place Is Good. This puppet was collected by F. H. Lem in Siela, Mali in the early 1930s. Indiana University Art Museum, 77.87. *Photograph by Michael Cavanagh and Kevin Montague.*

3.14. A Bamana performance of Kamalen Sogo, the Young Man's Antelope. 1979. Segou region, Mali. *Photograph by Lynn Forsdale.*

represent any particular antelope species. The troupe interpreted the character as a state-ment about young men as the heroes of the Sogo bò, an interpretation that is based on the character's name and its song (see below). Another character invented around this period and played in and around Kirango is Taasi Dòoni, Reflect a Little. In Kirango the character appears as a helmet mask representing a woman, while in several neighboring villages it appears as a rod puppet antelope head [Figures 1.18 and 2.18]. Dugu-duman-yiri-bi-wooyo, The Good Village's Tree Cheers, was also invented in this past generation by neighbors of Kirango and as far as I could determine it is limited to that single community. This masquerade appears in the form of an antelope, but its song under-scores the importance of solidarity and cooperation within the community.

3.15. A Bamana *maani* of Kuruntigi, the Boso Boatman. 1980. Segou region, Mali. *Photograph by Lynn Forsdale.*

More recently, characters such as Furusa Tile, Divorce Today, and Son-min-te-maa-na, the Character a Person Doesn't Have, are being performed in Kirango and a few neighboring villages. Divorce Today appears as a three-headed grass masquerade of no identifiable species while The Character a Person Doesn't Have takes the form of a rod puppet antelope masquerade.

Maani are always being constantly updated and characters like the farmer hoeing, women pounding millet and winnowing millet, the balafon player, and fishermen rowing boats have endured as part of the repertoire throughout this past century [Figures Pref.3, 3.9, and 3.15]. These puppets are not seen as historical anachronisms, but

3.16. Bamana *maani* of a European woman, probably an ethnographer. 1978. Kirango, Mali. *Photograph by Lynn Forsdale.*

3.17. Bamana *maani* of a European woman, probably a ethnographer. 1978. Kirango, Mali. *Photograph by Ly Forsdale.*

in fact do represent social types and daily activities that are still an integral part of rural life. Precolonial *sofa*, cavalry, *sòròdasiw*, African colonial soldiers, European colonial administrators, and even Western ethnographers have all been part of village repertoires for some time [Figure 3.10]. In some villages they still appear in the contemporary theatre while in other communities they have been replaced by more current representations. For example, beginning in 1968, Siriman Fane carved a group of maani representing Moussa Traore, the President of Mali, in his motorcade with his official motorcycle escort [Figure 2.4]. When I visited Siriman in 1978 this figure group was still part of his active repertoire of sculptures and still in demand.

In Kirango, in the 1950s and early 1960s, the troupe performed a small rod and string puppet representing a European woman who either smoked a cigarette or wrote with a pen into a notebook, the consummate ethnographer [Figures 3.16 and 3.17]. One wonders if this puppet may have been inspired by Germaine Dieterlen or one of her associates, who conducted interviews in this locale in the 1950s. As I sat there with pen and pad in hand, dying for a cigarette, I was struck by how perfectly the sculptor had captured the type. A Malian colleague informed me that in 1990 Numu Jon Diarra of Nienou had carved a small rod and string puppet representing me. I have yet to see the puppet, but when I asked my Malian colleague to describe it, his response was "it looks just like you."

A representative sample of masquerades that are found in many villages throughout the Segou region is contained in Table 3.2. Not all of them are played in every village and this table is not intended to be exhaustive. New characters are being continually created in communities throughout Segou at the same time that others are being modified or dropped from individual troupes' repertoires. Table 3.2, however, does serve to point up the diversity of characters and to suggest the range of sculptural forms that are currently being performed in the youth theatre. The link between character and form in Table 3.2, however, is not meant to represent any absolute.

Table 3.2 Segou Masquerade Characters, Sculptural Forms, and Costumes

The key to the sculptural form:

body puppet	= bp	grass masquerade	= gm
cloth masquerade	= cm	helmet mask	= hm
crest mask	= crm	miniature rod puppet	= mrp
face mask	= fm	rod puppet head	= rp

The key to the costume definition:

binsogo, grass costume = bin

finisogo, cloth costume = fini

An * after the masquerade name = widely distributed in the Segou region either historically or in the contemporary period

---

3.18. A Boso performance of Bama, the Crocodile. 1979. Kirango, Mali. *Photograph by Mary Jo Arnoldi.*

3.19. A Bamana performance of Dajè, the Roan Antelope. 1979. Segou region, Mali. *Photograph by Lynn Forsdale.*

Sogo (Animal)[7]

BAMANA NAME	ENGLISH NAME	FORM	COSTUME	
Bakòrò	Ram	rp	bin	
Bala*	Porcupine	gm	bin	
Bama*	Crocodile	cm, mrp	fini	[Figure 3.18]
Dajè*	Roan Antelope	rp	bin	[Figure 3.19]
Dankalankule*	Oryx	rp	bin	
Fali*	Donkey	rp	bin	
Gòn*	Baboon	fm	bin	
Jarawara*	Wildcat	rp	bin	
Juguni	Hedgehog	rp	bin	
Kalakadane	Antelope (no ID)	rp	bin	[Figure 3.20]
Kònkòrò	Reedbuck	rp	bin	
Koon*	Roan Antelope	rp	bin	[Figure 3.21]
Ma	Manatee	cm	fini	
Mali*	Hippopotamus	cm	fini	[Figure 3.22]
Mankalan*	Crowned Duiker	rp	bin	
Minan*	Bushbuck	rp	bin	
Misi*	Cow	rp, mrp	bin	
Nama*	Hyena			
Nama*		gm	bin	
Jado Nama		rp	bin	
Suruku Malobali		cm	fini	
Suruku Nama*		rp	bin	
Ngongo	Land Turtle	gm	bin	
Njona	Wildcat	hm	bin	
Nkoloni	Oribi	rp	bin	
Ntilen*	Giraffe	rp	bin	[Figure 3.23]
Sa*	Boa, Python	cm	fini	
Duguma Sa*	Snake (ground)	cm	fini	[Figure 3.24]
Sanfè Sa*	Snake (tree)	cm	fini	
Saalen	Nile Perch	cm	fini	[Figure 3.25]
Saga*	Sheep	rp, mrp	bin	
Sama*	Elephant	rp	bin	
Sensen*	Waterbuck	rp	bin	
Sigi*	Buffalo	rp	bin/fini	[Figure 3.26]
Sinè*	Gazelle	rp	bin	
Sogofin	Antelope (no ID)	rp	bin	
Sogoni Kelen	Antelope (no ID)	rp	bin	
Son*	Kob	rp	bin	
Sonsan*	Hare	rp, mrp	bin	
Tankòn*	Hartebeest	rp	bin	
Taw	Water Turtle	cm	fini	
Waraba*	Lion	hm	fini/bin	
Waraba Caco	Striped Wildcat	cm	fini/bin	
Waraninkalan	Leopard	hm	bin	
Wonto	Chimpanzee	fm	fini	

3.20. A Bamana performance of the one-horned Kalakadane, an Antelope. 1979. Segou region, Mali. *Photograph by Lynn Forsdale.*

3.21. A Bamana performance of the Boso character Koon, a Roan Antelope. 1979. Segou region, Mali. *Photograph by Lynn Forsdale.*

3.22. A Boso performance of Mali, the Hippo. 1979. Kirango, Mali. *Photograph by Mary Jo Arnoldi.*

3.23. A Bamana performance of Ntilen, the Giraffe. 1979. Segou region, Mali. *Photograph by Lynn Forsdale.*

3.24. A Bamana performance of Duguma Sa, the Ground Snake. 1979. Segou region, Mali. *Photograph by Lynn Forsdale.*

3.25. A Sòmonò performance of Saalen, the Nile Perch. 1979. Kirango, Mali. *Photograph by Lynn Forsdale.*

3.26. A Bamana performance of Sigimuso, the female Buffalo. 1979. Segou region, Mali. *Photograph by Lynn Forsdale.*

Kònò (Bird)

BAMANA NAME	ENGLISH NAME	FORM	COSTUME
Balakònònin	Crocodile Bird	rp	fini
Baninkònò*	Abdim's Stork	rp	fini
Duga*	Vulture	rp	fini
Kankari Kònò	Bird (no ID)	rp	bin
Kirina Kònò	Bird (no ID)	rp	bin
Kolanjan	Pelican (?)	rp	fini
Kònò Jolenjo	Bird (no ID)	rp	bin
Kònòsogonin	Ostrich	rp	bin
Nkuman	Crowned Crane	rp	bin
Sanin Kojan	Heron	rp	fini

Small birds are also frequently presented as miniaturized rod puppets attached to rod puppet animal heads and on the back of the larger masquerades.

Jinè (Genie)

BAMANA NAME	ENGLISH NAME	FORM	COSTUME	
Bilisi	Bilisi	gm	bin	[Figure 3.27]
Dasiri Sogo	Dasari Antelope	rp	bin	
Jinè-Faro*	Faro	mrp	fini	[Figure 3.28]
Jinè	Genie	all forms	fini/bin	
Jinèjan	Tall Genie	cm	fini	[Figure 3.29]
Mèrèn*	Mèrèn	bp, mrp	fini	
Sumusonin	Sorceress	gm	bin	
Wòkulò*	Bush Genie	fm, hm	fini/bin	[Figure 3.30]

Maani (People)

BAMANA NAME	ENGLISH NAME	FORM	COSTUME	
Balanin Fola	Balafon Musician	mrp	fini	
Barabara	Favorite Wife	hm	fini	
Cèkòròba*	Elder	bp, mrp	fini/bin	
Cikèla	Farmer	mrp	fini	
Conpe	Wanderer	fm	fini	
Donsocè	Hunter	mrp	fini	[Figure 3.31]
Fulacè	Fulani Horseman	mrp	fini	
Jobali*	Boso Woman	fm	fini	
Koorishena-muso*	Woman Cottoncarder	mrp	fini	
Kuruntigi	Boatman	mrp	fini	
Madame Sarata	Mrs. Sarata	bp	fini	
Maisa	Umu Assita (antelope puppet)	rp	bin	
Mònikèla	Fisherman	mrp	fini	
Moussa Traore	President Traore	mrp	fini	
Nafèlu	Policeman	fm	fini	

3.27. A Bamana performance of Bilisi, the genie. 1979. Segou region, Mali. *Photograph by Lynn Forsdale.*

3.28. Jinè-Faro, the female water genie. 1978. *Photograph by Lynn Forsdale.*

3.29. A Bamana performance of Jinè-jan, the Tall Genie. The masker performs on stilts. 1979. Segou region, Mali. *Photograph by Lynn Forsdale.*

3.30. A Bamana performance of Wòkulò, the Bush Genie. 1979. Segou region, Mali. *Photograph by Lynn Forsdale.*

3.31. An antelope rod puppet with smaller puppets of a hunter and a bird attached to the antelope's crown. During its performance the hunter raises its gun and fires at the bird. 1977. Gerald and Barbara Cashion collection. *Photograph by Lynn Forsdale.*

Nteke-dalen-be-Naje-kun	Naje (a woman)	hm	fini	
Nyò-susu-musow*	Women Pounding Millet	mrp	fini	
Nyò-surulan-musow*	Women Winnowing Grain	mrp	fini	
Sotigi*	Horseman	mrp, cm	fini	[Figure 3.32]
Tubabu*	European	mrp	fini	
Yayoroba*	Beautiful Woman	hm/fm/mrp/bp	fini	

3.32. A Sòmonò performance of Sotigi, the Horseman. 1979. Kirango, Mali. *Photograph by Lynn Forsdale.*

K'a ye (Imaginary Others)

BAMANA NAME	ENGLISH NAME	FORM	COSTUME	
Bèn Ka Di	Unity Is Good	rp	bin	
Bilanjan*	Bush Animal	gm	bin	
Bodakolon Kolon	Whirling Beast	gm	bin	
Cèw-ye-kelen-ye	All Men Are Equal	rp	bin	
Dugu-duman-yiri -bi-wooyo	The Good Village's Tree Cheers	rp	bin	
Falakani	Bush Animal or Boso Dance	gm	bin	
Furusa Tile	Divorce Today	gm	bin	
Kamalen Sogo	Young Man's Antelope	rp	bin	
Mali Bonyè	Celebrate Mali	hm	fini	[Figure 3.33]
Mali Kònò*	Bird of Mali	rp	fini	
Manyan	Manyan	gm	bin	
Pari	Credit Association (antelope puppet)	rp	fini	[Figure 3.34]
Soden Mali la	Malian Horseman	rp and mrp	fini	
Son-min-te-maa-na	The Character A Person Doesn't Have	rp	bin	

3.33. A Bamana performance of Mali Bonyè, Celebrate Mali. 1979. Segou region, Mali. *Photograph by Lynn Forsdale.*

Taasi Dòoni	Reflect a Little	fm, rp	fini/bin
Wagadugu Sa	Snake of Wagadu	cm	fini
Walè	Action	gm	bin
Yan Ka Di*	This Place Is Good	bp	fini

Men's Associations' Masquerades Performed in the Sogo bò

BAMANA NAME	ENGLISH NAME	FORM	COSTUME	
Ciwara	Ciwara association mask	cm	bin	[Figure 3.35]
Ntomo	Ntomo association mask	fm, rp	fini	[Figure 3.36]

The Contemporary Scene

BAMANA NAME	ENGLISH NAME	FORM	COSTUME
Avion	Airplane	cm	fini
Mobili*	Automobile	cm	fini

3.35. A Bamana performance of two Ciwara masquerades. 1987. Kirango, Mali. *Photograph by Mary Jo Arnoldi.*

3.36. A small rod and string puppet representing a Ntomo masker. 1990. Brussels, Belgium. *Photograph by Marc Leo Felix.*

Dancing, Drumming, and Singing

As the *Sogotigi*, owner of the masquerades, the youth association keeps detailed histories of the sculptural forms. Yet these sculptures and masquerades are only one of the expressive forms required to create a performance. Dancing (*dòn kè*), drumming (*dunun fò*), and singing (*dònkili da*) play equally important roles in bringing the masquerades to life and in creating and sustaining both the individual characterizations and the performance event.

Dance significantly contributes to creating the characterization, and most of the masquerades' dances are mimetic. Dancers draw their inspiration for animal characters from observations of the animal's behavior and movements in nature. The movement and gait of lions and wildcats emphasize their feline qualities, while the buffalo, the elephant, and the bovine assert their bulk and lumber slowly around the arena. The baboon and other monkey characters' movements are erratic as these characters dart to and fro and into the crowd, lunge at people as if to steal things, and scratch themselves and grab their private parts in an exaggerated manner violating any sense of acceptable social propriety. Fishing birds spread their wings and glide as if in flight, stopping to bob their heads up and down as if fishing the river.

Human characters' movements are drawn from a shared understanding of appropriate demeanor and comportment and are grounded in everyday life. Dancers either reproduce these culturally accepted movements or in a few cases they parody the norms associated with the person's gender or status. Cèkòròba, the Elder, generally moves solemnly and with great dignity and control [Figure 3.12]. When Yayoroba, the Beautiful Woman, enters the ring, the dancer drops down on one knee to bow to the assembled crowd in a gesture traditionally associated with a modest young woman's demeanor when she greets her elders [Figure Pref.4]. She moves gracefully, dancing with gently swaying hips in a style culturally associated with the appropriate demeanor for a modest Bamana woman. In contrast to Yayoroba, Kirango's Taasi Dòoni, a masked figure of a woman, gives a bawdy performance, moving seductively, brazenly, and quite suggestively [Figure 1.18].

Dancers create the movements of spirits and genies from their characterizations in stories, legends, and epics. For example, in the case of Jinè-Faro, the female water genie, the puppeteer periodically uses the puppet's hands to cover its face [Figure 3.28]. This gesture corresponds to a well-known legend that relates how when men gazed directly upon the face of Faro they were instantly struck dead.

This emphasis on mimesis in masquerade dancing is common to most performances in south central Mali and is not unique to the Sogo bò. The relationship that is established between the masquerade and its dance creates the character's identity. Some performers even said that the masquerade dance is actually more critical to the success or failure of the performance than is the sculpture. All of these mimetic dances are highly abstract, pulling only select phrasing from the larger universe of possible movements. Yet everyone agreed that the inspiration for these dances is based on the dancer's powers of observation and his understanding of the character in nature. We have no documentation on the historical development of these dances within Segou performance traditions, but it seems highly probable that hunters were instrumental in developing these forms. Hunters' knowledge and skills are based on a close observation of animal behavior. The mimetic skills valued in hunting are the same as those necessary to create credible characterizations in masked dancing throughout this region. Game is becoming more scarce in the Segou region and fewer young men train to be hunters. Without the opportunity to observe animal behavior firsthand, the dancers will draw their inspiration exclusively from past theatrical performances, rather than being continually renewed from the wellspring of experience in the bush. I would hypothesize that dances for animal masquerades might, therefore, become more conventionalized and stylized in the future.

Another type of dance performed by certain grass masquerades in the youth theatre and by power masquerades in men's associations involves continual transformations of the masquerade's shape. In these shape-shifting dances little attention is paid to the reproduction of mimetic movements of the animal in nature. The performance of Bala, the Porcupine, is a good example of this type of shape-shifting dance [Figure 2.16]. The masquerade at rest resembles a large undifferentiated haystack, but once it is in motion it becomes a whirling ball extending itself vertically and horizontally. These transformations are highly dramatic and awe-inspiring. They involve a series of quick acrobatic movements. The dancer tumbles, leaps several feet into the air, walks in a squat position, and rolls along the ground. These shape-shifting sequences require great physical prowess on the part of the dancer. It is no surprise that these performances are relatively short and usually involve a sustained doubling or trebling of the musical tempo.

In all three of the Kirango youth theatres the four original grass masquerades require this kind of performative transformation, as did the Bamana character Manyan, a grass masquerade that was a boli. Henry's description of the rod puppet Kòmò masquerade suggests that a similar emphasis was placed on shape-shifting in these performances (Henry 1910, 148). McNaughton's description of the bird masquerade performed by Sidi Ballo involved this same energetic display. Ballo turned the masquerade on its head and contorted its form into a variety of shapes. He even created the illusion that the masquerade was dancing of its own volition (McNaughton 1988, 47). The armature of the bird masquerade performed for descendants of the Diarra rulers in Koulikoro also lends itself to such dramatic contortions and shape-shifting. In a manner quite similar to the grass masquerades used in the youth theatre, this bird's body is constructed of a stack of three or four wooden rings in graduated sizes that are loosely connected to one another. By pushing and pulling on these rings, the dancer can expand or contract the bulk and height of the masquerade.

Besides the masquerade dances, the youth performances often include several other discrete dance events. In Kirango both young men and young women participate in circle dances that open the event. These circle dances are followed by acrobatic dance competitions between young men in the association. The men's acrobatic dance is called the *Bònjalan*. Throughout the afternoon and evening performances, young men and sometimes older women take the role of *kòrèdugaw*, clowns. Sometimes they wear an odd assortment of castaways, including old bottles, rags, and the like. They gather in the dance arena and perform with abandon. Their dances are often wildly impolite and, like the baboon and monkey masqueraders, they violate cultural standards of propriety, much to the delight of the crowd.

The masquerades and non-masked dances are always accompanied by drumming. Drumming is not an artistic activity that is restricted to professional musicians as is performing on either the *kòra*, a harp-lute, or the *balafon*, a xylophone, which is the purview of griots. During the Sogo bò theatre, there is generally one major drum team and several designated relief drummers. The Kirango Bamana troupe uses four drum types: the *dununba*, a large wooden kettledrum, several *bònkolow* and *kunanfaw*, medium sized wooden cylindrical drums, and a *nganga*, a small wooden handheld drum. The diameter of the large kettledrum is several feet across and the drum itself is quite heavy. It takes three strong men working together to stretch the cowhide for the drumhead and to tune this drum before each performance. The dununba drummer must be exceptionally strong, as the drum team is not stationary during the performance but continually moves around the dance arena. The weight of the drum is supported by means of a thick leather strap that passes across the lower back and hips of the musician. The low and resonant tone of this drum contributes to the distinctive sound of the farmers' performances and audibly distinguishes them from those of the Sòmonò and Boso fishermen.

Drummers, like masquerade dancers, can be selected from any social strata. The most celebrated drummers in the past several generations in Kirango have come from every segment of society. Drummers are chosen for their musical skills, their stamina and strength, and their knowledge of the body of different rhythms that are appropriate to particular masquerade characters and to specific dance events. While everyone could recognize differences in drum rhythms, I found that it was primarily drummers who knew the specific names for the different drum rhythms used in the theatre. We have little or no documentation about the history of the different drum rhythms used in the theatre. However, there is some indication that, like sculpture, drum rhythms moved independently from one performance context to another. Within the youth theatre there is a certain degree of local variation between the masquerade character and its chosen drum rhythm. Again, this suggests that, like sculptural form and theatrical characterization, some degree of latitude always existed in forging the artistic relationships between the masquerades and their musical rhythms.

The most frequently played drum rhythm in the Kirango Bamana theatre and in many neighboring farming villages is known simply as *sogo dunun*, the masquerade rhythm. Drummers play this rhythm for the majority of the theatrical characters, whether they are animal representations, personages, or conceptual masquerades. The Kirango troupe also plays a rhythm they call *Waraba Caco dunun*, Striped Wildcat rhythm, with their masquerade of the same name and for most of their hyena characters. There are also several other drum rhythms that the Kirango troupe has incorporated into the drama from other performance traditions. These include the Ntomo, Ciwara, Kòmò, and Dawòorò rhythms. The Ntomo rhythm and the Ciwara rhythm are played exclusively for the Ntomo and Ciwara masquerades, respectively. Kòmò dunun is played for several masquerades as well as for a theatrical reenactment of a Kòmò processional. The

Dawòorò rhythm is borrowed from the public dances following women's excision rites. The Kirango troupe has combined it with several masquerades representing female characters and for special animal masquerades.

Song is the primary verbal art form used in the youth theatre. In most communities, the masquerades are voiceless and their songs become the medium of verbal communication between the character and the audience.[8] Each masquerade character has a particular song associated with it and each of these songs has a distinct melody.

Female lead singers in the theatre are not considered to be professional singers, a definition reserved for griots in Bamana society. In Kirango, for example, neither Mei Diarra nor Nanyan Coulibaly, the two lead singers, is a griot. In contrast to amateur performers, griots are called *kumatigiw*, owners of speech, and they are considered society's premier verbal and musical artists. They recite genealogies, sing praises and epics, compose and perform poetry and stories, and provide musical entertainment during many public celebrations, including marriages and baptisms. Specialized verbal art forms they practice are the *balimali*, the recited or sung lineage genealogy (Hoffman 1990, 142–143), and the *fasa*, the praise song (Hoffman 1990, 92). Their performances are considered highly powerful because they can stir emotions and move people to action. For example, during the 1980s war between Mali and Burkina Faso, recordings of celebrated griots' performances, such as those by Basouma Sissoko, were played constantly on the government radio station. Barbara Hoffman reported that these heroic songs moved people in Bamako to take to the streets in a show of emotional support for the war effort.[9]

Griot language, *jelikan*, is a specialized form of speech. It can be inserted to varying degrees in a variety of performances and it is used extensively in the singing of genealogies and praises for heroic deeds (Hoffman 1990, 92). It consists of conjoined noun phrases, rather than complete sentences. As Hoffman noted, its simple syntactic structure renders its meaning obscure, making jelikan highly potent and powerful. She states:

> In my attempts to discover what it is about praise genres that is so powerful, a phrase-by-phrase examination of nobles' interpretations of praise lines revealed that they could not decipher the referential content of *jelikan*. Upon further investigation with griots, I was somewhat surprised to discover that a large proportion of any individual griot's repertory of phrases is empty of referential content to him/her as well. These phrases are usually not used in isolation, but in strings which may be many phrases long. The meaning of the individual phrase is thus its membership in the class of phrases that can be sung for a Traore or a Keita [hòròn lineages], it is not the sum of its parts. The obscurity of its referential content in the performance context is an important aspect of the *nyama* of griot language. (Hoffman 1989, 8)

While Sogo bò songs as a poetic form do contain metaphors and allusions, the singing of specialized fasa and the use of jelikan, verbal art forms that are reserved for professional griots, are not part of a youth association lead singer's repertoire. Griots may sometimes perform praise songs during the youth association event, although they are not considered to be performing under the auspices or direction of the youth association. For instance, when my praises were sung during the 1987 Kirango youth association theatre, it was a woman griot, not the association's lead singers, who performed my praises during the interlude between masquerade performances.

In his analysis of griots' performances of the Mande epics, John Johnson identified three different modes used in these events: the narrative mode, the praise-proverb mode, and the song mode. According to Johnson, the songs used within the larger performance differed from the other two modes in that, in the songs,

> the amount of aesthetic tension between the poetic line and the measure is the lowest for both melody and rhythm. Bard and instrument blend together more than in either of the other two modes. (Johnson 1986, 33)

The song mode is the primary verbal mode used in the Sogo bò theatre, the exception being in fishermen's youth association theatre. In certain fishermen's villages, Boso bards can be central to the performance and sing genealogies and praises for the lineage-owned masquerades, but never for those masquerades that are owned by the youth association. The same aesthetic blending of poetic line and musical measure that Johnson identified for the song mode in the epic performances is a characteristic feature of the songs sung in the youth theatre. In the performance of epics, songs serve to underscore important episodes (Johnson 1986, 32–33). The songs sung for the masquerades in the youth theatre serve a similar function. They first clearly identify the masquerade character and simultaneously draw the audience's attention to its performance.

While the female lead singers in the youth theatre are not defined by their society as professionals, they are highly talented singers and are expected to have control of an extensive body of songs in order to move the performance forward over many hours. The song structure and its performance are always antiphonal and the most basic songs consist of a single lead line or two that is then repeated in its entirety by the chorus. This verse and response may then be repeated twenty or more times during the masquerade's performance. Some masquerade's performances involve only the extended repetitions of what I am calling here the "masquerade signature song." The song and performance of Ntilen, the Giraffe, in the Kirango theatre followed this minimal structure and pattern of repetition [Figure 3.23].

LEAD SINGER   *Ntilen sogo ko sogojan*
               a cè ka nyi
CHORUS   *Ntilen sogo ko sogojan*
               a cè ka nyi

Throughout the evening the women perform other masquerade songs that are variations of this basic pattern. In the song for Misi, the Cow, the lead verse and its choral refrain were repeated for the first ten repetitions, then the lead singer introduced a new verse and the chorus responded not by repeating the lead verse but by introducing a different refrain. The lead singer then repeated the chorus's verse and the chorus responded to her call by repeating the verse again. Once they established this new pattern, they repeated it twenty more times [Figure 1.2].

LEAD SINGER   *Eee Misiw yoo oo*
               Misiw wilil'a
CHORUS   *Eee Misiw yoo oo*
               Misiw wilil'a (10 repetitions)

LEAD SINGER	*Eee Misiw yoo*
	Misiw wilil'a dan kolon na ee
CHORUS	*Eee Misiw yoo oo*
	Misiw wilil'a deliko la eee
LEAD SINGER	*Eee misiw yoo*
	Misiw wilil'a deliko la ee
CHORUS	*Eee misiw yoo*
	Misiw wilil'a deliko la eee (20 repetitions)

A common practice when singing the masquerade songs involves stretching the line to fit the measure. The singer accomplishes this by either stretching actual words or inserting nonsense syllables or onomatopoeic sounds leading into or finishing the sung line. Both professional griots and nonprofessional singers use this technique in a variety of performance contexts. In the Misi song, for example, the singer held or stretched the first and the last words in the line to complete the measure.

One critical function of the masquerade signature song is denotative. Each masquerade song must include the name of the character and this name usually appears in the first lead verse. This verbal information supplements the visual information communicated through the sculpture and dance and erases any potential for ambiguity about which masquerade is performing. Declaiming the masquerade's name functions as a form of praising. This praise line is instrumental, not merely informational. Singing the masquerade's name energizes the character and heightens the dancer's performance capacity. Publicly declaiming the character's name inspires the puppeteer/dancer in much the same way that a jeli's genealogical praise singing and hunters' bards' performances of heroic songs move those praised or their descendants to action. As Charles Bird has observed:

> Speech itself is considered to contain this energy as denotes the expression:
> *Nyama be kuma la*
> The energy of action is in speech.
> When a praise song is sung for someone, his energy to act is augmented, thus forcing him to act. . . . (Bird 1976, 98)

In the puppet theatre, although the leader singer is usually not a griot she does periodically interject praises into her songs with the same intention to move individuals and groups to action. However, she does not construct her praises using the powerful conjoined noun phrases of jelikan. At different points in the performance the lead singer will praise the assembled women as the singers or sing the praises of the young men as the owners of the masquerades. She may choose to praise particular sculptors who have created the masquerade, or she may praise the villages from whom a character was borrowed. She may also sing out the names of past and present leaders of the association and recognize by name or affiliation honored guests in the audience.

In the following song, recorded in 1979 during a performance outside of Kirango, Ahmadu Ballo, a blacksmith who carved the puppet head for the Kamalen Sogo, Young Man's Antelope, was publicly praised in a song that accompanies the masquerade's performance. People said that his mother had originally invented the song and that it has now become a regular feature of the performance[Figure 3.14].

LEAD SINGER   *A m'o ye*
                      Numuden Amadu kunbenna ni kamalenw ye eee
                      A m'o ye ee
                      Numuden Amadu kunbenna ni Kamalen Sogo ye

CHORUS   *A m'o ye*
                      Numuden, an ka taa o f'o ye
                      Na ni Kamalen Sogo ye ee

LEAD SINGER   Haven't you seen it
                      Amadu the blacksmith's child was met by the young men
                      Haven't you seen it
                      Amadu, the blacksmith's child was met with the Kamalen Sogo

CHORUS   Haven't you seen it
                      Blacksmith's child, let us go tell him
                      Bring the Kamalen Sogo

A few masquerade songs that are sung in the current theatre do contain a more elaborate narrative, although these songs are somewhat exceptional even today. One masquerade performed in Kirango, Jado Nama, is said to have been inspired by a song composed by a woman from the area that was popularized within the last generation. It tells the story of a celebrated woman singer, Ba of Sebedugu, who was diagnosed with *kènkònò*, which is a poison administered through food or drink (Bailleul 1981, 103). She was cured by Nama of Minjado, to whom this song is dedicated. The song now has been incorporated into the Kirango youth theatre and is sung for the performance of Jado Nama, a masquerade representing a hyena. The choice of hyena for the character seems to have been a conscious play on the healer's name, Nama, and on people's association of certain healing properties with hyenas. According to Zahan, in Bamana medical practices the intestines of the hyena are used as one of the best therapeutic agents against poisoning (Zahan 1960, 231).

In Jado Nama's song the lead singer develops the story in each successive verse and the choral refrain consists of the repetition of a praise line for the protagonist. A short excerpt from the song, translated into English, gives a sense of this narrative development.

LEAD SINGER   A yee I was stricken with sickness
                      I was stricken with the *kènkònò*
                      Let us thank Nama of Minjado

CHORUS   I have seen no one who can equal him

LEAD SINGER   i yoo Nama went into the bush
                      Nyakoro Jara went into the bush
                      He came out with the antidote for *kènkònò*
                      Let us thank Nama of Minjado

CHORUS   I have seen no one who can equal him

LEAD SINGER	i yoo For whom was this antidote intended
	It ought to be given to Ba of Sebedugu
	Let us thank the Nama of Minjado
CHORUS	I have seen no one who can equal him
LEAD SINGER	i yee Ba drank the antidote
	Ba drank this antidote for kènkònò
	I have begun to vomit
	Let us thank the Nama of Minjado
CHORUS	I have seen no one who can equal him
LEAD SINGER	i yoo What has come up with the vomit
	A toad has come out with the vomit
	Let us thank the Nama of Minjado
CHORUS	I have seen no one who can equal him

Other songs based on legendary characters, such as Sasali Bama, the Crocodile of Sasali, and Bilisi, a genie who appears in the epic of Da Monzon Diarra of Segou, are performed in Kirango's theatre and in a number of theatres in the region. In Kirango, the song for Bilisi, the genie, is sung for the performance of a grass masquerade intended to represent this legendary character [Figure 3.27]. While the Bamana of Kirango perform no crocodile masquerade, the song that alludes to the legend of Sasali Bama is currently sung for the character Bilanjan, a grass masquerade considered to be a tall bush animal [Figure 2.15]. In both these songs no extended narrative is developed, yet most everyone in the audience is familiar with the two stories from contexts outside of the youth theatre. The mere mention of the names of these legendary figures suffices to recall their stories for most members of the audience.

After the singers complete the character's signature song, they may fill out the masquerade's performance with songs drawn from other performance events. In the interludes between the different masquerade segments the lead singers choose songs which speak to critical social issues, including group solidarity, unbridled competition, marriage, and death. For example, many of the songs which Mei Diarra and Nanyan Coulibaly sang during the 1979 and 1980 Sogo bò were ones they had performed during the *Bara* dance events staged by the youth association during the dry season in 1979. Others I recorded in 1979 when Mei Diarra sang for the annual *kòlò susu*, the processing of fermented karité nuts into oil.

Of all of the Sogo bò's expressive forms, song demonstrated the most variation from village to village. While it is true that two villages may play many of the same animal characters, I regularly found that in these villages the women sang quite different songs for the same character even though the character took the same sculptural form and was accompanied by the same drum rhythms and by relatively similar mimetic dances. The greatest variation in masquerade songs seems to occur with those characters that have been a regular part of regional repertoires since the early days of the theatre. While one often finds that villages in close proximity to one another or tied through marriage relations often sing many of the same songs for identical masquerades, I was struck by the amount of variation in the repertoire of songs I found even in villages which share close relationships and also in those who have no history of exchanges. Songs for Dajè, the Roan Antelope, and for other animal characters that have been central to youth theatres for at least a century, can differ quite dramatically from one locale to another [Figure 3.19]. While we have little or no information about the history of these theatrical songs for most of this past century, the differences in masquerade songs that I was able to record in the region strongly suggest that the ability of singers to invent, modify, incorporate, and adjust these songs to changing local interests over time has certainly been a valued part of the Sogo bò's artistic history and part of what gives the theatre its continuing creative edge.

Because these songs are lyric poems, the verses are often enigmatic and ripe with allusions and metaphors. These songs contain multiple references which resonate with a host of verbal imagery contained in legends, animal tales, hunters' lore, and epics. At the most general level, people share a basic interpretation of particular animals. Many people used the allusions and metaphors in the songs to build upon shared interpretations in order to create more elaborate and finely textured meanings that were particularly relevant to their own life history, knowledge, and experience. Specific examples of the creative play of interpretation will be explored more fully later in this study.

The Movement of Forms and Their Incorporation into the Sogo bò

We do know from the ethnographic literature, from museum collections, and from contemporary commentary that similar expressive forms have been distributed across a wide variety of performance contexts within the region throughout this past century. The permutations and variations in the repertoire of Segou theatres strongly suggests that this movement of expressive forms and dramatic ideas is a longstanding artistic practice in the region. Rather than viewing the exchange or appropriation of forms as a recent phenomenon, or as evidence of the secularization of rituals, as Pageard suggested, it seems more fruitful to take the local view in order to understand these processes. From a local perspective no single expressive form in isolation defines any one performance context. It is the interrelationship of arts forged in performance that defines them as unique to one or another performance tradition.

The material, oral, and written record suggests that some constellations of forms historically moved as single performance units, while other art forms moved independently and more freely from one context to another. While it is difficult to reconstruct these histories it is, however, possible to develop some feeling for the regional flow of forms through time. Since my questions focused primarily on the Sogo bò, most of the examples of creative borrowing that people recounted highlighted the movement of particular expressive forms from outside youth theatre to within it. Sogo bò's primary definition as an entertainment and the high value that people give to innovation in the theatre have clearly contributed to the elevated tempo and increased scale of these borrowings. However, the invention and borrowing of forms to create boli such as Manyan in Kirango and Kirina Kònò, Jarawara, and Gòn in neighboring villages strongly suggest that these practices were not exclusive to performances defined as entertainments.[10]

Instances of borrowings and movements can be identified within the official history of the Kirango theatre. If we compare the Kirango case to other villages' past and current practices, a regional history begins to emerge that belies the still too often repeated notion that these artistic forms and their performance events are conservative and static.

According to oral traditions collected about the theatre in the Bamana quarter of Kirango, the earliest Sogo bò performances included grass masquerades borrowed directly from the Do bò theatre of the fishermen. In 1979 the Bamana and Sòmonò troupes performed these four grass masquerades. According to the official Bamana kamalen ton history, when the farmers adopted the theatre they did not take the masquerades wholesale, but transformed them into their own by creating new songs for them and by playing Bamana drum rhythms for their performances.

In the 1920s Shianro smiths introduced the rod puppet animal heads into the Kirango Bamana theatre. These smiths had for at least a generation been carving similar puppet heads for their own Cèko youth theatre. A decade later they introduced the characters Kalaka Sogo and Mèrèn into Kirango. Instead of incorporating these two masquerades, which represent community life, into the repertoire of the Sogo bò, the Kirango troupe used them in a totally different festival. It was only in the mid 1950s when the two separate performances were merged that the small rod and string puppets became part of the Sogo bò theatre. By 1950 Mèrèn was no longer being played. It was not until the 1960s when Siriman Fane introduced the character Yayoroba into the Kirango theatre that body puppets were reintroduced into Kirango.

The history of the Yayoroba body puppet is a particularly good example with which to demonstrate the dynamic movement of artistic forms and ideas within this region and beyond. Kirango's Yayoroba puppet was carved by Siriman Fane of Koke. He had already carved a Yayoroba puppet for his own quarter's theatre in the late 1950s. According to Siriman, whom I interviewed in 1980, his creation was inspired by the older Mèrèn body puppets. In 1987 when I interviewed other family members they said that although Yayoroba resembles the older Mèrèn body puppet, Siriman did not invent her. They said that Yayoroba was actually copied by Moussa Fane from a tourist sculpture made by a Wolof carver in Bamako. Both claims have a certain historical validity. Certain iconographic details of the Yayoroba puppet, such as its hairstyle, differ quite radically from that on Mèrèn puppets collected by Lem in Shianro in the 1930s (Lem 1949, 59 plate 13; Goldwater 1960, 35 plates 41, 42). These differences support the younger blacksmith's account that the Yayoroba figure was not wholly modeled after Mèrèn. However, by the late 1950s, when Yayoroba first appeared in Koke, Siriman had already produced a number of Mèrèn puppets for different villages in the Segou region. In fact, he claimed Mèrèn was the first puppet sculpture he carved as a young sculptor and he made it for the village of Siela in Shianro in the 1920s. According to oral traditions in Nienou, Mèrèn was already well known in the Cèko theatre by the turn of the century. Nienou smiths said that in this eastern zone the body puppet form was used not only for the character Mèrèn but for Yan Ka Di, This Place Is Good, and Cèkòròba, the Elder, among others. These early popular Mèrèn sculptures may have been the formal inspiration for the Wolof tourist piece carved in Bamako in the 1950s. If this is the case it would bolster Siriman's statement that Yayoroba was merely an innovation off of her older sister, Mèrèn. The movement of this body puppet from within the Cèko to a tourist art market, and then its reincorporation back into the youth theatre in Koke through the agency of Moussa Fane, a local smith, is a good example of this dynamic process. Nor is Yayoroba an isolated case.

Songs, drum rhythms, and dance also seem to have moved with a certain regularity. Between 1948 and 1950, the Kirango troupe introduced the masquerade character Maisa into their theatre. This character is still performed today and it appears as a roan antelope rod puppet masquerade. Several elder men who were members of the youth association during the late 1940s recalled quite specifically the circumstances surrounding this character's invention. They said that it was the Maisa song that was the original inspiration for the masquerade. This song was created as a praise song by an itinerant entertainer to honor the hospitality of a woman named Umu Assita who lived in a community south of the Bani River. The song was later popularized by singers traveling through the region. In Kirango it ultimately was plucked from these performances for use in the Kirango masquerade theatre. The Kirango troupe chose to combine this popular song with a roan antelope puppet masquerade and the theatrical character Maisa was born.

The troupe chose to play the Dawòorò drum rhythm for the Yayoroba masquerade introduced in 1960. The Dawòorò rhythm is played for the public celebrations following female excision when the young girls are brought back into the village and presented to the community. These young girls are now ready for marriage and are touted as beautiful and desirable. The ton's choice of the Dawòorò rhythm to accompany a masquerade representing a beautiful woman establishes an unambiguous link between the young unmarried women presented after excision and the masquerade character of Yayoroba. It ascribes to the masquerade character the same attributes and sense of potential that people associate with young girls preparing for marriage.

In Kirango, however, the Bamana troupe also plays the Dawòorò rhythm for Ntilen, the Giraffe. Playing the Dawòorò for a giraffe masquerade might initially seem to be puzzling. However, when I discussed the attributes of animals with different segments of the community, everyone immediately referred to the physical beauty and grace of the giraffe. Its dance in the youth theatre underscores these qualities. Ntilen's song includes the praise line *Ntilen sogo cè ka nyi*, the beautiful giraffe. *Cè ka nyi* translates specifically as physical beauty in this context. Thus the same attributes of physical beauty and grace that are associated with young unmarried girls during their public presentation are linked to the giraffe masquerade through the Dawòorò rhythm. These attributes are further reinforced through the masquerade's dance and are proclaimed in its song.

While the youth association never performs the Kòmò masquerade, the troupe does play the Kòmò drum rhythm for the reenactment of the Kòmò procession and for the masquerade character Mali Kònò, the Bird of Mali. In its original performance context, the Kòmò rhythm was played during the annual ceremonies of the Kòmò men's association. When the men's association masquerade moved through the village, all of the uninitiated, including women, children, and strangers, were required to stay hidden within their houses. Although participation at the Kòmò rites was restricted and only in-itiated men ever saw the boli masquerade, everyone else in the village could hear its distinctive drum rhythm. Kòmò was last performed in Kirango in the 1950s. Many of the young men, who are now in the association's senior age-grade, and most men who were members of the association in the years following Kòmò's demise, as well as many adult women in this village, remember the sound of the Kòmò moving through the quarter. Their association of this drum rhythm with an awesome and powerful force is still quite strong. Even younger people, who were born after Kòmò was abandoned and who never experienced a Kòmò performance directly or indirectly, are aware of this drum rhythm's history and legacy in their village. Its use in the Kòmò processional is intended to recall and heighten this memory.

Several former youth association members who were active when Mali Kònò was first introduced said that the kamalen ton's adoption of the highly charged Kòmò drum rhythm for this bird masquerade was intended not only to capture the audience's atten-tion but to heighten its appreciation of the character. They made it quite clear that the selection of this rhythm for Mali Kònò had been a deliberate and conscious one.

Another example of this movement of forms from one performance tradition to an-other is the performance of the Ntomo and Ciwara masquerades in the afternoon segment of the Kirango Sogo bò. I saw Ntomo performed during the 1978–1980 seasons, and when I returned in 1987 the troupe had added the Ciwara masquerade to the repertoire [Figure 3.35]. Recently in Brussels I came across a small rod puppet representing a Ntomo masker in the window of an African art gallery. Although I never saw a Ntomo rod puppet performed in Segou, its appearance as a small rod puppet was not in the least surprising considering the countless other mask forms that I had documented in the field that had undergone this same sort of transformation in their life histories within youth theatre [Figure 3.36].

An innovation that regularly occurs in the youth theatre involves the transformation of a well-established character into a new one by altering one or more of its artistic com-ponents. The rod puppet representing a large fishing bird known as Mali Kònò, the Bird of Mali, first made its appearance in the Kirango theatre in 1960. This rod puppet is similar to other bird masquerades, such as Baninkònò, the Stork, that had for years been popular in many fishermen's and farmers' theatres in the region. Creating the new character of Mali Kònò was accomplished by linking an already recognizable puppet form to a new song and a different drum rhythm. Its newly created identity as Mali Kònò underscores its link to a particular historical moment, that of national independence from French colonial rule in 1960.

Other changes in Kirango's theatre have involved structural changes in the festival itself. In the mid 1950s the troupe combined the original Sogo bò event with the spring festival's masquerade repertoire and with the Bònjalan dance competitions. Today every festival in the Bamana quarter opens with the dance events. These are followed by after-noon masquerades and then, after sunset, the original Sogo bò bush animal masquerades are performed.[11]

While it is often difficult to talk to people about the history of expressive forms in the men's associations, the Sogo bò theatre does provide a more fruitful avenue for investigating the dynamic nature of artist forms and performance in this region over time. Because the Sogo bò theatre is defined as play and entertainment, discussions of the theatre do not violate collective notions of secrecy, nor do discussions of these events and their constituent forms tread upon categories of knowledge and experience that people consider inappropriate for public explication.

Expressive Forms and the Evaluation of Mande Arts

Mande arts and performances, including those of Bamana and related groups such as the Malinke and the Kono, have been the subject of a growing number of perceptive studies since the 1970s. Although most studies have focused on different media and performance contexts, such as masquerade, epic and praise poetry, dance, and theatre, there is a growing body of evidence to support the claim that there are certain structural principles and key cultural values that organize the production and evaluation of artistic forms across media and across performance contexts (Arnoldi 1983, 1986, 1988b; Bird 1974, 1976; Brett-Smith 1984; Brink 1980, 1981; Ezra 1983, 1986; Hardin 1988; Hoffman 1990; Johnson 1986; McNaughton 1978, 1979, 1982, 1987, 1988; Zahan 1972).

These same structural principles and values find analogous expression in patterns of social organization and in social practices (Bird and Kendall 1980; Hardin 1993; Jackson 1982). These homologies of form across media and across contexts among Mande-speaking peoples throughout West Africa constitute an aesthetic framework or what Kaeppler has called "evaluative ways of thinking" (Kaeppler 1978 and 1986).

While different arts and performances have their own myths of origin, Brink noted that many of these myths follow a similar pattern. Art and artistic expression are generally said to have originated in the bush, a locus of extraordinary *nyama*, energy or life force. In many of these myths, including that for Segou's youth masquerade theatre, it was a hunter or other similarly endowed person who learned the arts from inhabitants of the bush (sometimes animals, sometimes genies) and brought them back into society. As Brink explains:

> Through the founder's transmuting acts the arts were made "good" and as such, they were made to embrace and express the principle of "goodness." They were given a cultural frame which subsumed the knowledge for their creation and evaluation and set the conditions for their social use. These aesthetic and social constraints, however, did not alter the arts' substantive connection with their bush origin, for this was the principal source of their energy and power, their *nyama*. (Brink 1981, 5)

All manner of things possess nyama.[12] McNaughton notes that Mande peoples believe that this energy embodies a sense of moral reciprocity. If nyama is released in massive and uncontrolled amounts it may even be deadly (McNaughton 1988, 15). It is this energy, released through the creative act of masquerade theatre, that participants acknowledge, both tacitly and discursively, must be clearly framed and bounded in time. Brink has suggested that for the Bamana the theory of aesthetic form, simply put, is "form managing power" (Brink 1981, 3).

An art's form, that is, its basic ordering characteristics, is encapsulated in the term *nyi* or "goodness." This nyi is made comprehensible through *cogo*, which has been variously translated as the manner, the way, the style. Cogo is the cultural knowledge necessary to "initiate, order, and identify" any art form or aesthetic expression (Brink 1981, 9). This cultural knowledge is passed down from the ancestors and gives the arts their moral authority. *Di*, tastiness, activates the nyama inherent in art through challenging and embellishing its form. Di encapsulates the sensate dimensions of artistic expression. In discussing the term di or diya, tastiness or sweetness, Kris Hardin noted that among the Kono, Mande-speaking people of Sierra Leone, the word di "is applied to song, a singer's voice, drumming, cooked food, and apparently other things that are ephemeral or impermanent" (Hardin 1988, 42). Form managing power might best be understood as the ability of performers to manage the dialectic tension between an art form's goodness and its tastiness, between the reproduction of a cultural form and its revisions in order to create and control its nyama (Brink 1981, 4).

In his study of Mande sculpture Patrick McNaughton discussed two terms, *jayan* and *jako*, that professional artist-smiths in south central Mali regularly used when evaluating sculptural form. Jayan refers to the core structure of form while jako [jago] refers to an embellishment or decoration of this core form (McNaughton 1988, 107–108). The features of form that correspond to jayan are realized through controlled composition and reduction and are encapsulated in two Bamana terms, *woron*, to husk or shuck, and *kolo*, kernel, nut, bone, nucleus, the essential structure (McNaughton 1979, 43). Jayan corresponds to the moral concept of nyi, goodness and knowledge, passed down from the ancestors. Jako, an embellishment or decoration, is what activates the cultural form giving it an immediacy and its quality of diya, tastiness or sweetness.

Smiths and non-smiths whom I interviewed often said that a good sogo sculpture, a *sogo nyana*, must include the appropriate cluster of diagnostic features, abstracted from the model in nature, which allowed people to unambiguously identify the character being represented. When discussing this representational verisimilitude, people frequently said that puppets and masks should be the *tògòma* of the living animal or person. Outside discussions of sculpture, the word tògòma identifies people generally of different generations who share the same first name. When a child is named after an adult, the child becomes the adult's tògòma, thus establishing a relationship between two individuals across generations. This relationship has a moral force. In evaluating youth masquerades people invoke this same moral force for these arts when they define these sculptures' "goodness" in terms of their tògòma relationship with the models in nature.

For sculptures of animals and birds, images that predominate in the youth theatre, both sculptors and non-sculptors alike identified similar clusters of features that carry the essential information. When animals are represented the features most often included the shape of the head and the muzzle or beak, as well as the length, size, positioning, and shape of the animal's ears or horns. Rod puppets representing the large variety of ruminants performed in the theatre are generally distinguishable from one another by the size of the head and the size and shape of the horns. In these sculptures, for example, Dajè, the Roan Antelope, has horns that are moderately long, strongly ridged, and curve backwards from the head [Figure 3.19], while Sinè, the Gazelle, has shorter straight horns with only the slightest curve at their tips [Figure 3.5]. Sigi, the Buffalo, is regularly distinguished from other animals by its large head and bovine muzzle and its massive horns [Figure 3.26]. Puppet heads of Misi, the Cow, always emphasize its bovine features and the distinctive shape of its horns [Figure 1.2]. In some communities, its costume often includes the characteristic hump on its back associated with the Zebu breed. Saga, the Sheep, has a distinct shape to its muzzle and characteristic curling horns [Figure 2.23]. Waraba, the Lion, and a whole range of wildcats stress feline characteristics in the shape of the head and the size and placement of the ears [Figure 1.15]. The sculpture of Sonsan, the Hare, emphasizes the animal's characteristic long ears, and Sama, the Elephant, is always shown with large, fan-shaped ears, tusks, and trunk [Figure 3.11].

Sogo bò sculpture stands out from most sculpture from this region because these masks and puppets are often boldly and brightly painted [Figure 2.21], decorated with patterned textiles in lieu of paint, or covered with embossed metal stripping, appliqués, and mirrors [Figure 3.37]. These embellishments heighten the dramatic potential of these objects, making them attractive and desirable and pleasing to the eye, *nye la jako* (McNaughton 1988, 107). People frequently mentioned the adoption of enamel paints for theatrical sculptures, which was probably introduced by the 1920s and gained more widespread use between the two World Wars, as an important innovation in the theatre. They felt that painting the object intensified the beauty of the carving and increased the sculpture's visibility during the performance. This surface decoration, however, is usually peripheral to the identification of the character. Some lion masks and elephant puppets, for example, are painted with bright polka dots [Figure 3.38] and bird puppets carry overall patterns of chevrons or stripes [Figure 2.20]. While Sogo bò sculptures may be flamboyantly painted in order to energize the masquerades, these decorations must never totally obscure the basic form. Shape-defining and shape-enhancing features must be kept in a dynamic balance.

The dialectic relationship between form and its revision encapsulated in the terms jayan and jako that people apply to Sogo bò sculpture also finds similar expression in the evaluation of dance, music, and song. People do invoke slightly different terms when discussing the evaluative criteria applied to the performing arts. In conversations about Sogo bò's music, song, and dance they regularly use the term cogo to describe the nyi or "goodness" of the form emergent in performance. They speak of *dònsen cogo* when discussing the pattern of the dance steps, and use the phrase *dunun fò cogo* to talk about the pattern of the drum rhythms. The melody and phrasing of songs are encapsulated in the phrase *donkili da cogo*. People use the phrase *nyènajè cogo* to talk about how the event is structured, organized, and patterned. In lieu of jako, performers often use the term *tèrèmèli*, bargain, or *tigè*, to cut, to describe how they revise and creatively play with the basic structure of a song, drum rhythm, or dance. Like the decorations applied to sculpture, the creative revisions of these expressive forms must not destroy or entirely obscure the basic pattern or configuration.

The Evaluation of the Arts Across Performance Traditions

The same link between the model in nature and its sculptural representation occurs in many other sculptures and masks used outside the youth theatre, although in some of the men's society masks, as in Kòrè and Ciwara, these modifications suggest a different intention from puppet sculpture. Early photographs published in Henry (1910) of Kòrè society monkey and hyena masks demonstrate that part of the inspiration for these masks was clearly the animal in nature. In the monkey mask the rounded head and ears and the shape of the muzzle link it to the monkey in nature; in the case of the hyena mask it is the shape and the length of its muzzle and its moderately long pointed ears (Henry 1910). However, unlike the Sogo bò sculptures of animals, these masks' animal features are overlaid with a long wedge-like nose form, a feature commonly used in representations of human beings and spirits in anthropomorphic form. As McNaughton noted, the combination of forms in these Kòrè masks thus renders their representation as neither totally animal nor wholly human (McNaughton 1988, 104).

The Ciwara masks from the men's association in the Segou region share features with the Dajè, the Roan Antelope, performed in the Sogo bò. Ciwara masks are often identified as roan antelopes. Like the youth theatre's rod puppets these sculptures emphasize the elegant backward sweep of this antelope's horns.[13] Yet sculptors regularly overlay human features on the head of the Ciwara mask [Figure 3.1]. This practice, however, is not common today in representations of roan antelope rod puppets in the contemporary youth theatre [Figure 2.24].[14]

Interpretative studies of Ciwara masks by Zahan recognize the link between the antelope figure and the roan antelope in nature (Zahan 1972, 1980). He notes, however, that a whole series of other iconographic elements are used in these masks. The symbolism of the Ciwara crests is far more subtle and complex than any simple reference to a roan antelope. In the case of Sogo bò animal masks and puppets, however, smiths and non-smiths always stated that the animal masks and puppets were intended to be unabashed portrayals of specific animals. The values so highly prized in the evaluation of animal puppets and masks in the theatre relate these sculptures to a distinctive category of speech, *kuma jè*, speech that is direct and clear. Kuma jè is the conveyor of truth, whose referential content is apparent and its meaning clear (Hoffman 1990, 92–94).

The high value given to straightforward and clear representation in puppet sculpture is conversely of little value in a number of other visual and verbal arts in these societies. The masks and objects defined as boliw and used in the men's associations such as Kòmò, Kònò, and Nama are not intended to be representations of a single animal in nature, but they are composite forms whose visual identification is unclear and ambiguous. The Kònò association mask is reported to be a composite of an elephant form and a bird form (Zahan 1974, 19). The Kòmò masks are sometimes described as hyena heads, but they carry bird feathers, porcupine quills, and horns from various animals attached to the core form [Figure 3.2]. Like the decorations on youth association sculptures, the additional attachments on the Kòmò masks are also referred to as *masiri*,

Pref. 1. A Bamana performance of Mali Kònò, the Bird of Mali. 1980. Segou region. *Photograph by Lynn Forsdale.*

Pref. 4. A Bamana performance of Yayoroba, the Beautiful Woman. 1979. Kirango, Mali. *Photograph by Lynn Forsdale.*

1.8. Bamana youth association members performing the circle dances. 1979. Kirango, Mali. *Photograph by Mary Jo Arnoldi.*

1.9. Bamana men performing the *Bònjalan*, the acrobatic dance competition. 1979. Kirango, Mali. *Photograph by Lynn Forsdale.*

2.1. A performance of the Sòmonò masquerade Soden Mali la, Malian Horsemen, at the Malian Independence Day celebrations in Segou. 1986. Segou, Mali. *Photograph by Ambassador Robert Pringle.*

2.4. Karankaw, People of Karan, created by Siriman Fane. The large animal is a giraffe. On its back are puppets of President Moussa Traore and his honor guard, a colonial officer on horseback, and a farmer wielding his hoe. 1980. Segou region, Mali. *Photograph by Lynn Forsdale.*

2.21. A rod puppet of Mali Kònò carved by Manyan Kumare circa 1968 for the Kirango Bamana. 1978. *Photograph by Mary Jo Arnoldi.*

3.34. A Bamana performance of Pari, the Credit Association, in the guise of an antelope. 1979. Segou region, Mali. *Photograph by Mary Jo Arnoldi.*

3.37. A Bamana Cèko antelope puppet carved by Numu Jon Diarra. 1980. Nienou, Mali. *Photograph by Mary Jo Arnoldi.*

3.38. Two Bamana Cèko puppets of Waraba, the Lion. 1980. Eastern Segou region, Mali. *Photograph by Mary Jo Arnoldi.*

5.2. A Sòmonò performance of Baninkònò, the Stork. 1979. *Photograph by Mary Jo Arnoldi.*

6.4. A Bamana performance of Sigi, the Buffalo. The Buffalo carries smaller puppets on its crown and horns and a set of small rod and string puppets on its back. 1980. Segou region, Mali. *Photograph by Mary Jo Arnoldi.*

an embellishment or a decoration. McNaughton observed that the quantity of decoration on these masks does indeed obscure the core form. Moreover, the surfaces of these masks are covered with sacrificial encrustations which are mixtures of millet gruel, animal blood, spittle, and other organic matter. This surface can be built up over a series of ceremonies and eventually the mask itself begins to evolve into an amorphous form which is unknowable, obscure, and impenetrable. In judging the masks, members praised those that were the most amorphous and heavily embellished (McNaughton 1979, 44). These masks are considered *a ye dibi la ko ye*, an affair of obscurity (McNaughton 1979, 44). As the blacksmith Sedu Traore stated, "The *kòmò* mask is made to look like an animal. But it is not an animal; it is a secret" (McNaughton 1988, 129). Their very obscurity, however, is their nyi, or goodness, therefore their appropriate culture form.

Although, as McNaughton suggests, the Kòmò mask violates the basic tenet of clarity and controlled decoration so highly prized in puppet sculpture, door locks, twin figures, and iron lamps, the masquerade's performances are judged in terms of their clarity. In his discussions of the Kòmò performances with a Kòmò member he recorded the following evaluation:

> The *kòmò* whose *Bamanaya* lies down outside, that is the sweet one, *Kòmò min ka Bamanaya mana da kènè kan, O de ka di*. By *Bamanaya* he meant the things of Bamana culture, everything that *kòmò* stands for. By "lies down outside" he meant reveals its capabilities most clearly. Kalilou [Tera] and I translated his sentence like this: The *kòmò* who knows the most and shows it most clearly, that is the best one. (McNaughton 1988, 144)

Kòmò masquerade performances, then, are power revealed. While the nature of the mask's power is a secret, there is no ambiguity about the intention of the mask's performance to reveal and to harness great stores of nyama for socially appropriate ends. Hoffman suggests that Kòmò masks and their performances are conceptually related to two specific categories of Mande speech: *jelikan*, griots' speech, and *dibikan*, diviners' speech. Like Kòmò masks and performances, these specialized forms of speech are obscure and their referential content is hidden. These speech acts are considered to release enormous amounts of nyama (Hoffman 1990, 91–92). Like Kòmò masquerades, jelikan and dibikan are about power that is controlled and directed by specialists, in this case by griots and diviners, for socially appropriate ends. The griots' praise songs are, as Hoffman explains, "power that moves, that enables" (Hoffman 1989, 5). The performance empowers both the griot and those whose praises are being sung. The syntax, pace, intonation, and volume of dibikan, although somewhat different from those of jelikan, function in the same way to obscure the referential content of the chanted phrases. It is later in the performative dialogue between the diviner and his client that clarity emerges. The diviner interprets the messages from the unseen world, which are transmitted in dibikan, through the use of kuma jè, ordinary, clear, and straightforward speech (Hoffman 1990, 93–94).

The visual ambiguity that is simultaneously an expression of secrecy and a revelation of great power in the case of the Kòmò masquerade seems initially to resonate with a small category of masquerades used in the youth theatre, the shape-shifting grass masquerades. Yet upon closer examination the grass masquerades share more affinities with other youth association sculptures than they do with Kòmò masquerades. While these grass masquerades do not carry the necessary visual clues to allow the audience to identify the animal being represented, their signature songs always contain this information. While they may be visually ambiguous, their link to an animal in nature is always made clear in their performance. This places them in the same category as the wooden masks and rod puppets used in the youth theatre.

While youth association masks, puppets, and masquerades may seem antithetical to the intentionally ambiguous artistic forms used and performed by specialists, at the most abstract level all of the Mande arts are related to one another through the ideology of aesthetic expression defined as form managing power. The cultural frame imposed on all expressive forms by their founders in the mythic past sets the conditions for their social use through time. It imbued all of these arts and their performance with a moral force. It is the interplay of nyi, goodness, and di, tastiness and embellishment, that releases energy for the collective good. The successful interplay between goodness and tastiness is the most important judgment rendered about any expressive form or performance. The performer's ability to manage and revise these forms in culturally appropriate ways is the ultimate test of artistic virtuosity, whether specialist or nonspecialist. It is what endows all Mande arts with their affecting power, their nyama.

CHAPTER FOUR

Time, Timing, and the Performance as Process

Notions of time, timing, and tempo regularly emerge as critical themes in discussions of the history and definition of the Sogo bò theatre. Multiple notions of time inform people's understanding of the masquerade form and they shape the construction and evaluation of these dramas. Time, as it marks the changing of the seasons and the lunar phases and sets the standard work week, contributes to people's evaluation of the appropriateness of Sogo bò events within the yearly cycle. Values that are associated with cultural knowledge and experiences which are located in past time, as well as the interface between these pasts and the present, clearly shape the form and content of these performances. By framing the performances as play and bounding them in time, the nyama or energy that is released through creative action is managed in socially productive ways. Finally, notions of timing and tempo underlie the articulation of artistry in these communities. They contribute in culturally specific ways to aesthetic evaluations of performers' competence and are critical in people's judgments of the success or failure of the event as a whole.

Timing and the Definition of the Sogo bò Theatre

The timing of youth association festivals within the annual cycle defines the social occasion for theatre. It contributes in perceptible ways to people's interpretations of these events as extraordinary and outside the flow of quotidian life. In most communities in this region, time, *tuma* or *waati*, is not conceptualized as an independent or formless variable but remains, as Grosz-Ngati has observed, firmly linked to the rhythm of activities (Grosz-Ngate 1986, 129). In Kirango and elsewhere everyday activities, from greetings to agriculture and fishing practices, as well as extraordinary events, such as ceremonies of the men's associations, marriage rituals, and youth association theatre, are organized according to diurnal and/or seasonal patterns.

In the late twentieth century both the Islamic calendar and the Gregorian calendar operate alongside the diurnal and seasonal rhythms that organize people's daily lives in more rural settings. The Islamic calendar, which has become ever more prominent in people's lives throughout this last century, organizes religious activities on a daily, monthly, and yearly basis. It defines the calls to prayer and fixes the dates of major religious celebrations. The national calendar, based on the Gregorian calendar, defines the standard work week, sets the scholastic year, and fixes the dates for a whole host of national holidays, including Independence Day (September 22) and New Year's Day (January 1). For at least a generation in many rural communities like Kirango, both the Islamic calendar and the national calendar have begun to play an increasingly more important role in shaping the timing and duration of the youth association festivals. However, despite an accommodation to other calendars, the Sogo bò has not yet become fully divorced from its original seasonal timing.

Throughout the region, the year, *san*, is divided into two seasons: *samiyè*, the rainy season, and *tilema*, the dry season. *Samiyè da (daminè)*, the rains begin, or *san yèlèma*, the year turns over, begins in late May and opens each new agricultural and fishing year. The New Year (January 1) as set by the national calendar does not as yet play any significant role in defining the year in most rural communities. During the rainy season the energies and activities of the majority of adult men and women in Kirango and other rural communities in the region are still fully devoted to these pursuits and this labor-intensive period extends from the first rains in early June through October.

Kawule begins in late October with the fonio harvest. This transitional period marks the end of the rainy season and the onset of the dry season, which extends from November through May. Following kawule, the quarter shifts its primary orientation away from agriculture and fishing to various other productive activities. These include hunting, masonry, weaving, smithing, and potting, as well as the production and reproduction of social relationships through a variety of rituals and entertainments. For example, during the height of the dry season, between January and May, communities still hold the majority of weddings. This period is also designated as the culturally appropriate time for young boys' and girls' initiations and for the annual ceremonies of men's associations such as Kòmò, Kònò, Nama, Ciwara, and Jara. People also perceive the dry season as the appropriate time for a whole range of village entertainments, including the Sogo bò, the Bara and other dance events, the Kotèba theatre, and performances by itinerant singers and musicians.

While many nyènajè, including the Kotèba theatre, are not fixed to any particular moment within the dry season (Brink 1980; Meillassoux 1964, 1968), the youth association's masquerades are still only performed at the beginning and at the end of the dry season. The timing of these Sogo bò events does seem expressly aimed at heightening, through elaborate artistic means, people's awareness of the transformation in the seasons. This transformation shapes the activities and rhythms of their daily lives in the months that follow the festival.

The youth association festivals self-consciously alter the tempo of daily life. During the festival period, which may last a single day or several days, most people in the quarter or village usually do not go to their fields nor do they travel to markets outside the community, etc. During the morning, critical activities such as women's household duties and tasks such as feeding livestock and watering gardens do continue apace. Performances begin only in the late afternoon hours. Other, less pressing activities are temporarily suspended for the duration of the festival. Everyone, except elder men, gathers his or her physical and mental energy and devotes the afternoons and evenings to fully participating in the entertainments. Many villages' festivals, including those in Kirango, now also accommodate the Islamic prayer times. Afternoon events generally begin only after *selifana* (about 2:00 P.M.) and usually end around *laansara* (about 5:00 P.M.), although in many villages these late afternoon performances continue until just after sunset. The evening masquerades, however, usually begin after *saafo* (about 8:00 P.M.). By comparison, the occasion and duration of baptisms, marriages, and funerals are quite different. These events involve a more limited group of people and the suspension of regular daily activities takes a more limited form. These family events have more impact on the activities of specific households over others in the village.

From at least 1896 to about 1981 in both the farming and fishing quarters in Kirango, the youth association masquerades were regularly performed during kawule. This festival lasted for only one day and people linked the celebration to the end of the rainy season and the onset of the dry season. More specifically in the Bamana quarter today, the theatre is closely associated with the rhythm of agricultural practices. Among the farmers, their festival is known alternatively as *Fini tigè nyènajè*, fonio harvest festival, or *Daba bila nyènajè*, setting down the hoe festival. These festival names specifically acknowledge people's efforts during the rainy season and signal the impending changes in the kind of activities and the tempo of village life in the coming dry season.

Yet, more important for understanding the orientation of repertoire of the early theatre between 1896 and the years prior to World War II, the timing of the Bamana quarter's Sogo bò during the kawule focuses attention on these communities' historical investment in hunting, which was one of the most important dry-season activities for men. Many elders credited the original inspiration for the masquerade repertoire to hunters' stories and legends concerning animals in the bush. This hunter/warrior ethos, rather than one oriented specifically to agriculture or fishing, still predominates in performances even today. Theatrical traditions collected in both fishing and farming villages in the region, who have been performing the masquerade theatre for a century or longer, confirmed that until relatively recently the Sogo bò, the Do bò, and the Cèko were always scheduled just prior to the hunting season. It is noteworthy in this regard that it was in the month of September in 1878 that Soleillet attended the fishermen's Do bò performance along the Niger River. According to a survey I conducted in 1978–80, villages in eastern Segou regularly performed the Cèko during kawule. In Kirango, Bamana and Sòmonò historians also declared that their theatres were originally performed during kawule. In 1979, the Bamana quarter performed its masquerades on November 3, while the Kirango Sòmonò troupe had already performed the Do bò twice before: the first performance on October 7 and a second performance as part of the Islamic festival of Tabaski on November 1.

Since at least the first decade of this century the Kirango Bamana quarter has organized a major quarter-wide festival in late May to celebrate the arrival of the rainy season and the beginning of a new year. The spring festival is sometimes called san yèlèma, the year turns over, or *Samiyè da [daminè] nyènajè*, the rainy season entertainment. Samiyè da, the beginning of the rainy season, is the focal point of the rural calendar and plays an important role in both men's and women's lives. People use each new rainy season as the measure for calculating a person's age and for determining the number of years a woman has been married into her husband's household (Grosz-Ngate 1986, 130). For young men and women it has always been the period that marks each age-set's move into, through, and out of the kamalen ton. In the past it also marked men's movements into and through certain initiation associations like Ntomo and Kòrè (Henry 1910; Zahan 1960).

The original spring entertainment, which featured dance and song events and no masquerades, may have always been oriented more specifically toward the community's new investment in agriculture. One of the alternative names for this spring festival, *Daba taa nyènajè*, taking up the hoe festival, does specifically link the celebration to agricultural rhythms. Until the mid 1920s no masquerades were performed during this spring festival. However, when the quarter did introduce two masquerades, Mèrèn in the 1920s and Kalaka Sogo in the 1930s, into the afternoon entertainments, they were not bush animal characters, but representations of people and community life. Until the late 1950s people did not consider the spring festival masquerades to be part of the Sogo bò masquerade repertoire. When, in the mid 1950s, the kamalen ton deliberately incorporated its Sogo bò theatre into the New Year festival entertainment, the troupe merged the once separate masquerade repertoires into one. Today the festival includes both afternoon and evening masquerades and this event is called the *Tonko nyènajè*.[1]

In Kirango today, the spring festival is the largest and most important of the two festivals staged by the youth association. The festival lasts for four days, a traditional Bamana week, in contrast to the one-day festival held during kawule. During the four-day festival nonessential activities are suspended and the quarter gathers together for special meals, daily dances and musical events, the Sogo bò masquerades, and an all-night musical vigil, which follows the first evening's masquerade performances.

The contemporary identification of the spring festival specifically with the kamalen ton underscores the fact that since the mid 1950s the youth association has gradually assumed more of the responsibility for the staging of the four-day festival events. The ton now prepares and distributes the festival meal for the quarter. Wives of ton members brew the millet beer which is consumed during the festival. The association also organizes a late morning procession through the quarter to bring New Year greetings to every household head, and it produces all the musical and masquerade entertainment for the quarter. The association has also taken over the production of the all-night musical vigil as an exclusive ton event.[2]

Today, depending on the local history of the theatre, the youth association might perform the Sogo bò masquerades only during kawule or, as in some communities, like the Boso community of Kirango, they may perform the masquerades only at the beginning of the rainy season. A troupe might choose to play the masquerades twice annually, as was the case in the Bamana quarter in Kirango for thirty years between the mid 1950s and the mid 1980s. Yet no village that I visited or that people talked about was in 1987 performing the masquerade theatre arbitrarily within the seven-month dry season. These performances continue to be restricted to one or both of the transitional periods that mark seasonal changes. In 1979, when the Sòmonò troupe reprised their theatre as part of their celebration of the Islamic festival of Tabaski, the feast day fell within the period of kawule and they defined the performance as an authentic Do bò event. Most people that I interviewed still strongly felt that masquerade performances held outside the transitional periods—for example, performances given upon the request of visiting government dignitaries (such events are documented for the precolonial, colonial, and postcolonial periods) or those staged for the regional and national arts festivals or for visiting film crews or tourist groups—were not *Sogo bò yèrè yèrè*, authentic or real theatre. People's perception of these latter performances as being "inauthentic" was based on their being held outside their customary time.[3]

When people state that playing the theatre during kawule and/or at samiyè da is their *laada*, custom or tradition, they are investing the very timing of the theatre with a moral authority that derives its force from past practices. Knowledge and practices deemed customs or traditions are those that have been handed down from the ancestors and that are clearly associated with past time. People's definitions of tradition do not mean that there have been no changes in theatrical practices, as the oral histories of the Sogo bò, Do bò, and Cèko throughout the Segou region make clear. Rather, changes in the theatre have their own temporal rhythms. Once these changes are initiated, accepted, and successfully repeated over time, they begin to lose the quality of novelty and take on the characteristics of laada.

Discussions of the two transformations in theatrical timing in Kirango, the first initiated in the 1950s and the second in 1981, provided insights into the way that theatrical practices become custom over time. In the 1950s the troupe decided to put on two performances each year. When I lived in Kirango between 1978 and 1980 people saw these biannual performances as customary. However, following a severe drought in 1981 the association troupe abandoned the Sogo bò festival during kawule. The decision to abandon the kawule performance was still being debated in 1987, and, in terms of theatrical timing, it was open to contestation.

People's positions within the debate were based on their age and their different experiences and investments in the theatre both past and present. In discussing the history of the theatre, men over the age of sixty still emphasized that kawule was the customary timing for the masquerades. They supported this claim by invoking the traditional theatrical practices of their own fathers and grandfathers. In 1987, many older residents saw the decision to abandon the kawule performances as temporary. They considered it a legitimate response to current drought conditions and they pointed out that in the past when there had been a bad harvest or a poor fishing season the theatre was not played. Yet they always insisted that when conditions improved, the theatre had been reprised. Their definition of the theatrical timing remained firmly tied to the period of kawule. Men around the age of fifty had been members of the association when the masquerades were first introduced into the spring festival. They supported the older men's definitions by stating that indeed kawule remains the customary timing for theatre. They continually spoke of the spring masquerade theatre as a new innovation, although they clearly expected that the current youth association would continue this pattern of biannual performances. Young men who had been young children in the mid 1950s and who are now in the senior age-sets of the current association did not define the spring festival as new, but defined the biannual performances of the Sogo bò as theatrical custom. Their concern to reinstate the kawule performance was based on this broader definition.

The youngest age-sets in the current association, who entered after 1981, have performed the masquerades only during the spring festival. These young men and women, who are still in their teens, were aware that the theatre was once played during kawule, but they seemed less involved in the debates and more thoroughly committed to investing their artistic efforts in the production of the Tonko nyènajè, the spring festival. Although these junior members currently expressed no burning commitment to restoring the kawule performance, the outcome of these definitional debates clearly remains open. Ultimately it will be this latter group and the generations moving into the association in the coming years who will resolve this issue. Their choices will influence how their own sons and daughters will come to define what is the customary timing for the Sogo bò theatre within the year.

While the striking increase in village entertainments during the dry season months can be understood as a response to the changes in the rhythm and nature of activities during this season, choosing the date for the youth association theatre remains at least partially tied to lunar phases. In Kirango, as in most rural villages in the region without electricity, dry season entertainments are still regularly held during the period of the full moon. Throughout this season the full moon is the moment during the month when everyone, except the really aged, gathers on the streets in front of their compounds or in the public plazas to talk and relax, or to participate in the more formalized entertainments such as puppet masquerade theatre, Kotèba, dance events, or performances by itinerant storytellers and musicians. The nighttime sights and sounds, which are normally obscured and muted, and the streets and plazas, which are usually deserted at that time, come alive. During the period of the full moon, people temporarily suspend their commonly held feelings, beliefs, and attitudes toward the night as a locus of danger. Throughout this area both men and women expressed their ambivalence and trepidation about the night. The association of night with danger emerges as a theme in stories, legends, and personal narratives. People generally associated the daytime with sociability and the night with secrecy, antisocial behavior, and treachery. During the full moon the separation between day and night becomes less pronounced. Both day and night become appropriate times for all manner of public entertainments, from children playing games in the streets to highly formalized cultural performances such as the puppet masquerades.

In Kirango by the mid 1970s all three troupes—the Bamana, the Boso, and the Sòmonò—had begun to adjust the timing of their festivals within the transitional seasons to correspond to the standard work week. A fair number of men from the village worked for various government services in neighboring Markala or in Segou city. Today, the masquerade festivals regularly begin on Saturday afternoon and last through Monday afternoon.[4] Monday afternoon's performance is generally quite abbreviated and the audience consists of only women and children, since many adult men have by then returned to the workplace.

It was also during the 1970s (around 1974) that both the fishermen and the farmers began borrowing portable generators and electric lights from government offices in Markala to use for the performances. The Kirango troupes' ability to artificially illuminate the dance arena gave them the freedom to adjust the timing of the festivals to accommodate the current needs of their residents. In contrast, even in 1987 most of the villages located at some distance from towns and government centers were still regularly scheduling their performances during the period of the full moon. In these villages troupes do not have strong ties to the government industrial sector, and the majority of young men are not so fully integrated into this labor system. Consequently, these troupes are not pressured to adjust their festivals to a standard work week.[5]

At the local level, an individual village's theatrical history can also influence the timing of these performances. In Kirango, for example, during the 1979 kawule season, the Sòmonò performances took place several weeks before the Bamana performance. The priority that farmers give to fishermen in Kirango is based on the collective memory of the Sòmonò's original ownership of the masquerade. The farmers still respect the fishermen's right of first performance despite the fact that since at least the eighteenth century the Bamana quarter has dominated the political life of this village.

The Kirango Bamana quarter also once participated in a special theatrical relationship with three other local farming communities. According to farmers in Kirango, their ton enjoyed the right of first performance within this grouping, followed by the tons of Djamarabougou, Tiongoni, and Bambougou. The theatrical history that determined the order of performance among these four villages, however, bears no relationship to other histories, such as the founding histories of villages or their position in the dynastic history of the precolonial Segou state. This suggests that it was probably based solely on when each village adopted the theatre in the past. By 1978 the four villages no longer seemed to follow this order of performances. However, an echo of their shared theatrical history was still in evidence as young men from these villages regularly attended each other's performances and these four villages' basic masquerade repertoires were still quite similar. Sometimes young men from these four villages performed in their neighbors' festivals. For example, in June 1980 the Kirango drum team was invited to perform for the Sogo bò in Djamarabougou. Their appearance in the Djamarabougou festival was a direct expression of the shared artistic histories of these two communities.

Becoming a Performer in the Sogo bò

In his approach to the study of performance, Richard Schechner shifts the orientation away from the performance event as a product to an analysis of these events as part of a larger performance process. He defines this larger process as including training sessions, workshops, rehearsals, warm-ups, the performance event itself, and postperformance events. Although he recognizes that not all genres of performance, nor all cultures, emphasize or give equal weight to every phase of the performance process, his orientation does extend the inquiry over a much larger temporal and spatial field (Schechner 1985, 16). Adopting Schechner's definition of performance as a process rather than a product allows for an examination of the specific ways in which Sogo bò actors generate performance knowledge. By extending the time frame beyond a single event, we can begin to understand how performance knowledge is transferred and modified from one performance to the next and across generations.

Performers in the youth association theatre do not fit the model of performers in Western art theatre or of Bamana griots, who acquire their performance skills over years of formalized training. Every young person is expected to become a performer in the youth association theatre during his or her tenure in the kamalen ton. The performance biographies of men who participate in the Sogo bò theatre extend for the culturally defined period of their youth from about the age of fourteen until the age of forty-two. The performance biographies of women, especially those who become lead singers, differ from men. These women often perform in the theatre well beyond the period of their youth, which is defined as ending at their marriage. Several lead singers in Kirango, for example, performed for thirty or more years and continued to be active even after they assumed elder status.

These singers' careers occasionally overlapped and it was common for two lead singers of different ages to perform together for a number of years. For example, Nanyan Coulibaly and Mei Diarra performed together in 1978–1980. Both women started performing when they were young and both are now grandmothers. In 1978 Nanyan was probably in her late forties and Mei was probably in her mid forties. A decade later, in 1987, both women were still performing in the June festival [Figure 2.12]. In 1992, Nanyan Coulibaly did not perform in the Tonko festival.

Over their performance lifetime, whether as singers, dancers/maskers, and/or musicians, both men and women become increasingly more knowledgeable about the theatre. They develop and refine their performance skills through regular participation in public performances. Formal training, workshop settings, and rehearsals are virtually nonexistent for the Sogo bò. Performance plans and strategies are negotiated in an ad hoc and informal manner. For example, throughout the year and especially in the weeks leading up to a festival, young men do discuss performance strategies and they often work in informal groups to develop new masquerades. In the morning on the day of the festival, dancer-masqueraders may try on the finished masquerade costumes and run through an abbreviated dance performance. This exercise is intended more to check the sturdiness of the construction and provide the dancer with a feel for the costume's weight and flexibility. It is not a formal rehearsal for the theatre.

Sogo bò performers begin to familiarize themselves with the theatre and its dramatic plans and strategies as young children. By the age of fourteen, when young boys and girls become active members of their youth association, they have already taken the first steps to becoming proficient performers in the Sogo bò theatre (Ottenberg 1975,

1989). The process of becoming a performer begins at a very early age in Segou communities. In Kirango, for example, I observed infants being introduced to songs, rhythms, and dances from a variety of local performance events. In informal play settings in the household, a mother or an infant's older sisters will hold the infant and clap the child's own hands in basic rhythm sets. Later, when the child can sit up and has gained a modicum of dexterity, the adults or older siblings will place an overturned container in front of the child and first beat out a rhythm and then encourage the child to imitate it. These games are informal, constructed as play, and last until either the adult or the child loses interest in the activity. Learning proceeds initially from the direct manipulation of a child's body. Later the child self-consciously imitates other performers, whether they be older children or adults.[6] Mauss described this second type of learning process as "prestigious imitation," stating that:

> The child, [or] the adult, imitates actions which have succeeded and which he has seen successfully performed by people in whom he has confidence and who have authority over him. The action is imposed from without, from above, even if it is an exclusively biological action, involving his body. The individual borrows the series of movements which constitute it from the action executed in front of him or with him by others. (Mauss 1979, 101–102)

Through "prestigious imitation" and not verbal instruction, children slowly begin to embody the formal principles that organize the production of various expressive forms. This embodiment eventually allows the children to generate these forms and to recognize formal patterns in others' movements and actions. Learning through "prestigious imitation" is not restricted solely to the mastery of artistic forms. It is employed in teaching children all manner of skills, from farming to domestic activities and from culturally appropriate postures and gestures to ritual activity (Hardin 1987, 180–191).

By the time that children become members of the youth association, when they will be expected to perform and be evaluated publicly, they already have a fairly sophisticated knowledge of the structure and much of the basic content of the masquerade theatre. Throughout their childhood boys and girls experiment with theatrical forms. Out of these play experiences their own judgments about skills emerge and are refined. More important for understanding the affective nature of art in these communities, children not only learn to generate form, they also embody the culturally specific framework which makes these forms and movements meaningful and relates them across contexts to other domains of experience and action. As Bateson and Mead noted in their studies in Bali, mimetic learning is not all form; to a great degree it involves the mastery of content (Bateson and Mead 1942). Children who are in the process of learning songs, drum rhythms, and dances in Segou communities not only learn to reproduce more and more complex formal configurations, they learn to reproduce them in culturally appropriate ways and in culturally appropriate contexts. They are not only learning to sing, play music, or dance, but they are also learning through praxis the culturally specific evaluative criteria applied to these expressive forms.

In discussions of bodily practice in Kuranko initiation in Sierra Leone, Jackson demonstrated through a number of specific examples how "what is done with the body is the ground for what is thought and said . . . bodily practices mediate a personal realization of social values, and immediate grasp of general precepts as *sensible truths*" (Jackson 1983, 337; the emphasis is mine) These sensible truths are generally not open to verbal exegesis but are practical habits and truths. In Jackson's words, "Bodily self-mastery is thus everywhere the basis for social and intellectual mastery" (Jackson 1983, 337). In the last several decades Mande scholars have analyzed this essential link between knowledge, ethos, and practice in a variety of contexts, including daily work activities, rituals, and entertainments (Bird and Kendall 1980; Brink 1978; Grosz-Ngate 1986; Hardin 1987, 1993; McNaughton, 1988).

A child learns that control over his body, i.e., control over his actions in interactions with others, is the outward manifestation of control over his interior state, his self. A graphic example of the importance placed on self-mastery and of the link between bodily actions and mental and emotional states was revealed to me in the following incident that took place in Kirango in 1979. One day in front of a friend's compound a three-year-old child was acting out a temper tantrum, yet no adult raised a hand to physically restrain him. His mother and the other adults who were present responded by laughing at him and ridiculing his behavior through verbal insults and gestures that only infuriated him even more. Thoroughly frustrated at their response, the child began picking up stones and sticks and flinging them at the adults. They made no move to stop him. They continued to laugh at him and insult him until he was shamed into calming down and bringing himself both physically and emotionally under control.[7] The emphasis placed on learning self-control in this particular instance underscored the importance assigned to the mastery of self in relationships with others in every domain of adult activity.

Adult men and women are expected to maintain control over their emotions in many public contexts. I once attended a funeral for a newborn that had died. After paying my condolences to the grieving mother inside her house, I joined the women sitting in the family courtyard and, touched by the tragedy, I began to cry. Later several women teased me for crying at the public funeral for an infant's death. They let me know that my response was culturally inappropriate. In private conversations with women friends in the village that evening we talked about the incident and I explained that I was not crying for the child but for his mother who had carried him for nine months. Their response was immediately empathetic and they each began talking about grief and the personal tragedy of losing a child, an experience that every woman present had had in her own lifetime. I came to understand that while a mother's grieving for a lost infant was expected and appropriate in private and in the company of close women friends, gestures of grief for the loss of a baby had no place in the public arena. Women were expected to show self-control and a certain stoicism during the public portions of the funeral.[8]

Becoming aware of and mastering one's body as a performer while simultaneously acquiring the knowledge of the culturally appropriate ways of acting, thinking, and feeling in the Sogo bò theatre is an essential part of becoming a competent performer. Mastery of self involves much more than a mastery of form. It involves an individual's understanding of how theatrical action fits with the definition of the Sogo bò as ludic. It includes an awareness of the social identity and the nature of relationships among actors and between performers and their audience that is based on culturally defined notions of gender and relative age. It calls for the recognition and reproduction of appropriate behavior within the theatrical setting.

At the early stages in the acquisition of expressive skills, there does not seem to be any significant difference being made between genders. As adults, however, gender lines will be more clearly demarcated in public performances as in most every field of productive activity, including domestic, agricultural, and ritual spheres. Adults encourage both boys and girls to learn the same set of rhythms, sing the same songs, and perform the same dances. All children are introduced to a full range of dance movements. Through association with specific rhythms which are beat out, clapped, or sung, these young children eventually begin to experience particular dances and rhythm sets as single units. Once children have gained even a perfunctory competence in the various dance movements, they are encouraged to experiment with the basic patterns, embellishing them through a process of trial and error. The most adept among them will soon begin to outpace their peers. Adults informally track the progress of children in their mastery of these skills. When I asked adults how masked dancers, lead singers, or drummers were chosen for the adult theatre, it was clear from their responses that adults track talented individuals by observing their performances in these childhood games. They knew before a young person's entrance into the youth association which children were developing an interest in performing in the theatre. They had already identified which children had the talent and the aptitude to take on more specialized roles in the masquerade theatre.

As young children, individuals begin to learn to distinguish bodily movements and dances that are associated with particular classes and genders. Through daily interaction with peers and adults, they also become attuned to which of these attitudes and dances are appropriate for specific contexts in their communities. For example, much dance is a gendered art form. Dancing, which is defined as male, tends to emphasize mastery of gymnastic skills and often contains abrupt transitions between passages. Many women's dances feature encircling gestures and emphasize fluid transitions between movements. It is my impression from watching children's play activities that both boys and girls have a practical knowledge of each others' dance styles and that most children were more than capable of reproducing both styles.

As adults, appropriate public contexts for displaying the mastery of the other gender's style are severely limited. Young women have few opportunities for performing male dances in a public forum. However, in the context of teaching younger siblings to dance, it was a male toddler's sisters who most often demonstrated the various male dance steps for their younger brothers. When playing together, preadolescent girls often perform acrobatic dances as part of their games, and adult women occasionally take on male roles in certain theatres and rituals. Among the Kuranko, Jackson observed that during performances associated with female initiation women often imitated dances and bodily attitudes and gestures defined as belonging to men (Jackson 1983, 335–336). In Kirango during the *woloma*, a women's ritual that takes place during marriage events, one woman dresses as a warrior/hunter and presides over the events, taking the role of *Bamanaya*, literally Bamana-ness. Her costume, gestures, and comportment imitate that of male hunters. I also attended several performances of a women's theatre in another community, where women took the male parts and parodied the gait, posture, and gestures of men.

Taking on the roles of female masked characters within the Sogo bò theatre affords men the opportunity to display their knowledge and mastery of women's dances. Although the masker's male identity is concealed, everyone tacitly recognizes that it is a man performing under the masquerade. The performances of female characters often result in a friendly competition between the masked dancer and young women from the association. During the masquerade performance one or two young women may be emboldened to enter the arena to dance alongside the character. I also attended performances where individual young women danced with Gòn, the Baboon, and Wòkulò, the Bush Genie. Perhaps these young women won their audience's approval not only for their artistic virtuosity, but because in their boldness they had overcome social constraint and were seen to be acting heroically.

In addition to gendered dance styles, people draw distinctions between the dance and performance styles of different classes within Bamana society. Men and women of different classes perform several of the same dances in the theatre, especially during the dance prologue that opens the afternoon festivities. However, at certain points in the performance, class differences in performance styles are emphasized. More emotive license in terms of exaggerated gestures and dance movements is the birthright of members of blacksmith, bard, and leatherworking groups, as well as descendants of former slaves. Individuals from these groups enter the ring and dance while praising the masquerades. This same performative license is extended to the young men and to women who take on the role of kòrèdugaw, clowns.[9]

Men's and women's knowledge and practical mastery of each other's dance styles and their knowledge of drumming and song have implications for understanding how aesthetic evaluations are made about performances in the Sogo bò. As Jackson notes for Kuranko society,

> . . . the principle of sexual complementarity in Kuranko society can only be viable if Kuranko men and women periodically recognize the other in themselves and see themselves in the other. Mimesis, which is based upon bodily awareness of the other in oneself, thus assists in bringing into relief a reciprocity of viewpoints. (Jackson 1983, 336)

In the youth association theatre, women who praise the drumming or dancing of a male performer are basing their aesthetic evaluations on their practical knowledge of these skills, not as untrained observers. The reverse is also true. Men's evaluations of women's dancing and their imitation and parody of women in the theatre demand a practical knowledge of women's dance forms. For a masked dancer to successfully embellish women's dance movements, sometimes giving them a bawdy or comic interpretation, he must have mastered the original dance being parodied.

From their attendance at the adult puppet theatre and through the games which children devise to imitate the theatre, young boys and girls learn from a very early age to conceptualize particular constellations of drum rhythms, dances, and masquerades as units and to associate these units with particular dramatic personae in the masquerade theatre. Children's growing awareness of the theatrical relationships forged between specific verbal and visual artistic forms was clearly expressed in their responses to photographs of the masquerades and to recorded music from the theatre. Children around the age of four or five responded enthusiastically to a photograph of a masquerade not only by shouting the name of the masquerade but by initiating the appropriate theatrical song and by dancing in imitation of the character's performance in the theatre. These young children generally had mastered only one or two lines of the song or part of the dances. When I played a recording of a puppet song, children invariably responded by joining in the singing and by dancing the masquerade's dance, overlaying their movements with hand gestures that imitated the movement of the puppet head. For example, for Ntilen, the Giraffe, children would generally extend their hand above their heads then lower their arm to the ground to imitate the character's performance in the theatre. One afternoon I played the taped music from a performance for a group of children in my household. Kogo, a twelve-year-old boy, was inspired to make a series of drawings of the masquerades that were based on these masquerade songs. Although he was not yet a

member of the youth association, his drawings clearly revealed he had a well developed working knowledge of the theatre and he had correctly associated individual masquerade forms with their proper songs and musical rhythms. His drawings included one of Bilanjan, a generic bush masquerade with long extended appendages [Figure 4.1]. Another drawing was Waraba Caco, a large, distinctive, barrel-bodied wildcat with great teeth and a beard [Figure 4.2]. He also made drawings of Misi, the Cow, Gòn, the Baboon, and Mali Kònò, the Bird of Mali.

Following the millet harvest in January, boys between the ages of five and ten made toy masquerades from millet stalks and bits of cloth that they begged from women in the household. In constructing these toys the boys were concerned with representing what they understood to be the critical formal elements that identified each individual masquerade. Among their favorites were cattle, giraffe, buffalo, and roan antelope [Figure 4.3]. These miniature masquerades were then incorporated into more elaborate games which became mini-masquerade performances. Women or older girls often would stop their work and join in for a few minutes, providing the boys with

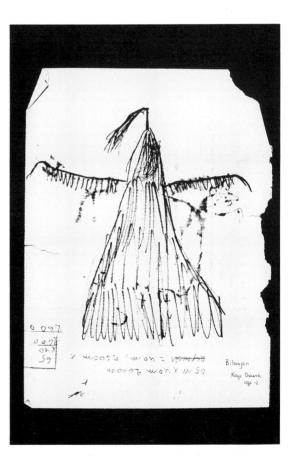

4.1. A drawing of Bilanjan, a generic bush animal, by Kogo Diarra, age 12. Kirango, Mali.

4.2. A drawing of Waraba Caco, the Striped Wildcat (the large figure) and Misi, the Cow (the small figure) by Kogo Diarra, age 12. 1980. Kirango, Mali.

the appropriate vocal and rhythmic accompaniment.

Several preadolescent boys in the Bamana quarter owned wooden masks that had been carved expressly for them by local blacksmiths.[10] One of these masks was a scaled-down version of Gòn, the Baboon, a comic character who opens the masquerade event in the adult theatre. In 1979 several weeks prior to the festival, a group of young boys and girls began to play with this mask on the street outside of one of the compounds. They invested time in refurbishing the mask and in creating a grass costume. During their performance they exhibited a thorough understanding of how the adult masquerade performances were organized. The boys assigned appropriate performance roles to various of their playmates, including masker, attendant, drummers, and crowd control. They placed the girls together in a group as the women's chorus. They assigned the role of audience to the youngest of their siblings and seated them in a circle in order to demarcate the dance arena. One of the boys, the owner of the mask, danced the Gòn. Adults did not participate in these games, although they did watch unobtrusively from the sidelines. Adults encourage children to become involved in these play activities. They see them not only as the training ground for the theatre, but as part of a general training directed toward becoming socially competent adults.

Timing and the Production of the Masquerade Event

There is ample evidence in this century to support the hypothesis that expressive forms moved with a certain regularity between the puppet masquerade and other performance genres within Segou. The current similarities among these various performances, however, are not reducible to constellations of shared expressive forms. They derive rather from the specific aesthetic notions that guide the production of form and performance and contribute to aesthetic value.

Most of the adult participants in the Sogo bò share a common definition of the theatre and of its artistic forms and have practical knowledge of these performances as both performers and audience. They bring to each new performance a number of the same expectations about the theatre and the way the event should unfold. Success in the theatre not only involves being able to reproduce last season's performance and metaphorically all past performances, but it requires a well-developed facility for creatively playing with audience expectations in appropriately artful ways. Over the many hours of the performance the troupe must constantly reshape and adjust its performance among the various performance units in response to its audience in order to engage its participants in this collective enterprise. Through their artistry actors, singers, and musicians must arouse people to respond and to participate. Sustaining this audience involvement over a period of four or more hours requires careful orchestration among the three performance units in order to achieve a lively balance between expectations and innovations. This is the performative dilemma to which every troupe devotes its creative energies.

The dialectic tension between nyi and di, goodness and tastiness, and jayan and jako, cultural form and embellishment, energizes the performance. Creativity lies in the opening up of the cultural form at any given moment (Drewal 1991, 43). The Bamana notion of artistic virtuosity, kènèya, suppleness, recognizes

4.3. Baisu Diarra with his toy masquerade representing Dajè, the Roan Antelope. 1979. Kirango, Mali. *Photograph by Mary Jo Arnoldi.*

that cultural form and its revisions are fundamentally linked in the production of art. Managing the interplay between goodness and tastiness constitutes an indigenous theory of performance. In the production of Sogo bò performances, actors continuously assess and act upon the possibilities opened up through this process. The moral force of nyi, the cultural form and the conditions for its use, brings the past into the present and constructs the illusion of an unbroken flow of time from generation to generation. The features of di that energize cultural forms privilege the present moment and support the high value given to innovation in the puppet masquerade theatre. To be sure, an ontological priority is always given to the past, expressed through theatrical tradition or custom, but cultural forms in process are always open to the potential for modification and revision. In creating the Sogo bò performances, troupes employ various strategies to generate and negotiate the dialectic tension between the past and the present, between kòrò, the old, and kura, the new, and between the repetition of an expected cultural form and its embellishments and revisions. Tempo and timing play a central role in establishing the performance frame and moving the action forward to its conclusion many hours later.

In most villages the troupes generally used the same set of characters from season to season to open and close their performance event. In Kirango the theatre is divided into two segments, the afternoon segment, beginning about 4:00 P.M. and ending just after sunset, and an evening performance, beginning after prayers and continuing well into the night until around 2:00 A.M. In the 1950s, when the Kirango troupe combined their two festivals, they were faced with the problem of having to institute and bring the dramatic action to closure in two separate segments. Currently, they open the afternoon segment of the event with Gòn, the Baboon, and close it with the performance of Jobali, the Boso Woman. The evening segment opens with Nama, the Hyena, and closes with Ntilen, the Giraffe. The community considers all of these characters to be *sogokòròw*, old masquerades. Their association with past time gives them the moral force to both initiate the dramatic frame, thus bringing people temporarily into the imaginary world of theatre, and subsequently to dissolve the frame, thereby returning performers and audience to the everyday world. Troupes and their knowledgeable audience are keenly aware of the power of this framing device. When Gòn first enters the ring, he darts around the circle and quickly exits. His arrival alerts the audience to the start of the masquerade performances. While his initial entry grabs the attention of the crowd, his quick retreat creates an aura of anticipation that is both physically and audibly palpable as people in the audience begin shifting in their seats straining to catch the arrival of the masquerades. The Baboon then reenters and gives a more extended performance, but the tempo remains brisk and energetic, pulling the crowd into the action and ensuring that the dramatic frame is established. In the evening segment Nama, the Hyena, opens the event [Figure 2.13]. As in the Baboon's performance, the tempo of the Hyena's performance is brisk and his energetic shape-shifting dance draws the crowd firmly into the dramatic action.

The afternoon segment generally ends with Jobali, although this was not the case in the 1979 spring performance in Kirango [Figure 1.16]. Obviously the troupe does not always adhere to this pattern, although people regularly said that if you arrive at the afternoon performance and Jobali is being played you know you are near the end of the event. The use of Jobali to bring closure to the afternoon events has now worked itself into the very interpretation of this masquerade character in Kirango.

The evening segment generally closes with Ntilen, the Giraffe [Figure 3.23]. When Ntilen was brought out in the 1979 performance in Kirango, you could see the audience begin to shift and disengage from the dramatic action. As the Giraffe was led out onto the dance arena, people started to gather up their belongings and began to leave the plaza even before the drummers and singers fully wound down. Men in the Kirango troupe were also quite adamant in stating that if they brought out Ntilen in the middle of a performance their audience would think the Sogo bò was finished and get up and go home.

The afternoon and evening masquerade program is organized according to a hierarchy of masquerades based on their age. In both segments the dramatic action always begins with several of the oldest masquerade characters. In 1979 in Kirango, for example, during the su fè sogo, the evening segment of the kawule performance, Nama, the Hyena, opened the event [Figure 2.13]. His performance was quickly followed by Falakani, a generic bush animal, and Bala, the Porcupine [Figures 2.14 and 2.16]. These three grass masquerades are considered the most traditional masquerades in the current theatre. Prior to the mid 1980s, the grass masquerades were not performed during the spring Tonko festival. In the 1979 Tonko performance, for example, the troupe opened the evening segment with Suruku Nama, a rod puppet masquerade representing a hyena [Figure 1.11]. In 1979 the song that was sung for the grass masquerade in the kawule festival was also sung for the rod puppet version played in the New Year festival. While the masquerade forms differed, the song established the link across seasons and between these two representations of the Hyena, allowing the newer rod puppet version to take first position in the spring performance. In 1982, the troupe quit performing the kawule season Sogo bò. When I returned in 1987 for the spring Tonko performance, Nama the grass masquerade was brought out to open the su fè sogo segment. The rod puppet Suruku Nama, the Hyena, which had opened this event in 1979, was only performed much later in the program.

The initial organization of the masquerade program according to the age of the masquerades seems consistent throughout the region. It constitutes a performance principle that is invested with a specific cultural meaning understood by both performers and audience through their past participation in these events. In Kirango it organizes people's understanding of the historical relationship between fishermen's and farmers' theatres in their community and between the two original festivals now combined into a single spring performance. This principle also resonates profoundly with people's lives outside the theatre. Age hierarchy organizes a whole complex of social relationships that unfold within the household among men and among women, in lineage, quarter, and village affairs, and even between villages. The high value given to maintaining this principle in the opening sequences of the event imbues these artistic productions with the same sense of correctness and moral authority that is reproduced and manifested in everyday and ritual practices.

Once the opening sequences establish the frame for the event, the masquerade program is no longer overly determined by custom, and the troupe begins to play with the masquerade program. Their concerns about timing and tempo emerge as more critical to their notions of artistry than is the maintenance of the principle of age hierarchy in masquerade presentation. Both afternoon and evening sequences open in fast time with the intention of engaging the audience and instituting the performance frame. Once the frame is established, the tempo of the afternoon segment slows down and it proceeds at a generally slower pace than does the evening performance. However, in both segments, once people are thoroughly engaged the troupe begins to alter the tempo of the event in order to play with their audience's expectations and to make the performance tasty.

One strategy the troupe uses to alter the tempo is to manipulate the order of the masquerade program. For example, when the troupe wants to accelerate the tempo of the event, they generally bring out various antelopes, whose performances are appropriately brisk and energetic. When they want to slow the pace they play characters such as the Buffalo, the Elephant, or the Cow. As the performance unfolds, the troupe must rethink and readjust its strategy to be sensitive to the moment and to take advantage of the crowd's reactions.

There is a customary pattern to how troupes organize these performances that consists of masquerade performances separated by musical interludes. In constructing any actual performance, however, the troupe often revises this pattern, as well as playing with the internal tempo within each of these segments. In the evening performances of the 1979 kawule festival in Kirango, the Bamana troupe first established the classic pattern of masquerade–musical interlude–masquerade and repeated this pattern for the first hour.

The event opened with the masquerades Nama, Falakani, and Bala. While each character was different and was performed with its own masquerade song, the individual performances were all energetic and consisted of shape-shifting dances. The three masquerade performances each occupied relatively the same length of time. Between these three masquerades there were musical interludes. The lead singer sang several different songs in each interlude, but the length of the musical interludes was consistent, lasting somewhere between five and ten minutes. The troupe then brought out Dajè, the Roan Antelope masquerades [Figure 2.24]. These masquerades slowed the tempo only slightly but enough that it was perceptible to the audience. As these masquerades were exiting, in burst Suruku Malobali, the Shameless Hyena [Figure 2.17]. It darted into the ring, ran around the perimeter of one side of the dance arena, then retraced its steps and quickly exited. The speed of its entry and exit pushed the limits of performance acceptability and the masquerade was in the arena for barely two minutes. Its appearance, however, did radically alter the tempo and seized the attention of the crowd. Almost before the crowd or the singers and drummers could adjust their responses, the Shameless Hyena was gone.

The lead singer then took control of the performance and settled the audience back into the tempo that she had established in the previous musical interlude. The masquerade Kònònin, the Bird, then entered, and gave an energetic performance. As Kònònin exited the troupe brought in a second antelope pair, aborting the musical interlude between the two masquerade sequences and altering the expected pattern. After the antelopes exited, the troupe again revised the pattern as the Shameless Hyena dashed into the arena, made his way once around the circle and exited, causing an audible stir from the crowd. This time the lead singer and drummers had been cued to its entry and they immediately switched into the Shameless Hyena's song and drum rhythm. Following Suruku Malobali's departure the lead singer and her chorus radically slowed the tempo by singing the narrative song for Jado Nama, even though the masquerade itself was not performed. This song lasted for about ten minutes. The troupe followed this extended musical interlude with a set of four masquerades—Kònò Jolenjo, the Bird, Bilanjan, a generic bush animal [Figure 2.15], Sigi, the Buffalo, and Sogoni Kelen, the Antelope [Figure 2.22]. With these four masquerades, the troupe reestablished the pattern of masquerade–musical interlude, but each of the four masquerades performed at a different tempo and for a different length of time. The duration of the musical interludes, however, was almost identical, each lasting under five minutes. The first two masquerades gave fast-paced and brief acrobatic performances. Sigi, the Buffalo, then slowed the pace and gave an extended performance. In marked contrast to Sigi, Sogoni Kelen moved the performance into fast time with an energetic acrobatic performance that brought many people in the audience to their feet.

By this time the performance was well into its third hour. After a short musical interlude, Suruku Nama, the Hyena, entered and established a tempo that was almost midpoint between that of the lumbering Buffalo and the energetic small Antelope [Figure 1.11]. As the Hyena exited, the chorus launched into a song, and following this interlude the troupe brought in the masquerade Bilisi, whose performance tempo mirrored that of the Hyena [Figure 3.27]. When the Genie exited, the women sang the praises of both the masquerades and the young men in the association. All the young men not directly involved behind the scenes rushed into the ring and danced exuberantly. As the drummers cut the music, the troupe brought in Waraba Caco, the Striped Wildcat [Figure 1.19]. This massive masquerade lumbered around the ring in an extended performance that cooled the performance down. Suddenly the Shameless Hyena again darted into the ring and, never one to stay long, it quickly left again. The women began a song, but it was short-circuited by the entry of two masquerades. These masquerades, a second version of Dajè, the Roan Antelope, gave an energetic performance, with their heads shooting up several feet into the air then dropping suddenly to a 90-degree angle to their bodies. The chorus's musical interlude was again truncated and the antelope Maisa, Umu Assita, entered and slowed the tempo. Maisa was followed almost immediately by Misicè and Misimuso, the Bull and the Cow masquerades [Figure 1.2]. Their dances were even slower and more measured than was Maisa's.

The theatre was now at the end of its fourth hour. The troupe then completely altered the tempo of the performance by bringing out three fast-paced masquerades, Bakòrò, the Ram, Sinè, the Gazelle, and Njona, the Wildcat, one right after another, cutting out the musical interludes completely. After this performance burst, the masquerade Sumusonin, the Little Sorceress, entered and gave an extended performance lasting for nearly fifteen minutes [Figure 1.12]. The performance was in its fifth hour. Sumusonin exited and the troupe brought in Ntilen, the Giraffe. It performed for only a few minutes, during which time the audience disengaged and began to leave the plaza.

Embellishing or subverting the expected pattern of the performance by manipulating its internal tempo involves the constant interaction of performers and audience. A troupe's successful manipulation of the pattern and tempo of the performance is critical in these performances. Their use of performative strategies to create redundancy and novelty depends on the performers' individual and collective artistic skills, experience, and knowledge of past theatres. Things can go awry, as in the two cases I documented in 1979 outside Kirango. In one village, midway into the performance there was a long hiatus between masquerades and the musical interlude extended first ten, then fifteen, then twenty minutes. The drummers and singers successfully held the audience's attention for nearly fifteen minutes, which seems to be the outside limit for these events. After fifteen minutes, however, no masquerade appeared and both the audience and the singers and drummers began to lose interest. There was a real danger that the performance would collapse. In desperation the masquerade troupe sent out a young man to perform acrobatics on the handlebars of a bicycle, which I might add was quite a feat as he was riding the bicycle in sand. The crowd was at once intrigued and amused and the singers and drummers and audience reengaged. When the cyclist exited, the troupe immediately brought in a masquerade and the performance picked up and moved confidently toward its climax several hours later. My Kirango companions were sympathetic to the performers' dilemma but they were delighted that the troupe had made this timing faux pas.

In a second village, another timing error, not nearly as potentially catastrophic, however, did point out the necessity for troupes to constantly adjust their performances to their audience responses. In this instance the troupe brought out a masquerade that was clearly a crowd-pleaser. The troupe was so involved in the performance that they lost sight of their audience. After the masquerade had made its way around the dance arena, its attendants decided to lead it around for a second performance. Half way through this second circuit, it was clear that the audience was losing interest; people began to disengage and move around and the choral accompaniment was certainly halfhearted. To their credit, the troupe soon adjusted their performance, rushed the large masquerade out of the arena and aborted the expected musical interlude. They changed the tempo of the performance by reintroducing the comic character of Gòn, the Baboon, into the ring for a fast-paced dance. The crowd approved and the troupe won back its audience. After Gòn exited they continued with other masquerades, but they did not attempt to push the audience's tolerance again. Redundancy, in this case, led not to increased involvement, as is sometimes described for trance, but had the opposite effect, resulting in restlessness and boredom. As a corrective, the novelty of replaying a comic character like the Baboon in the middle of the performance pulled the audience back into the theatrical action.

Just as improvisations in the tempo and timing, which are based on the audience's expectations and responses, shape the masquerade order during each event, they play an equally critical role in establishing the performative relationships among the dancers, drummers, and singers. There is always tension between the remembered and the performed and between the reestablishment of cultural form and its revisions. It is this tension that gives all these arts their aesthetic edge. As each Sogo bò masquerader enters the arena, he is expected to establish the identity of his character through appropriate mimetic movements. Felines stalk, cattle lumber, and birds glide. Once he establishes the cultural identity of his character, the dancer is then free to extend the performance and to play with and embellish the basic movements. This play between form and embellishment in the masquerade dances generally involves altering the tempo of the dance. Within this basic jayan/jako framework, troupes develop their own performance styles. For example, in Kirango, where the audience for the theatre may swell to several thousand people, the dance arena is quite large. The common practice is for the masquerades to make one circuit around the perimeter of the dance space. The masker generally locates himself several yards inside the perimeter of the circle. As he moves around the arena, he stops at four points in the circuit roughly equidistant from one another. Each time he stops he breaks into a fast-paced dance [Figures 4.4 and 4.5]. This convention, in effect, allows the entire audience, no matter where they are located, to view the masquerade's performance. In those communities where the audience is much smaller, the masker generally goes directly to the center of the arena, where he will perform the basic slow/fast sequences several times from relatively the same position in the circle. For most of the large rod puppet masquerades, it is during the fast time of the performance that the puppeteers bring the puppet head into full animation. For those masquerades who carry small puppets on their backs, the costumed animals come to a full stop and drop to the ground, and then

4.4. A Bamana performance of Nama, the Hyena. 1979. Segou region, Mali. *Photograph by Lynn Forsdale.*

4.5. A Bamana performance of Nama, the Hyena. 1979. Segou region, Mali. *Photograph by Lynn Forsdale.*

the puppeteer animates the small puppets. Farmers hoe, boatmen row, women pound millet and card cotton, hunters raise their rifles as if to fire, and soldiers raise and lower the flag. When they perform the grass masquerades, dancers in Kirango still follow this same pattern but the overall tempo of the dance is generally quicker than for the rod puppet masquerades, which do not involve extensive acrobatic shape-shifting.

In Kirango when the masquerade completes one circuit of the dance arena it falls back into a tempo somewhere midway between the slow and fast tempos and it exits. There are exceptions that are clearly meant to violate this pattern. The most radical departure in the Kirango theatre is certainly the Shameless Hyena character. In other villages the convention of moving between a slow and a fast tempo also holds, but the number of repetitions may be longer or shorter, or the troupe may have developed a signature style for entry or exit. For example, among the Kirango Boso, once the masquerade makes a complete circuit of the dance arena it often moves backward about a quarter of the distance just covered, stops and plays another fast sequence, and then quickly exits.

The average costumed masquerade weighs forty or more pounds and in Kirango the fully costumed Mali Kònò, danced by a single young man, weighs considerably much more than that. Despite this weight the dancers must be able to move with grace and agility, without falling or slipping. In the grass and rod puppet masquerades the dancers cannot see from underneath the costume. They are either guided by an attendant who rings a bell or by a group of male attendants who keep the masker on track, often shouting directions to him. From the vantage point of the audience, the din of the music and the songs now amplified by microphones drowns out any stage directions that might be being shouted to the masquerader by his attendants.

The lead singer's knowledge of the appropriate songs is one criteria by which people evaluate her performance. The quality of her voice and the way she embellishes a song's phrasing and melody constitute the jako of her performance. These are the qualities that distinguish her performance from that of every other female singer. There is also a second level of this jayan/jako interplay that involves the lead singer and her chorus. While the lead singer generally sets the verse, the chorus can also invert this pattern by introducing a new verse. The lead singer also injects praises for groups or individuals who are in attendance. Part of the singer's skill is her awareness of who is in the audience, whether they are visiting dignitaries, past association leaders, sculptors, or men who had invented particular masquerades played that evening. This knowledge is critical and allows the singer to compose and insert praise lines at appropriate places during the event. In Kirango neither of the female lead singers was a griot. The praises they sang were not lineage histories, but were generalized praises for the accomplishments of individual men and women or particular groups present at the event.

Drummers perform as a team. At the onset they first establish the basic rhythm and then the lead drummer or several of the drummers embellish and improvise off this established rhythm. If the lead drummer is very skilled, he may improvise off a "hidden rhythm." This "hidden rhythm" might have been one previously established by the drummers but which currently exists only as a memory from moments past. In other cases the "hidden rhythm" might be carried forward by the clapping of the women's chorus, the melody of the song, or in some cases by the bell rung by the masquerade attendant. This process is fluid and quite complex.

The puppet theatre is structured so that an inexorable bond is created between the visual and verbal components of the drama. Performers consciously struggle to maintain a unity among the various art forms during the event. One judgment of a performer's competence, whether he or she is a dancer, a drummer, or a singer, is how quickly he or she can identify and pick up on the cues that pass between the different units and that orchestrate the event. These cues can be instigated by any one of the performers and this process is always rapid and in flux. In the musical interludes singers and drummers share the primary responsibility for moving the performance forward in time. Usually the singer introduces a song and the drum team follows her lead. Occasionally the drummers introduce a new set of rhythms and the lead singer (singers) keys off the rhythm and breaks into the new song.

In the masquerade portion of the event cueing involves all three performance units—singers, drummers, and masqueraders. For example, during one sequence the female singer was alerted to the entrance of the masquerade character before the drummers were aware of its entrance. She cued the drummers to its arrival by switching into the puppet signature song, yet for a few moments the tempo of the singing was out of sync with the drumming. Almost immediately, however, the drummers adjusted the rhythms and the sequence moved into high gear. Sometimes the masquerade attendants take the lead in cueing the other performance units. In Kirango in the 1987 performance, young men led each masquerade into the dance arena singing its signature song. The tempo of their songs was always slow, even dirge-like, and resembled the tempo of songs sung by bards in the fishermen's performances. When the lead singer took over the song, she adjusted the tempo to accommodate the character's dance. In a 1979 performance in the Boso quarter in Kirango, two small puppets on the back of the character Soden Mali la, the Malian Horsemen, began bobbing up and down wildly and clapping their hands together. In this case it was the puppeteers, hidden inside the costume, who were signaling to the singer and drummers that they wanted to shift the tempo. The drummers responded and the singers followed in short order. In the Bamana performance that year, Mali Kònò wanted to begin the short acrobatic dance sequence but the drummers were not immediately aware of the dancer's intentions. The dancer began to move forward and backward and repeated this movement several times. After about fifteen to twenty seconds, the drummers focused on the action, correctly interpreted the dancer's cue, and responded by doubling the tempo of the drumming. This in turn cued the singers to increase the tempo of the song, thus bringing the three units back into a performance unity.

At various points in the performance, individual performers are pulled forward into the limelight. At these moments individual virtuosity is appropriate and elicits praise from the audience. The musical interludes provide singers and drummers with opportunities to display their skills, while the puppet sequences shift the audience's focus to the dancers. When spectators are moved by the performance, they react by entering into the action, showering the performer or a performing unit with verbal and gestural praise. I have often seen young men and more rarely women enter the ring to praise a masquerader's dance or an especially virtuoso drum performance, or stand in front of the lead singers to shower them with praise.

However, when a performer or a performance unit becomes so enamored of its own virtuosity that it ignores the other performers, such self-absorption threatens the unity of the performance and is judged negatively. I attended one performance where a drum team became so involved in its own playing that it ignored both the singers and the masquerade. An astute lead singer assessed the situation and intervened by abruptly changing songs and leaving the drum team afloat. The drummers quickly got the message and refocused their attention on the business of the drama. During another performance, the chorus, tired of repeating the same refrain, rebelled and started a new song. For a minute or two the lead singer and her chorus were completely out of sync. The drum team resolved the issue by picking up on the chorus's song and forcing the lead singer to comply. In both these cases, unchecked competition among or within the performance units and an individual's self-promotion threatened the performance. Although at different times during an evening's event one performer or group may hold sway, the ultimate success of the theatre depends upon everyone's knowing when to give individuals the limelight and when to share it with the entire group. A *nyènajè nyana*, a good performance, then, must include the competent displays of singing, dancing, and drumming that are considered integral to the definition of the genre. People state very emphatically that once a masquerade is in the arena, the dance, drum, and the song rhythms must be brought into unity.

Actors are sensitive to the interplay between the forces of tradition and innovation, between old and new forms, and between individual artistic virtuosity and collective action. Their adult audience is made up of former actors in the theatre and at each performance every troupe knows implicitly that their efforts and artistry will be judged against past performances and the achievements of former troupes. While these performances are defined as play and entertainment, they are serious play. Each troupe knows it will gain its place in the theatrical history, or be forgotten, not only in terms of its predecessors' artistic achievements but in light of the performances of its successors, the boys and girls in the audience, who wait in the wings eager to take on the role of performers in these events. Local definitions of appropriate time and timing determine the periodicity of these events within the year. Theatrical practices in time shape and define becoming a performer and the transfer of theatrical knowledge. Finally, notions of timing and tempo orchestrate the production and appreciation of these events. There is, however, another element, that of style, that is equally critical in the production, evaluation, and interpretation of these events and is related to the various notions of time discussed above. Style, in this sense, emerges and is shaped by each group's claims to different histories, identities, and practices. In the theatre this style manifests itself in the distinctiveness of each group's music and dance, and through its choice of masquerade characters. These expressive forms and masquerade characters contribute to the subjective and objective recognition and appreciation of these performances as belonging to one ethnic group or another within the broader context of a shared regional performance tradition.

CHAPTER FIVE

Bringing the Past into the Present in Masquerade Theatre

Youth association masquerade performances are important public settings for the production of historicity and group identity in Segou. Four ethnic groups regularly perform the theatre in the Segou region, the Bamana, the Boso, the Sòmonò, and the Maraka. To a large extent people's sense of themselves as a group, their *si*, is based on their perceptions of a shared past. These pasts can be differently invoked and interpreted, depending upon the social occasion and upon which group controls historical expression.[1] People consider the past to be a rich and authoritative cultural resource. In the Sogo bò theatre actors selectively use imagery referring to different pasts to explore, construct, and intensify their own group identity and, by extension, their relationships with other groups (Bloch 1977; d'Azevedo 1962; Peel 1984). Contemporary masquerade troupes draw historical imagery from the full spectrum of the past, from mythic time to the present, and allude to shared pasts through the form and style of their expressive forms and by means of specific dramatic personae.

In the Segou region these reference groups are relatively fluid and have changed over time depending on the context. Any discussion of ethnic identity and ethnic groups as they emerge within contemporary puppet masquerade theatre must be attentive to the role that the colonial administration and the community of scholars have played in reifying ethnic groups in Mali. Throughout the first half of this century certain criteria and features were selected and valorized over others in the process of defining the different ethnic groups. These group definitions have become naturalized and until quite recently uncritically repeated in most scholarly and popular publications.

To some extent, but not entirely, these colonial constructions have also shaped Malians' own popular discourse about their ethnicity in the late twentieth century (J. Bazin 1985).[2] As a prelude to this study of how troupes use artistic forms and imagery in the production of contemporary identity, it is imperative to examine the cluster of different historical traditions that are current among the four major groups who regularly perform these masquerades today.

It is noteworthy that throughout Segou's history people living in this region have been profoundly affected by their geographical location, by the impact of long-distance trade, and by the processes of state formation that began in the Western Sudan in the early centuries of the first millennium A.D. All of the precolonial states which at various times controlled this region shared certain structural and organizational features. The sociopolitical organization of these states was based on the kinship system (clans and lineages). Each state history reads as the rise of one group or subgroup over others and over neighboring peoples. In the Western Sudan the territorial base of many of these precolonial states was extensive. Their histories are marked in both oral traditions and written documentation as ones of formation, consolidation, expansion, crisis, alliance, and either abrupt or gradual decline. The earliest states included the medieval polities of Ghana and Mali. These states extended their authority over much of present-day Mali, including major portions of the Segou region. Later, from the sixteenth century to the late nineteenth century, various states, including Segou and Masina, controlled all or portions of the Segou region. Smaller polities arose within the Segou region. These included Karadougou, Shianro, Kala, and Djenne, who at various times were independent of the larger states and were either allies or adversaries.

In the process of expansion, these precolonial states all seemed to follow a similar pattern. They generally left local political structures intact, but placed state administrators and military in key areas to protect their interests. Slavery was important in the history of these states. Although slaves were at various times an important export commodity, they also clearly provided essential labor in local production sectors. In the military, captive men often formed the core of the standing armies that were maintained by these states. In the state administration, freed slaves or the ruler's personal slaves, whose loyalty was invested in his person, are often remembered as achieving prominence in state affairs. Throughout the centuries, the extraction of tribute from subjugated communities and the control of lucrative trade routes were critical to the maintenance of the state.[3]

The memory of these precolonial states plays a significant role in the present constitution of contemporary group identities. Whole communities or segments of a community may choose to identify themselves with one or more of these precolonial states. Many Bamana and Sòmonò identify with the precolonial Segou state, while some Boso identify themselves with the ancient state of Ghana. Certain Maraka retain historical memories of their association with the ancient state of Ghana, while others identify more closely with the precolonial state of Mali. In the context of puppet masquerade theatre, troupes often make direct or oblique references to these precolonial states in fashioning their group identity.

Throughout the last century in scholarly reconstructions of these precolonial states, ethnic labels were regularly used to characterize the different states. These states are now popularly known as the Soninke state of Ghana, the Malinké state of Mali, the Songhay state of Gao, the Bamana and Toucoulour states of Segou, the Bamana state of Kaarta, and the Fulani state of Masina. With few exceptions, however, the population of each state was quite diverse and at its apogee each had extended its influence well beyond the core area of its formation. A perusal of some of the more common oral traditions that people hold in this area about their historical relationships to various precolonial states clearly reveals the essential heterogeneity of groups who today call themselves or are identified by outsiders by a single ethnic name.

The large body of oral histories, myths, and legends about the precolonial past held by the different groups in Kirango and in other communities throughout the region if woven together result in a complex and often contradictory narrative. In the puppet theatre, as in other social contexts, a group or segment of a group may draw its current identity from one or more of these pasts. Among Kirango groups, for example, people construct part of their group identity from a perceived association with one of the precolonial states that once controlled the Segou region. Yet, in many other communities within the region these state histories are rarely invoked in the theatre. In these cases different criteria dominate the discourse about identity. In reconstructing their past, these communities may choose to emphasize origin myths and migration histories of resident lineages, rather than any larger state history.

In addition to state and local political histories, people create part of their current identity from their investment in a particular religion. During the performances most communities also emphasize their investment in either agriculture or fishing as an identity marker. In any analysis of historical imagery in puppet masquerade theatre, it is essential to recognize and to appreciate the diversity of traditions found within each group and community. At the same time that people define themselves as either Bamana, Boso, Sòmonò, or Maraka, the multiplicity of historical traditions that emerge both in the theatre and in other social contexts underscores the range of diverse pasts available to people as they forge their identities within these masquerades.

A Survey of Historical Traditions in the Segou Region

This brief survey of historical traditions of the four principal groups who perform the puppet masquerade theatre does not pretend to be exhaustive, nor is it my intention to promote the historical legitimacy of the claims of one group or segment of a group over others. It is also not my intention to produce any coherent master narrative. These competing traditions are not viewed as misrepresentations or distortions of some objective historical truth; rather, their very diversity underscores the dynamic processes at play in the production of historicity within the puppet masquerade theatre.

THE BAMANA

The Bamana are the dominant ethnic group, numerically, politically, and culturally, within the Segou region. The Bamana, or Bambara, have been the focus of many historical and ethnographic studies over the past century. Outsiders have characterized them variously as lazy or industrious. They have described them as peaceful people strongly invested in agriculture, or as a people habituated to warfare and pillage. They have reviled them as stupid and superstitious or have conversely praised them as great metaphysicians (J. Bazin 1985, 87–90).

Within Bamana communities in Mali, regardless of their different traditions of origin, individuals are classified as belonging to one of three social categories. These categories include the *hòròn*, freemen, the *nyamakala*, blacksmiths and bards, and the *jòn*, descendants of slaves. Descent and historical circumstance determine an individual's membership in one of these categories. An individual's social classification as either hòròn, nyamakala, or jòn may be critical in a variety of contexts, for example in marriage negotiations and in establishing political or ritual leadership. However, within the context of the youth association and during its puppet theatre, these social categories, while never wholly ignored, are usually never explicitly invoked.

In the production of historicity, the greatest ambiguity surrounds the definitions of the category of slave. While jòn describes the domination of master over slave, some Bamana communities also classify the descendants of the *tonjòn*, the precolonial military class, as slaves. This includes the descendants of the populations of Segou town and of the Segou state, as well as the descendants of the ruling Diarra lineage. Those groups who define the tonjòn as slaves assert that they themselves are the "authentic or real" Bamana. In their eyes true Bamana are those farmers who resisted domination by the powerful Segou state and who historically refused to adopt Islam (Lewis 1979, 87–89). However, as Jean Bazin makes clear, the term jòn and the term tonjòn imply quite different orders of domination:

> . . . although some consider all the Segou-Kaw (people of Segou) as a body, to be jon as instruments of royal will, the latter have the right to consider themselves "free" since they are in the public service of the warrior community and not the instruments of production of any private person. (J. Bazin 1974, 111)

Not surprisingly, the Bamana living in Kirango, who trace their descent from the Diarra dynasty and from Segou's military class, the tonjòn, do not define *Bamanaya*, Bamananess, in the same way as do the Bamana groups that John Lewis interviewed. While today they are proud to be farmers, they take great pride in their descent from the Segou state and its military class and they certainly do not consider themselves descendants of slaves. Kirango was a royal Diarra village and a military stronghold on the Niger River. One of the community's ancestors, Kirango ben Diarra, became the head of the Segou state in the mid nineteenth century. Bamana in Kirango call themselves *Segoukaw*, people of Segou, and more specifically *Ngolosi*, descendants of Ngolo Diarra, the founder of the Diarra dynasty. Moreover, I have regularly heard contemporary hòròn and nyamakala in Kirango and elsewhere in the area describe themselves as *Allah ka jònw*, slaves of Allah. This term is the public expression of their Islamic faith. Like their claim to descent from Segou, Kirango Bamana are proud of their new Islamic identity and the term slave of Allah in no way suggests that they have renounced their historical claims to being descendants of Segou warriors or to being hòròn or nyamakala.

THE BOSO

The Boso are a small group of fishermen currently living along the Niger and Bani rivers within the Segou region. These Boso always describe themselves as both fishermen and master hunters. Their own historical traditions relate them to fishing groups living on the river north of Segou, who call themselves Sorko.

Today most Segou Boso speak the Bamana language and they share with their Bamana neighbors many of the same cultural values and social institutions. Yet despite a shared language and a number of shared cultural practices, Boso consider themselves and are considered by their neighbors to be a distinct ethnic group.

Throughout this zone, the Boso are universally recognized as the original inhabitants of the floodplains that lie on either side of the Niger and Bani rivers from Lake Debo south into the Segou region. These floodplains lie within portions of the historical polities of Segou, Masina, Karadougou, Shianro, Djenne, Sokolo, and Kala. In most villages in these areas, the histories of the farmers generally acknowledge that the Boso were the first inhabitants of the area. These farmers accept that the Boso were already established in this area when their own ancestors migrated into the region.

Oral traditions concerning the Boso collected from Malinke and Bamana in the late colonial period support these fishermen's current claims and reflect the longstanding interaction among farmers and fishing groups. According to one version of the Mande creation myth, the Boso are descendants of the eldest twins born of Faro, the creator of the world. The rest of mankind are the descendants of the union of the second set of twins and the woman Muso Koroni. The descendants of Muso Koroni suffered the contamination that their mother inflicted on her descendants by her transgressions. The Boso, who were spared this contamination, enjoy a special relationship to Faro.

In another fragment of the myth, Faro transforms himself/herself into the Niger River and floods the area in order to reclaim the fonio seeds which Muso Koroni had stolen. The Boso followed Faro in his/her transformation as the Niger River and thus became the first settlers along this river and in the floodplains (Dieterlen 1957, 132). In many villages along the river, the titles of *murukalatigi*, owner of the knife handle, and *jitigi*, owner of the water, two important ritual offices, remain the prerogative of Boso families. These ritual offices reinforce the fishermen's claim to a special relationship with Faro and to first occupancy in the region.

While the Segou Boso relate themselves in certain contexts to Sorko fishermen living north along the Niger River, they also preserve an elaborate internal system of differentiation that is based on migration traditions and on dialect.[4] Some Segou Boso trace their ancestral homelands to Dia and ultimately to the ancient state of Wagadu or Ghana.[5]

Other traditions held by the Boso and their neighbors recall the Boso's political subjugation to the rulers of the precolonial states of Mali and Segou. Although the Boso claim to be the first occupants of the region, it is clear from oral traditions that the empire of Mali and that of Segou held political sway over these fishermen. Boso stated that before French colonial rule they did not have an internal system of chieftaincy and their historical relationships to these two precolonial states are always framed in terms of either alliances made with specific rulers or subjugation by a ruling group.[6]

The political subjugation of the fishing communities to the Segou state remembered in Boso oral traditions also appears in the Segou epic. According to the epic, Segou rulers brought many Boso groups from outside the region into the area to fish for the state.[7] Boso elders in Banankoro echoed this tradition by stating that their ancestors were forced to settle into Segou from Dia during the reign of Da Monzon Diarra (1810–1827). According to these elders, while some fishermen from the village chose to return to Dia in the early colonial period, many remained in Banankoro.[8] Today, the descendants of those who stayed in this village preserve the history of their origins through the names of the four fishing quarters in Banankoro, which are said to be the names of their villages of origin in the region of Dia (Banankoro Boso, 1980).

Within the larger Segou region, local polities also established political control over fishing villages. According to elders in Shianro, during the precolonial era their port on the Niger River was the Boso village of Gomitogo.[9] Local traditions recall that later, during the period of the Toucouleur state when Tijani Tall ruled the Masina region, he forced many nomadic Boso from the north to settle in permanent villages around Mopti (Gallais 1967, 98).

THE SÒMONÒ

The Sòmonò are the largest group of fishermen living in the Segou region today. Some neighboring groups claim that the Sòmonò were former slaves of the precolonial Segou state while others characterize the Sòmonò as a casted group attached to Bamana and Malinké farmers. Unlike the Boso fishermen, subgroups of the Sòmonò claim origins not only from the Bamana and Malinké but from the Maraka, Fula, Minyanka, and Bobo. Sòmonò hold the most diverse histories of origin, and in the construction of a group identity shared traditions of ancestry are less important than either their investment in fishing as an occupation or their Islamic heritage.[10]

Boso and Sòmonò fishermen draw distinctions among the two groups based not only on their different traditions of origin but also on critical differences in their fishing technologies. While these distinctions are not always clear-cut today, in the past Sòmonò tended to use large undifferentiated nets to drag the river while the Boso used smaller specialized handheld nets that they adapted to particular species of fish. Consistent with these differences in fishing technology, the Sòmonò organized collective fishing expeditions, while as a rule the Boso tended to fish individually or in small family groups. The Sòmonò prefer deeper water fishing, while the older Boso methods were better adapted to the shallower waters of smaller tributaries and marshes (Daget 1949, 18–73; Gallais 1967, 413–433; and Kirango Sòmonò, 1980).

Certain Sòmonò groups describe themselves as longtime residents of the region, and Sòmonò living around Segou city claim that they were the founders of the city (Pageard 1961c, 17). References to the Sòmonò appear regularly in Segou state chronicles, where they are mentioned as warriors, councilors to the ruler, and mediators in court affairs. They also played a critical role in transporting Segou's armies across rivers during various military campaigns (Monteil 1976 [1924]). The traditions of Segou city Sòmonò concerning the origin of the puppet masquerade link it to the reign of Biton Coulibaly. These traditions support the Sòmonò's claim to a special historical relationship with the Segou state.

The Sòmonò were early practitioners of Islam and their long association with Islam in the Segou region serves to set them apart from historically non-Islamic groups like the Bamana and the Boso. Today, even though many Bamana and Boso villages along the rivers have converted to Islam, many of the imams that serve these communities are Sòmonò.

THE MARAKA

Maraka is an ethnic label almost entirely limited to the Segou and Kaarta regions. In Segou, people with quite different histories of origin identify themselves as Maraka. The term is used by people around San in eastern Segou who claim a Soninke origin in the state of Ghana; by those groups in the eastern zone who claim a Malinké origin and a historical relationship to the medieval state of Mali; and by diverse groups for whom being Muslim is the most important feature of their contemporary group identity.

Within the larger group who call themselves or who are designated by outsiders as Maraka, people make certain internal distinctions: Maraka jè (white Maraka), Maraka kan folow (those who speak the Maraka language), Maraka fin or Maraka da fin (the black Maraka or the black-mouthed Maraka), and Maraka jalan (the dried Maraka) (Roberts 1978, 5).

The Maraka jè or the Maraka kan folow consider themselves the "authentic" Maraka. These Maraka claim descent from the Soninke who migrated from Ghana into Segou. According to one etymology of Maraka, the term means to command, to govern, and this etymology is used to bolster their claims of historical political ascendancy (Roberts 1978, 5). Throughout Segou, Maraka jè are known as traders and indeed from all accounts their ancestors established important precolonial commercial centers at Sansanding, Djenne, and Segou well before the emergence of the Segou state.[11]

A second etymology sometimes given for the term Maraka is Mali-ka, People of Mali (Gallais 1967, 83). In the eastern portion of the Segou region, certain Maraka groups who are farmers and not traders claim origin or historical allegiance to the medieval empire of Mali. Chieftaincy in many of these villages is still invested in Traore lineages, who claim descent from the Mande heartland.[12]

Both the Maraka who claim origins in Ghana and those who trace their descent to Mali are considered to be longtime adherents to Islam, and for the latter group it was their religious affiliation that played a significant role in differentiating these farming communities in eastern Segou from non-Islamic Bamana with whom they share a number of cultural and linguistic affinities.

Maraka da fin, or Maraka fin (black-mouthed Maraka, or black Maraka), is the name used for people whose origins are said to have been Soninke but who over the centuries have come to be assimilated into the dominant Bamana culture in the Segou region. Though identified as Maraka fin by those claiming to be Maraka jè, these groups generally call themselves Bamana.

Maraka jalan, the dried Maraka, is a term commonly used by Maraka jè for people of diverse origins in and around San who converted to Islam in the nineteenth century. Maraka jalan often identify themselves simply as Maraka. The adoption of a Maraka ethnicity by these groups is intended to distinguish themselves from their non-Islamic neighbors. Roberts follows Gallais and translates the term Maraka jalan as dyed Maraka (Roberts 1978, 5; Gallais 1967, 84, 109–110). However, most people I spoke to translated the term *jalan* as dried as in *jege jalan*, dried fish. They used the term pejoratively and explained that Maraka jalan referred to people who had abandoned their own traditions and are dried, i.e., without nyama, energy or life force.

I found that the term Maraka jalan was also used in a more limited area in and around Segou city to identity the descendants of the followers of El Hadji Oumar Tall. In this particular context it referred to their Islamic heritage and to the etymology of *mara ka*, to govern. Bamana also often refer to this group as Futakaw, people of the Futa.

Historicity, Ethnicity, and Style in Masquerade Performances

In puppet theatre the play of these different group histories opens up people's construction of their identity. Within any performance the troupe continually draws and redraws different boundaries that circumscribe a we/them, insider/outsider claim. Members of the audience, who may be either residents or nonresidents of the quarter or village, either share an identity with the performers or they distinguish themselves from the troupe through their interpretation of different dramatic personae and their identification of the theatre's artistic forms and styles.

Among all four groups certain points of convergence in the history of the theatre, in its organization, and in its timing within the year contribute to people's sense of these masquerades as part of a common regional historical experience. Since Independence in 1960 this regional identity for the puppet masquerades has been bolstered through the participation of Segou troupes in the national arts competitions. In these festivals, the primary identity of the masquerade troupes is a regional one and the differences among the performances of the four groups become secondary and of lesser importance than when these performances are played in their local settings.

Another factor that contributes to people's sense of a shared theatrical past is the common sculptural style for masks and puppets used by all four ethnic groups. Interestingly, the style of these puppets and masks is variously called Bamana, Maraka, or Boso in the Western art historical literature. A shared sculptural style certainly dates back to at least the turn of the century, if not earlier. The blacksmith artists who carve most of the masks and puppets for the youth masquerade identify themselves and are identified by their neighbors as Bamana. These smiths carve not only for Bamana troupes but for Boso, Sòmonò, Maraka, and even some Bobo communities who have recently begun to play the theatre. While everyone recognizes that the fishermen are the progenitors of the theatre, everyone also grants that the farmers through their affiliated blacksmiths have been a central force in the sculptural development of these masquerades.

Much of the African art in Western museums and private collections has little associated field documentation, although pieces continue to be confidently labeled as representing one group's artistic style over others. Recently Kasfir and Frank, among others, have demonstrated the problems with these museum attributions (Kasfir 1984; Frank 1988). In the case of museum holdings of Segou puppets and masks, those with metal decorations are regularly identified as Maraka sculptures even though other groups in eastern Segou share with the Maraka a distinct preference for sculptures decorated with metal [Figure 3.37]. Many of the puppets and masks that are boldly painted are identified as Bamana although again all of the groups living in western Segou communities tend to favor painted pieces over those decorated with metal [Figure 2.20]. It is equally true in the late twentieth century that boldly painted puppets and masks can be found in the repertoires of some eastern Segou villages, while ones decorated with metal bosses and appliqués can be found in western villages (Arnoldi 1983, 191–193).

The majority of sculptures which were collected after the 1930s and have been attributed variously to either the Bamana, the Boso, the Maraka, or the Sòmonò on stylistic grounds were in fact most probably all sculpted by *cikènumu*, who local communities identify as Bamana. Unlike Western art historical classifications based on sculptural style, in Segou individual puppets or masks are defined as belonging to a particular group by virtue of their inclusion in a particular performance event, where they are inexorably tied to the style of music, dance, and drumming. It is performance style, not sculptural style, that participants themselves use to draw distinctions among different groups' theatres.

While people recognize and openly discuss the cross-fertilization among ethnic groups in the development of the theatre, it is performance style that actively shapes the participants' investment in different ethnic identities within the performance event. Drumming, song, and dance always accompany the appearance of the masquerades, and each of the different groups claims to have a distinct style of singing, dance, and music. When people discussed these differences they themselves generally invoked ethnic terms as a way of distinguishing among performance styles. For example, people spoke of a Bamana dance, or a Maraka song, or a Boso drum rhythm. Performers also made broad generalizations about each group's performance styles. In Kirango for example, Bamana performers described their own song style as having a faster tempo than songs sung by the Boso and Sòmonò. They judged the Bamana songs to be crisper and more succinct. Their descriptions of a quintessential Bamana song style correlates with their descriptions of Bamana drum rhythms and the style of Bamana dancing. Among all of these groups the maintenance of a unity among the different expressive forms is an aesthetic ideal and it is the ultimate criterion for judging the success or failure of any performance.

People's consciousness of different ethnic styles is heightened in those communities, like Kirango, that are multi-ethnic. In villages with mixed ethnic populations, when one troupe or the other "borrows" masquerades from their neighbors they often consciously set out to modify the song, dance, and drum style to reflect their own group's performance style in order to transform the "borrowed" masquerade into one of their own. This was the case when Bamana troupes at the turn of the century borrowed the four grass masquerades, Nama, Falakani, Bilanjan, and Bala, from the fishermen's theatre [Figures 2.13, 2.14, 2.15, and 2.16]. Bamana and Sòmonò troupes often play three or four of these characters today. Although the masquerade forms are identical across troupes, the Bamana and Sòmonò sing different songs, perform different dances, and play different drum rhythms for these characters.

This process is not unique to Kirango. In a neighboring village, the Bamana troupe "borrowed" the character Koon, the Roan Antelope, from their Boso neighbors [Figure 3.21].[13] While they kept its original form and its name, they changed its song, dance, and drum rhythm to reflect its new Bamana identity. At the same time, then, that a shared masquerade can herald a common origin, its performance style works to emphasize differences between groups. Since the audience at the Kirango performances include spectators from all three ethnic groups, individuals may momentarily share a sense of identification with the performers through shared masquerades while simultaneously associating or disassociating themselves with these same performances based on their knowledge of performance style. People's knowledge of their own and other groups' performance styles is primarily a practical knowledge. It derives first and foremost from their own performance biographies in youth theatre and secondly from their lifelong attendance at other ethnic groups' performances.

During the 1989 performance in the Bamana quarter in Kirango, differences between farmers' and fishermen's performance styles were openly acknowledged and celebrated in the event itself. In this performance the troupe decided to play the Boso masquerade character Koon, the Roan Antelope, in addition to the Bamana masquerade Dajè, also a version of the Roan Antelope. Unlike the neighboring Bamana troupe, which had effectively transformed the Boso character Koon into their own, the Kirango Bamana troupe's intention was clearly not to assimilate the character into the Bamana repertoire. The troupe did not purport to claim its performance as their own. What they did instead was to invite the Boso female lead singer, Maimuna Thiero, to sing for Koon. They also invited the Boso association's drum team to play for the masquerade's performance. Koon's appearance alongside that of other Bamana masquerades accentuated people's perceptions of the differences in the two troupes' performance styles. After the event, people interpreted the troupe's conscious retention of the masquerade's Boso identity and performance style as theatrically innovative. The performance of Koon also allowed the Boso in the audience to identify with the larger performance event and spoke quite eloquently to the current amicable relationship between the two rivals. In the 1992 spring performance, the Bamana troupe again performed the character Koon and added the performance of Saalen, the Nile Perch. Again, Maimuna Thiero sang the songs for these two characters and the masquerades performed in a style that the audience associated with the fishermen's theatre.

Collaboration between individuals from different troupes is not unheard of in Kirango, and young men who are friends but members of rival troupes do talk to one another about theatre and exchange ideas and advice on matters relating to masquerade construction, etc. In the mid 1950s it was Ousmane Diarra's friend from Djamarabougou who helped him construct the Shameless Hyena character. In 1978 one of the members of the Bamana troupe, who was an electrician by training, helped the Boso troupe to install battery-operated eyes in their masquerade of the turtle. While this type of collaboration is fairly common, it was the inclusion of fishermen's masquerades in a farmers' performance in 1989 and in 1992 that I had not seen a decade before in Kirango.

In another village, whose residents identify themselves as either Bamana or Boso, I was initially surprised to find that the two groups cooperated in the production of their annual puppet masquerade theatre.[14] They bring the masquerades to the village in boats and the fishermen and the farmers perform their masquerades together in one afternoon and evening during the full moon just prior to the onset of the rainy season. While everyone agreed that the fishermen were the original owners of the genre, they stated that in this community both groups have been performing together since the 1920s. I wondered if ethnicity was a much less important factor in their theatre than it was in Kirango. Yet a closer look at the performances revealed that although the two groups perform together in a single event, each group continues to retain ownership of particular dramatic characters. The troupe has adopted the convention of fishermen playing the first character and then following it with a farmers' masquerade and continuing this sequence throughout the event. Moreover, like the Kirango theatres, the farmers and fishermen retain distinct performance styles that serve to distinguish one group's masquerades from the other's. Fishermen and farmers cooperate to stage the festival, thus publicly acknowledging a shared artistic heritage. Yet these same actors simultaneously maintain ethnic diversity as a critical artistic feature within each performance.

Historical animosities within villages whose residents all identify themselves as members of the same ethnic group can also lead to the construction of different group identities in performance. In one village near Kirango two different quarters who identify themselves as Bamana to outsiders retain distinct group identities based on their historical circumstances. One quarter identifies itself as the original inhabitants of the village. The other identifies itself as descendants of Ngolo Diarra and the Segou warrior state. Today, a descendant of the conquering Diarra lineage is the *dugutigi*, the village chief. The residents who claim descent from the founders of the village see the Diarra lineage as usurpers.

In this community each quarter's claim to a different group identity was not benign and found expression in the puppet masquerades. Each of the two residential quarters organized its own separate youth association and each association performed a separate puppet masquerade in the village. One of the resident blacksmiths, who was aligned with the ruling Diarra lineage, carved many puppets and masks for his quarter. However, he categorically refused to carve for the other quarter's theatre. It is by the inclusion or absence of this blacksmith's sculptures that local residents and visitors could distinguish one quarter's theatre from the other in this village.

The thinly veiled acrimony between the two quarters asserted itself very pointedly when I was working in this community. In October 1979 I attended and photographed a masquerade performance in the first quarter. My first round of post-performance interviews with the troupe went very well and the association was quite open and eager to discuss the theatre with me. A few weeks later I was introduced to the blacksmith sculptor who lived in the other quarter and I conducted an interview with him. A week later when I attempted to schedule a second series of interviews with the first quarter's troupe, it was made very clear to me that I would have to make a choice between the two quarters, as neither could support my working with both of them. In the end I chose to work with the sculptor and abandoned my research in the other quarter.

Certain pre-theatre spectacles and ceremonies can also make public the particular identity of the masquerade performances that follow. In Kirango during the late morning preceding the beginning of the afternoon performance, the Sòmonò troupe parades several of their puppet masquerades in boats in full view of the village. While this parade effectively alerts the village to the coming festivities, it also clearly marks the event and its masquerades as a fishermen's theatre. This parade of masquerades is a regular feature in many fishermen's festivals along the Niger River and has a long history. Soleillet described one of these pre-performance spectacles in 1878. The parade of masquerades on the river is indeed visually spectacular and over the past century it has become a signature feature of Segou fishermen's theatres (B. N'Diaye 1970, 438; Arnoldi 1977, 10). In more recent government-sponsored celebrations in the colonial and postcolonial period, Sòmonò and Boso troupes have been regularly invited to participate in the afternoon entertainments. In these contexts the opening parade has taken on a performance life of its own, divorced from the larger masquerade event [Figure 2.1].

In the Bamana quarter in Kirango, the youth association opened its 1989 spring festival with the Dònkan ceremony. This ceremony is expressly intended to recall the quarter's historical allegiance to the precolonial Segou state and to invest the troupe in their warrior heritage. Oral traditions state that the ceremony took place on the evening before warriors departed for battle. Today, an hour before the masquerade performance begins, the troupe plays out this ceremony in the association meetinghouse adjacent to the plaza where the masquerades will be performed. The timing of the ceremony coincides with the hour before the masquerade performance when the general audience is settling itself around the dance arena. Although only youth association members participate in this ceremony, the general audience arriving for the masquerade event can easily hear the songs and music being performed inside the house. While the association members perform the songs, a group of older men enter the meetinghouse and proceed to give the assembled association officers encouragement and advice. They are followed by a group of elder women who enter the house and extol the young men to be brave in the coming "battle." The advice of the elders and the songs that are sung refer to the precolonial warrior-heroes of Segou. This ceremony forges the link between the assembled young men and their warrior ancestry. The Dònkan ceremony emphasizes an important dimension of the Bamana quarter's group identity that derives from their claim to descent from the Segou state.

Troupes also use songs and individual dramatic characters to make direct or indirect claims to different precolonial historical traditions and spheres of influence. These songs and masquerades actively contribute to the creation of group identities within these events. For example, in one Maraka farming village in the Shianro area the chorus sings a praise song for the masquerades that alludes to this community's claim to descent in ancient Mali. A phrase in the song refers to the public plaza as "Papa Tarawele ka fèrè" or "Our father's (founding ancestor's) plaza." Praise lines in songs sung in the Bamana quarter in Kirango make references to the glory of Segou and to their warrior heritage.

While contemporary troupes throughout the region perform many of the same masquerade characters, individual communities often perform one or more characters that serve as a testimony to their historical identity within the region. In Kirango, for example, among the Boso, who claim origin in Dia and ultimately in Wagadu, the troupe performs a large python masquerade known as "the snake of Wagadu." The myth of the sacred python of Ghana is well known throughout Mali, and the Boso troupe asserts publicly its claim of descent from Wagadu through this masquerade's performance [Figure 5.1].[15]

5.1. A Boso performance of Wagadu Sa, the Snake of Wagadu. 1979. Kirango, Mali. *Photograph by Mary Jo Arnoldi.*

In a number of Maraka villages in and around San, the character Nkolokun, a face mask covered with metal appliqués or merely painted yellow, is regularly performed. People said it represented the legendary golden mask of the ancient empire of Ghana. Like the "snake of Wagadu [Ghana]" performed by the Boso in Kirango, this Maraka character asserts these communities' claims to descent from Ghana. As one moves further away from San, the songs that accompany the Nkolokun masquerade assert a quite different claim. In these Maraka villages Nkolokun's song makes the people's claim to ancestry in the Mali empire.

In the Bamana quarter of Kirango, the troupe performs the character Bilisi, a genie that appears in the epic of the Segou empire [Figure 3.27]. In Kirango, Bilisi is a more recent masquerade. Their version does not follow the verbal description of Bilisi in the epic, but takes the form of a three-headed beast made entirely of grass. Like the other grass masquerades from the earlier period, Bilisi is played in total darkness and is a shape-shifter. His song and dance speak to the awesome powers of the genie and reinforce the quarter's heritage as Segoukaw, people of the Segou empire.

One of the most important characters in Kirango's Sòmonò performances is Baninkònò, the Stork [Figure 5.2]. Costumed in yards of gold lamé cloth, this masquerade is called *Do Mansa*, King of Puppets. This masquerade is nearly identical in form to another bird masquerade currently played by the Sòmonò in Segou city. Kirango Sòmonò trace their origins to families in Segou city, and local Sòmonò historians claim that sometime before the rise of the Segou state a fishing village was founded on the present site of Kirango by the Sòmonò Thiero from Segou.[16] The performance of the Stork in Kirango links these Sòmonò with those in Segou city, thus asserting their claim to a share in the central role that the Sòmonò have played in the political history of this region.

In Kirango and in neighboring fishing communities troupes perform a set of masquerades that represent large river game such as the hippo [Figure 3.22], the manatee, and the crocodile [Figure 3.18]. In farming villages troupes also represent important bush animals such as the lion [Figure 1.15], the buffalo, and the elephant [Figure 3.11]. While both sets of animal characters celebrate hunters as society's heroes, these groups' different choices of animals assert their claim to different spheres of experience and influence in the bush.

Within the Boso theatre and in certain Sòmonò communities the performance of water animal masquerades celebrates the histories of individual lineages within the village. These particular masquerades are owned by individual lineages and their performances are distinct from those masquerades owned by the association as a whole. In the Boso quarter of Kirango, the masquerades Mali, the Hippo, Ma, the Manatee, and Bama, the Crocodile are the property of individual lineages. Only young men from these lineages have the right to dance these characters in the annual theatre. Moreover, when the lineage masquerades are performed they are accompanied by a male lead singer, not a female lead singer. Their performances begin with the songs for the great Boso hunters of the distant past. The male singer then inserts the names of great hunters from the resident lineage who owns the masquerade into this illustrious list. Finally he sings the names of lineage members who have danced the masquerade in the past. Two well-known singers in the area, Budagari Coulibaly [Figure 2.2] and Vadama Traore [Figure

5.3], had regularly been invited to sing for fishermen's performances in Kirango. The tempo, style, and length of the songs for lineage-owned masquerades are quite different from those of songs sung by the women for the association-owned masquerades. The performances of lineage-owned masquerades are closer in tempo, style, and length to the epics sung by specialist griots among the Bamana.[17] While the Boso or Sòmonò women lead singers sing praises for themselves or sing praises for individual men and women in the audience, the masquerade songs they sing are always universally interpreted as songs for the animals.

Despite the differences in choice of big game represented in fishermen's and farmers' theatres, correspondences do exist across these groups in their interpretation of the import of hunting and the powers resident in the bush. All of these groups share the belief that animals have powerful nyama. A hunter's prowess stems not from mere physical ability, but depends on his knowledge of the bush and his mastery over the nyama released at the death of these animals. An emphasis on the hunter's knowledge and his ability to control these forces was evident in how both the Bamana and the Boso troupes played out hunting scenes in their 1979 performances. The commonly held beliefs about the bush, animals, hunting, and hunters allowed both farmers and fishermen in the audience to construct a shared interpretation of these scenes that cuts across the ethnic boundaries that troupes establish by their choice of a particular animal character.

In Kirango several masquerades heighten the quarter's investment in its Bamana patrimony. In 1979 the troupe played the mask Ntomo [Figure 1.13], a character borrowed from the boys' initiation association of the same name, and they performed the Kòmò dance [Figure 1.14], associated with this powerful men's association. In 1987 they performed the masquerade Ntomo and added a performance of the Ciwara masquerades from the men's association of the same name [Figure 3.35].

During the 1979 Ntomo sequence, the masker led the dancers into the arena and his attendants appeared dressed in the short blouson pants and sleeveless vests associated with Ntomo members, the bilakorow, young uncircumcised boys. Most of the dancers in this sequence were from the junior age-sets of the youth association but were still well beyond the age of Ntomo initiates.

In the 1979 Kòmò dance procession, all the dancers wore long robes and some wore *bamada* hats, once a common hat type worn by

5.3. Vadama Traore, a Boso singer, from Walentigila. 1980. *Photograph by Lynn Forsdale.*

adult Bamana men in this area. These young men wore costumes intended to represent those of elder men, and the drum team played the Kòmò men's association rhythm. The mask once associated with this powerful association, however, was not performed. During the processional, one of the young men led a tethered goat round the arena. At the dance's climax, he mimed sacrificing the animal.[18]

The Ciwara association and its signature crest masquerades, representing a male and a female roan antelope, have a long performance history in Bamana villages in this region. These masquerades were once performed in this men's association's public rituals. The masquerades danced for a competition among the young men tilling the fields. In the 1987 performance of these masquerades in the youth association theatre, a line from the song that accompanied their performance reads: "the steed of the communities is the hoe." This song line alludes to Ciwara's original performance context and it celebrates farming as the most noble pursuit for the Bamana.

These different men's associations were active in the quarter up until the 1950s, and even though most of the current actors were never initiated, the memory of these associations is still an important part of the quarter's history and its current identity. No one interpreted their re-presentation in the youth masquerade as ludic or satirical. The Ntomo and Ciwara masquerades and the Kòmò procession served as powerful references to the quarter's heritage and intensified and celebrated the quarter's Bamana identity.

In 1979 and 1980 both the Kirango Bamana and the Kirango Boso troupes also performed versions of a large antelope masquerade, out of whose back appeared several smaller puppets. The Bamana version included representations of a farmer with his hoe and of women pounding millet. The Boso masquerade included a small puppet representing a crocodile. Underlying these celebratory displays of farming and fishing there is always an implicit recognition of the tensions which exist between these two groups in the village. Bamana claim that farming is the most noble of activities, while Boso and Sòmonò assert the counterclaim that fishing is the first activity of mankind. In his ethnography of the Niger River fishermen, Ligers published a Boso adage that illustrates quite graphically this tension: "If you see a Boso bending over in a field, don't believe that he is farming, he is only vomiting" (Ligers 1964, II: xi).[19]

I once naively praised the fishing skills of one of the adolescent girls in the household when she had brought home a bucket brimming with *ntinenin*, a type of African tetra. These tasty small fish are considered a delicacy and each year when they run in the Niger River even farmers harvest them. Saiyo was not amused when I praised her abilities as a fisherman, and she swung around abruptly and bristled, "I am not a Boso."

While each of Kirango's theatres celebrates a distinct group identity, they also play characters that speak to their shared colonial and postcolonial experiences. In Segou the colonial period begins with the fall of Segou city to the French in 1890 and ends at Independence in 1960.[20] The colonial and postcolonial periods offer the community a set of images and references that are widely shared across groups and with which each group can build a sense of group solidarity with its neighbors. Many villages, including Kirango, play small puppet figures representing colonial officials or colonial militia, a direct reference to their shared history under colonialism. In and around Siela, in eastern Segou, people interpreted the large body puppet Yan Ka Di, This Place Is Good, as a veiled critique of the French policy of forced labor [Figure 3.13]. Elders in Ngarababougou said they first played the character during the period when the French conscripted local men and women as laborers to build the road from San to Djenne. One image in the masquerade's song referred to the French colonial supervisor on this work project.

Other masquerades that have been popular for at least several decades, such as the automobile and the airplane, speak to the changes wrought more generally over the last century in people's experiences. In one 1979 performance of the airplane masquerade, the masquerade attendant turned to the audience and invited them to board Air Mali, which was scheduled to leave for Gao, a city in the northern region of the country.

In Kirango both the Boso and Bamana troupes play characters that celebrate Malian independence from the French. The Bamana character Mali Kònò, the Bird of Mali, was adapted from earlier bird masquerades [Figure 1.17]. In the Boso quarter, the character Soden Mali la, Malian Horsemen, makes a direct reference to the modern republic [Figure 5.4]. All three Kirango troupes decorate the area with bunting in the colors of the Malian flag and in a number of villages in the area troupes use flag-shaped cloths in the national colors as part of many of the animal masquerade costumes. In 1978–80 several Bamana troupes in villages around Kirango performed a set of puppets that represented Moussa Traore and his presidential honor guard. These images and references to the new nation-state assert each community's claim to a share in a national Malian identity.

Among all of the groups that perform these masquerades, the past is compartmentalized and knowledge of the past is often defined as the property of particular subgroups

5.4. A Boso performance of Soden Mali la, the Malian Horsemen. 1980. *Photograph by Mary Jo Arnoldi.*

within the community. Norms governing the ownership of the past set limits upon who has the authority to declaim certain traditions and on what occasions their expression is considered valid and appropriate (Appadurai 1981; d'Azevedo 1962; Peel 1984).[21] What is especially interesting about the play of different histories in youth puppet masquerade theatre is that many of the constraints that limit historical expression outside the theatre are essentially ignored during these performances. Sogo bò performances open up history rather than circumscribing it. Within the temporal flow of these events, the performance offers the community repeated opportunities to negotiate and renegotiate group identities based on these histories, no matter how fleeting or broadly imagined these shared pasts may be defined at any single moment.

This historical license might well be explained by the fact that the dramatic representations of these different pasts are always fragmentary. Youth association performances are never intended to constitute any master narrative. Masquerade performances, therefore, cannot be read as the dramatization or reenactment of the creation myth as Dieterlen suggested (Dieterlen 1957, 136). Because the performances are defined as play and entertainment, they do not constitute any official chronicle about the past. Multiple references to diverse pasts are organized within an interpretative frame that effectively diffuses the potential for any serious debate over the validity of competing claims.

Although the four groups recognize that they share a performance tradition and a similar style of masks and puppets, farmers and fishermen assiduously maintain distinctive performance styles that they assert to have been passed down unchanged from their ancestors. Each of these groups maintains a set of masquerades that celebrate and intensify its unique claim to a share in the precolonial history of the region. While performance style and historical imagery play important roles in establishing people's sense of their group identity, that sense of identity is only one part of what is being communicated within these events. Under the guise of play, the Sogo bò performances offer the participants the opportunity to imagine and comment upon the moral universe, the nature of social relationships, and the ambiguities and uncertainties that they experience in their daily lives.

CHAPTER SIX

The Production of Meaning and the Play of Interpretations

Every day people in Segou experience the fragility of their social relationships. Discussions of crises, altercations, and tensions in the community are communicated and critiqued in private conversations among kin and friends. In the public context of youth theatre, however, the masquerade arts effectively depersonalize this critique. These entertainments recast actual incidents in more general terms and subject them to a more universal moral commentary. In the youth theatre, animal characters, representations of people and community life, and masquerades of powerful bush spirits and genies explore the intricacies of this moral universe. Like folktales and other theatrical forms, these masquerade performances throw cultural values and social relationships into high relief and open them up for public scrutiny. Youth association theatre is a fictional world and an imagined reality defined as play and occupying a special time and place. The community's definition of these events allows participants to ponder the full range of possibilities, opinions, desires, anxieties, and fears and to engage in a creative dialogue about the dynamics of social relationships and the nature of their everyday lives (Beidelman 1986, 1; Jackson 1982, 263–265).

Bamana Nyama and Malo: Why Elder Hòròn Men Don't Play the Sogo bò

That young men's and women's performances are deemed culturally appropriate to their age and/or gender constitutes an important interpretative frame for the youth association masquerade.[1] In much the same way that the definition of youth association masquerades as entertainment and play opens up the production of historicity and group identity, the Sogo bò's play frame gives voices to young men and to women to explore and comment upon the nature of the relationships among men, between men and women, and among women. Masquerade troupes, whose members are regularly denied a public voice outside theatre, use the arts to legitimate and extol or to subvert and challenge through parody, irony, and satire the official hierarchies of age, status, and gender. While their perspectives often coincide in the theatre, young men and women do not always speak with one voice. Within any performance the men and women may choose to take oppositional positions in the ongoing and lively debates about the nature of their relationships. The simultaneity of different and sometimes discordant voices is made public through the affecting power of art.

Malo, social constraint, defines social roles and supports the hierarchy among hòròn, freemen, *nyamakala*, professional specialists, and jòn, descendants of slaves. Malo also reinforces the hierarchical relations between age groups and between genders. While malo has regularly been translated as shame, Brink noted that rather than implying guilt or bad conscious it is interpreted as "a condition in which the person is 'controlled by another's eye,' that is, socially constrained by another's authority, power or social position, and ambivalent about how one's behavior might be interpreted and reciprocated" (Brink 1980, 419).

Malo guides most everyday practices, from greeting behavior to the organization of production. A more- or less-developed capacity for malo is one way that society characterizes the differences among hòròn, nyamakala, and jòn. Malo also organizes relationships between elders and youth and between men and women.[2]

Society ascribes to the hòròn the most developed sense of malo while jòn, because of their historical servitude, are often characterized as *malobali*, without shame. Grosz-Ngate suggested that the very definition of jòn in essence denied this group access to full personhood (Grosz-Ngate 1989, 170).[3] Unlike the master/slave relationship, the relationship between hòròn and nyamakala is not based on conditions of servitude. Recent analyses of the interdependencies of these two groups reveal the asymmetrical relations of power and authority that organize their interactions (Hoffman 1990; Kendall 1982; McNaughton 1988; Wright 1989). While the former master/slave relationship was clearly hierarchical, the relationship between hòròn and nyamakala is much more subtle and complex and is based on these two groups' differing capacities and control of nyama, life force or energy.[4]

Among the Bamana the two nyamakala groups which play important roles in a variety of performances include the jeli, bards, and the numu, smiths.[5] The smiths have played a central role in the artistic history of the Sogo bò by providing theatre troupes with most of the masks and puppets that are used in these performances. In contrast to the blacksmiths, it is the bard's absence from any central role in the youth theatre that is particularly noteworthy.

Griots are the society's professional verbal artists and musicians and they are the owners of specific verbal and musical forms and a number of musical instruments. People consider griots' performances of *balimaliw*, recited or sung genealogical histories, to be one of the most nyama-laden verbal art forms (Zahan 1963, 134; Hoffman 1990, 142–143). This distinctive form of praise singing is decidedly absent from the youth association's Sogo bò performances.[6] The lack of any central performance role for griots in the Bamana youth theatre suggests that people have an indigenous definition of professional and amateur artists and of professional and amateur performance genres in these communities. Among the Bamana the Sogo bò theatre falls within the category of amateur arts. This is not to deny the power of these arts, since according to myth all Bamana arts originated in the bush, which is the locus of extraordinary energy and power. Rather, it suggests that people recognize differences in the capacities of those arts that are made and performed by specialists and those that can be practiced by anyone.

Both blacksmiths and bards, by virtue of their heritage, possess potent *nya* or means to engage successfully in nyama-laden activities such as praise singing, ironworking, woodcarving, etc.[7] Hòròn's inherited means, however, are reputed to be much less powerful than that of the nyamakala. As Bird and Kendall point out, hòròn must seek daliluw to protect themselves from the effects of this energy through a boli, amulets, or talismans that they acquire from nyamakala (Bird and Kendall 1980, 16–17). While there is a clear ambivalence among hòròn toward nyamakala, most hòròn remain dependent on nyamakala in every domain of their lives.

The more highly developed sense of malo, associated with hòròn, is manifested in the very public behaviors people have come to recognize as *hòrònya* (literally, hòròn-ness): generosity, humility, passiveness, patience, and submission (McNaughton 1988, 17). These hòrònya behaviors act as a sort of dalilu to protect hòròn from the nyama of others (McNaughton 1988, 17; Cisse 1964, 200). Hoffman notes that "These dalilu, available to anyone, are often the only dalilu nobles can muster on their own to combat the effects of nyama" (Hoffman 1990, 139).

Hòròn behaviors and those of the nyamakala stand in sharp contrast to one another on public occasions, a contrast that is clearly recognized, understood, and acted upon by both groups. In discussing the hòròn and jeli relationships, Hoffman observed that

> In general, nobles love what griots do in performance, but they loathe the idea of doing it themselves. As a result, nobles—noble men in particular—tend to make a conscious effort to refrain from behaving in ways that could be perceived to be griot-like: they try to avoid raising their voices, using elaborate or "flowery" speech, and showing emotion. (Hoffman 1989, 5)

Hòròn children who are being loud and boisterous are often reprimanded by their elders for acting like nyamakala. As Hoffman observed, hòròn women can be criticized publicly by jeli elders for dancing too much like griots (Hoffman 1989, 3).

While hòròn criticism of jeli behavior has been widely reported in the ethnographic literature, jeli's evaluation of jeli behavior is quite different. Hoffman writes: "Practicing griots, on the other hand, are almost never ashamed of the behavior they are criticized for; in fact, they are taught to be *ashamed* of being ashamed of that behavior" (Hoffman 1989, 3).

Although the behavior that defines the distinctions between hòròn and nyamakala on many public occasions is relatively unimportant in performing youth theatre, the artistic roles that nyamakala play in the larger society do not go unrecognized. Numu, as important agents in the production of masquerade forms, are regularly praised during these performances. Jeli's status as professional singers and musicians is occasionally recognized through the use of small rod and string puppets that portray them as musicians. Yet, despite society's recognition of the contributions of numu as sculptors or jeli as professional musicians, they are not called upon to take any central performance roles in the youth theatre. In this amateur entertainment, beliefs about age and gender and the corresponding definitions of the capacities for malo among different age groups and between men and women shape the theatrical content and determine the artistic biographies of the Sogo bò performers. Today in Segou very old men rarely participate in village entertainments. Theirs is a gradual detachment from these events, and this process can at least partially be understood in terms of malo. The concept of social constraint associates particular activities with the *kamalen waati*, the time of youth, and others with *kòrò waati*, the time of elders.

People believe that elders have a more highly developed capacity for malo than do their juniors and men more than do women. These beliefs naturalize the superior status of elders over youth and of men over women. These status differences are maintained and manifested in ritual and everyday practices (Grosz-Ngate 1989, 168). To a large extent these same social hierarchies of age and gender determine who participates in the Sogo bò and during what period of their lives.

Males move through four age categories in their lifetime: *bilakoro*, uncircumcised boy, *cèmisèn*, male youth, *kamalen*, young man, and *cèkòrò*, elder man. For females the three critical social ages include *npogotigi*, unexcised and/or unmarried girl, *muso* or *musomisèn*, woman or married woman during her childbearing years, and *musokòrò*, elder woman. Passage through these social ages follows different temporal rhythms and has different implications for the lives of Bamana men and of Bamana women.

Until relatively recently young uncircumcised boys were organized as a group within the Ntomo association. This initiation association included three age-sets from age six to about age fourteen. Passage from one age-set to another within Ntomo was marked by annual ceremonies (Pâques 1954, 56–57; Zahan 1960, 53–73). In his final year in the Ntomo, a boy underwent circumcision and transformed into a fully male person, cè (literally man, in this context) and moved from bilakoro to cè or kamalen, youth. The category of cèmisèn, male youth, as it is used today, encompasses the period of early adolescence, a transitional period between childhood and full manhood.[8]

The age category known as kamalen includes both young bachelors and married men. A man is called a kamalen from about the age of fourteen until his mid forties. Entry into the village youth association, kamalen ton, coincides with this age category and a man continues to be active in the youth association from his late twenties to his late thirties or early forties, depending on local custom.

Formerly in Kirango and in many other communities in the Segou region, the youth association existed alongside various other men's initiation associations. Boys from the age of about seven until age fourteen were members of the Ntomo association, which was responsible for preparing and initiating these boys into the first stage of manhood. However, even when Ntomo was operational, the kamalen ton and its masquerade festivals were also perceived by these same communities as important in this larger socialization process (Zahan 1960, 12n3). Today in many communities these men's initiation associations are no longer operational. The kamalen ton has become the primary social institution that concerns itself with socializing young men into adulthood.[9]

The age category of kamalen clearly refers to males in the prime of their life physically and sexually. The ethos of the kamalen is directed toward assertiveness, bravery, and courage translated into actions that will win each young man his *tògò*, reputation or name. A man's transition from kamalen to cèkòrò, an elder, is achieved gradually and begins when he formally leaves the youth association. However, there is no formal association of elders that corresponds to either the Ntomo association for boys or the kamalen ton, the youth association for young adult males.[10] People address elder men in their late sixties or older as *cèkòròbaw*, literally, big or great elders. The cèkòròbaw, not the kamalen, are perceived to be the guardians of tradition and it is this guardianship that gives moral authority to their actions and speech. As elders they bring ancestral time and contemporary time into alignment. Elders are said to be oriented to the past and to the maintenance of society. Kamalen, by contrast, represent the present and are oriented to change and innovation.

Among females the category of npogotigi includes all girls from the age of puberty, when they are excised, until their marriage. Following excision rites, young girls are presented to the community in public ceremonies as fully female and as potential brides. Today, excised but unmarried females are active members of the kamalen ton and the female wing of the association is called npogotigi. Unlike boys, whose status changes from bilakoro to cè or, more specifically, kamalen upon circumcision, a girl's status does not change to that of a woman, muso, until she marries. Female sexuality is much more tightly controlled than that of males, who are sexually active as kamalen whether they are married or not. While formerly it was more common for young girls to marry only a few years after they were excised, today many of them do not marry until they are in their late teens. Despite this shift in marriage practices, an important group of gifts which are presented to the bride's family by the groom's family is still called *boloko fènw*, excision things (Grosz-Ngate 1989, 170).

While men in the household and within the village are ranked according to their age based on the principle of birth order, a female's status as a muso, woman, is based on the number of years she has been married into her husband's household. Following menopause, a woman's status changes to that of musokòrò, an elder, but this status change is not marked by any public celebrations or rituals. Each stage in a man's or a woman's life represents a distinct moment in the socio-moral career of the individual (Grosz-Ngate 1989, 173). As people move through each of these phases, they acquire more cultural knowledge and are expected to act upon this knowledge to organize their interactions with others. When a person violates norms associated with his or her age and acts inappropriately, people sometimes level the criticism that the person is acting "outside his or her time." In these cases, the individual may be subject to private or public ridicule or censure.

In this strongly patrilineal society, women are ranked lower than men and men regularly appeal to myths to support their claims to superiority over women. These myths link women's current inferior position to their inability to keep secrets (Grosz-Ngate 1989, 174). Men see the consequences of shameful acts, which include speech acts, as a form of social death. Women, however, because of their less developed capacity for malo are perceived as not experiencing shame to the same degree as do men. Grosz-

Ngate relates a proverb that men frequently used to support their claims to having a more highly developed sense of malo than women do:

> If you find a woman in trouble, help her. But if you find her in a shameful situation, leave her because she will get over it. If you find a man in trouble, leave him because he can get out of it on his own. But if you find him in a shameful situation, get him out of it because otherwise he will die. (Grosz-Ngate 1989, 171)

Within this cultural milieu, men are women's social superiors. They are responsible not only for their own actions, but for those of women who are under their authority. For example, a husband can be shamed not only by his own misplaced behaviors, but by those of his wife (wives).

When a woman passes into the category of elder, *musokòròba*, attitudes toward her change. Like male elders, musokòròbaw are said to have *barika*, power, grace, or moral force. Elder men and women are often referred to as *maa sèbèw*, serious people, a term rarely used to describe either children or young adults, whether male or female (Grosz-Ngate 1989, 175–176). While people believe that elder women, because of the "natural" differences between men and women, still have less capacity for malo than men have, elder women, like elder men, enjoy a superior status over their juniors. Because of their barika, both elder men and elder women are often asked to give advice and blessings on various social occasions, for example, during the Kirango Dònkan ceremony that precedes the Sogo bò performances.

Despite their redefinition as musokòròbaw, elder women can and sometimes do take an active part in the village youth theatre, while cèkòròbaw now rarely do. In Kirango, women remembered that Assista Coulibaly, who married into Kirango from a village around Yamina probably in the 1940s, performed as the lead singer in the theatre from the time she was a young bride until she was quite an old woman. Likewise, during the 1979 performances many older women participated with the younger married women in the women's dance celebrating their identity as members of the resident lineages in the quarter.[11]

For men, hòròn and nyamakala alike, the kamalen waati is considered to be the appropriate age for dancing, playing music, and participating in a variety of entertainments, including the Sogo bò. Practicing bards and blacksmith-sculptors, who society defines as professionals, can, if they choose, continue to perform or carve sculpture into their old age. Gifted bards and smiths often gain regional, national, and even international artistic reputations. Hòròn men rarely perform in the youth theatre after they leave the association.[12]

In their youth, hòròn men, however, often achieve a certain notoriety as actors, dancers, and drummers. However, once they move out of the youth association and into the category of elder, many of these men begin to disassociate themselves with their artistic achievements. For example, I once jokingly addressed the head of my household, a hòròn man in his early sixties, by a praise name he had won as a drummer during his youth. He became visibly embarrassed, saying quite emphatically that he had put these activities firmly behind him. While his age-mates, his wives, and his family remembered his musical reputation (it was his wives who told me his praise name), his youthful reputation as a master drummer no longer remained part of his public self-image as an elder.

Since there are no formal rituals marking men's change of status from youth to elders, individuals have a certain degree of latitude to decide for themselves whether and how long they will continue to attend and participate in the youth theatre. While elder men categorically state that theatre is appropriate to the kamalen waati, men in their late forties and well into their fifties do still regularly attend the performances, although only on rare occasions do they actually dance. In Kirango in 1987, during the first day of the Tonko festival the lead singer began to sing the praises of the former association leaders who were in the audience. These men were in their late forties and fifties. Her singing did move them to participate and they entered the circle and began to dance exuberantly if only for a short time. The participation of these elder men did not seem to seriously undermine their new status as maa sèbèw. In the 1992 performance, one of these older men entered the ring to dance. Some people in the audience clearly appreciated his participation and called out encouragement. But, I also noticed that several younger men in the youth association were not pleased. They obviously did not think his participation was appropriate and they even began verbally to raise a protest.

However, it was rare indeed to see hòròn cèkòròbaw, who are well into their sixties and older, at the theatre. Unlike musokòròbaw, these elder men are expected to exhibit the most highly developed emotional restraint on public occasions. James Brink related to me that in his discussions of Kotèba theatre with old men who no longer attended this youth theatre in the Beledougou region, elders often characterized the theatre as disrespectful, irreverent, and impolite. When he asked them what it should be, one old man replied that it should be everything it is.

Conversion to Islam in Kirango and other communities may have greatly accelerated older men's distancing themselves from public entertainments since participation in dancing and theatre is not seen as appropriate conduct for Muslim elders. Grosz-Ngate reported that in villages in Sana province in Segou elder men said they no longer attended these entertainments because millet beer was served during the events. She related that

> They [elder Islamic men] explain this change by pointing out that they might take offense [at the serving of alcohol] and intervene in the proceedings whereas nonconverts, who drink on those occasions, and older women do not exhibit the same sensibilities. Alcohol makes nonconverts oblivious to possible injurious behavior and older women, in contrast with men, are given to amusement just like their children and grandchildren. (Grosz-Ngate 1989, 171)

Whether elder men explain their reasons for not attending the theatre in terms of its disrespectful content or the fact that alcohol is served, implicit in their statements is their awareness that to take offense and disrupt these events violates the very definition of the Kotèba and Sogo bò as play and amusement. Elders are also keenly aware of the power of art to touch and engage senses and emotions, thus potentially pushing a person to react in an unhòrònlike manner.

There is, then, a bittersweet quality to aging for most hòròn men. This may have as much to do with society's expectations about appropriate behavior for these elder men as it does with any individual man's recognition of his own diminishing physical or sexual prowess. As Jackson noted for the Kuranko, and this is certainly true for the Bamana as well, "Moral propriety is a matter of living up to the expectations of a role" (Jackson 1982, 25). The weight of malo is on these elder hòròn men's shoulders and while their authority in the household and in the village increases with age, there is a price to be paid. Many hòròn cèkòròbaw today no longer see the public expression of their emotional and sensory selves through participation in the arts as an option open to their age group.

Kamalen and Cèkòrò: Relationships between Men

Depending on the context, malo, social constraint, might be described as enabling or as potentially paralyzing and ultimately destructive. Bamana society is equally dependent upon the mass of people who contribute to the maintenance of the status quo and upon those exceptional individuals, the heroes, whose actions move the society forward. Too heavy an emphasis on unity can lead to stagnation, and too heavy an emphasis on competition can lead to chaos. An imbalance in either direction threatens the continuity of the society.

Among the Bamana, behavior is often discussed through the invocation of two concepts, *badenya*, mother-child-ness, and *fadenya*, father-child-ness. *Baden*, mother's child, is a kinship term used to identify full siblings, children of the same mother and father. *Badenya* refers to those ideal qualities that underlie the relationship between full siblings, i.e., amicability, cooperation, and solidarity. Baden and its derivative *balima*, most often translated as kin, are also used metaphorically to distinguish one's kin from non-kin, fellow villagers from strangers, and at the more general level to separate Malians from foreigners. Direct and indirect references to badenya are invoked in puppet masquerade theatre through various expressive forms and stand as metaphors for the high value that people place upon unity and cooperation among any number of individuals who classify themselves as a group.[13]

Faden, children of the same father, includes half siblings and the children of classificatory fathers. A child addresses his father's brothers as *fa*, father, and their children as his faden. Half siblings, like full siblings, are prohibited from marrying and the relationship between half brothers embodies the potential for genealogical schism and competition for inheritable resources through the patrilineage. Fadenya denotes the quality of this relationship. The jealousy, rivalry, and competition which characterize the relationship between half brothers are also extended to include the relationship between consecutive generations, i.e., between fathers and sons. Like badenya, the concept of fadenya is extended beyond the domain of kinship relationships to note any rivalry, even that between unrelated households or between villages or nations. In 1959, for example, Senegal and Mali were joined in the Mali Federation, but in 1960 this partnership was dissolved due to differences over political and economic issues. Senegal, which had been Mali's baden during the federation, was reclassified in the political rhetoric of the day as Mali's faden.

Understanding and managing this dialectic tension between badenya and fadenya are important aspects in the socialization of young men into adult society and find expression in the activities of the kamalen ton. The values associated with badenya, i.e., social solidarity, respect for authority, cooperation, and with fadenya, i.e., rivalry, assertiveness, courage, individuality, define the dimensions of a socially competent male person. Bird and Kendall have suggested that the dialectic between these two orientations constitutes an indigenous theory of social action (Bird and Kendall 1980, 14–15). The dialectic relationship between badenya and fadenya, which shapes social relationships, resonates with that between the aesthetic concepts of nyi, goodness, and di, tastiness, which guide people's evaluations and interpretations of the arts. The tension between an orientation toward values associated with the collective, badenya, and one toward the values associated with the individual, fadenya, finds frequent expression throughout the youth association performances.

During the kamalen waati the emphasis is placed on a young man's physical prowess, on acquiring cultural knowledge, and on attaining knowledge of self. In the past, these sets of youthful concerns, behaviors, and activities were acted upon and honed in both men's initiation associations and the kamalen ton. Because many villages have now abandoned the men's initiation associations, the kamalen ton has become the most important local institutional context for this socialization process. It is during the kamalen waati that young men develop as social actors and acquire the skills that society deems necessary to function as competent adult men (Brink 1982a, 417). It is within the youth association and its activities, including the production of entertainments, that young men organize their behavior around those values associated with both the badenya and the fadenya axes.

Within the youth association, men's membership is organized both by age-sets and by activity groups. Today in Kirango, for example, an individual enters the kamalen ton as a member of an age-set that includes all young men born in the village between a span of from three to four years.[14] An individual remains a member of this age-set throughout his tenure in the association and by extension throughout his entire adult life. Young men tend to draw many of their friends from their age-set, and when the kamalen ton is invoked these informal relationships become formalized.[15]

Hierarchy among the age-sets within the association and each set's rights and privileges follow the principles of age ranking among men operative within the society as a whole. Authority over the membership is invested in the office of *tontigi*, owner of the ton, who is ideally the eldest male in the senior age-set. This jural structure reproduces that of the village at large and of individual households. Authority in the village is invested in the *dugutigi*, the owner of the village, who is, at least in principle, the eldest male in the founding lineage. In the household this position is held by the *dembayatigi* or *dubatigi*, owner of the household, who is generally the eldest male in this resident lineage. The tontigi is assisted by members of the senior age-set, who act as his advisors in much the same way that the village elders advise the village chief. At meetings of the ton I attended while living in Kirango, age-set hierarchy was made visible in the seating arrangements for the meetings. The officers from the senior age-set sat facing the assembled group, with the remaining members of the senior age-set seated directly opposite the officers. The other age-sets were seated in descending order behind the senior set.

Beginning in the mid to late 1950s, each age-set in the Kirango Bamana association chose a different costume for the Sogo bò festival.[16] In the circle dances that open these events, the young men organize themselves by age-sets with the senior set taking the first position in the outer circle, followed by each age-set in descending order. The age-set costumes publicly call attention to and clarify the principle of age-set hierarchy.

Paralleling the age-set organization is a second one, which revolves around what I call "activity groups." Membership in one of these groups cuts across the age-sets and selection is based on an individual's personal skill and his potential as perceived by the ton leadership. In theory, inclusion in an activity group is negotiable throughout the period of tenure in the ton, while membership in an age-set is fixed. Activity groups are invoked during the preparation and presentation of the masquerades in the youth theatre. When the young men who have prepared a masquerade dance with it during its performance, these attendants include individuals from the different male age-sets in the association.

As in all human endeavors, however, there is often disjunction between ideology and practice. For example, while ascribed status based on an individual's membership in either the hòròn or the nyamakala class is generally overlooked within the youth association, a nyamakala from the senior age-set may be chosen for the leadership position of ton spokesman by virtue of his heritage and his personal skill as an orator. Additionally, while the eldest man in the senior age-set should be chosen as the tontigi, another man in this age-set who has demonstrated exceptional leadership qualities might be selected to lead the association. In this case the principle of age hierarchy is manipulated to take into account an individual's potential in the best interests of the ton.[17]

Movement through the association is vertical, and in theory the entry of a new age-set displaces the set above it, thus resulting in the retirement of the senior age-set. However, depending on the demography of the village and its labor needs, this movement can be manipulated by the elders. The senior age-set's exit out of the association can be delayed and this accounts in part for the variation in the age distribution of kamalen ton members from one village to another in the region. It may also partially account for historical differences in the number of years young men spend within the association.

In many villages, unmarried women are considered part of the kamalen ton. Unmarried girls in the association are addressed as npogotigi and not as muso. The most senior of this group takes the role of *npogotigi kuntigi*, the leader of the women's section, and she is the spokeswoman for the women's interests in all association business. The superior status of men over women is underscored during the ton meetings in Kirango, where the women's group always sits behind the most junior of the men's age-sets. At the first meeting I attended, the officers seated me with the senior men's age-set, directly facing the officers. After becoming a member of the association I was given the honorary title of *npogotigi kuntigi*, head of the women's section. It was clear at subsequent meetings that I was now expected to take my place with the women, behind the men's sections.

The women's section, like the men's, is organized by seniority based on birth order, and the young women are divided into different age-sets. During the Sogo bò in Kirango each age-set wears a wrapper and blouse made from different patterns or colors of textiles. In the circle dances the women's section constitutes the inner circle and the senior women's set takes first position and is followed by each set in descending order.

Association women provide the water and food for the men during a number of ton work activities. In Kirango, for example, in 1978, the elders asked the ton to provide the material and labor to repair the tomb of Diarraja, a descendant of Kirango ben Diarra. The men made the mud bricks and did the construction, while the women hauled the water from the river for mixing the mud mortar. The women also provided the men with drinking water. During the spring festival, the women's section cooks the festival meal and makes the lemon ginger beverage, while wives of ton members prepare the millet beer.

Farmers' and fishermen's youth associations share a similar structure and engage in a similar range of activities. Youth associations are not unique to groups living in the Segou region; they are quite widespread throughout West Africa (Paulme 1969). John Lewis observed that many studies of age groups in West Africa have focused on the basic contradictions and tensions between the lineage form of organization and the community-based age groups. Those studies which predict an ultimate resolution of this conflict tend to favor one or the other form of social organization as triumphing. However, in his analysis of the Segou Bamana ton, Lewis found that there seemed to be a positive correlation between the strength of the lineage organization within any one village and the strength of its kamalen ton (Lewis 1980, 18–19). This correlation supports an interpretation that emphasizes the essential complementary relationship between the two at the village level.[18]

The publicly stated raison d'être for the kamalen ton and its activities, including the masquerade theatre, is to promote *jè*, unity, within the village. Yet despite the publicly acclaimed integrative function, the association in fact institutionalizes the competition between consecutive generations of men, the youth and the elders. All young men are classified as baden, kin, within the context of the kamalen ton. In their activities, i.e., communal farming, public works, and entertainment events, an individual's affiliation to a particular patrilineage/clan takes a secondary role to his allegiance to the association. In purely functional terms this realignment of alliances within the association can mediate the rivalries between faden, half brothers, of the same household or lineage. It is not unusual for faden of nearly the same age to be members of the same age-set, or for faden in consecutive age-sets to cooperate in the same activity group. An individual's allegiance to a particular age-set or activity group can temporarily obscure tensions experienced between himself and his faden outside the association. In extreme cases it might even favor the resolution of open hostilities. In the process of reclassifying all young people in the village as baden within the kamalen ton, the community temporarily suppresses the rivalry among peers by emphasizing the rivalry between consecutive generations.

It is during the kamalen waati that young men begin to actively seek to surpass the accomplishments of their fathers. Bird and Kendall noted that

> In the Mande world, a name must be won not only in the arena provided by one's peers, but also in that abstract arena created by one's ancestors. This conception of the patrilineage as competitor is captured in the proverb: i fa y'i faden folo de ye, Your father is your first faden. (Bird and Kendall 1980, 14)

In the context of generational relationships, the rivalry between a young man and his father is extended to include the competition between young men and elders. In the rural areas in the Segou region young men represent over half of all the incorporated males within the village, yet they remain jural minors in lineage and village affairs. According to the 1987 census figures for the region, approximately thirty-four percent of males are between the ages of fourteen and forty-four and only seventeen percent of the male population is over forty-five. Males under the age of fourteen number about forty-nine percent (La République du Mali 1990, vol.4: 7–9).[19] In these communities elders remain the jural authority. Despite changing conditions, they still control, to a large extent, young men's labor, their access to wives, through control of bride wealth, their access to land, through control of the lineage organization, and their access to power, through control of history and certain domains of knowledge. The kamalen ton diffuses the elders' control over their sons. The ton provides young men with a number of contexts sanctioned by tradition within which they can take the lead and act as *nganaw*, heroes. Within these contexts they can cast aside social constraint and pursue their reputation.

As a social institution, the ton has an identity apart from other village institutions. While the kamalen ton recognizes the authority of the elders, it simultaneously claims a certain autonomy. In Kirango and elsewhere in the Segou region, the kamalen ton's claim to autonomy is seen as its legacy from Biton Coulibaly and the *tonjòn*, the warrior class.[20] It is the male ethos of warrior/hunter that young men emphasize when they invoke this legacy. It is this ethos that empowers them to act within the context of ton activities.

Despite this claim to a warrior legacy, the youth and the village elders do engage in formal behaviors in order to lessen the possibility of overt conflict between the two groups. The kamalen ton performs a number of activities in the community. At the request of the village chief, it undertakes public works projects, which include clearing of public places and construction and repair of public buildings, roads, dams, and bridges. For this work the association is not remunerated. During the farming season, youth have the obligation to provide the community with the labor necessary to ensure success in agricultural and fishing activities. Bamana farmers use labor-intensive methods of agriculture and the household farming unit is often not sufficient to meet labor needs during critical periods in the cycle, especially during the harvest. For these tasks individual households can augment their own labor force by requesting the participation of the kamalen ton. Although the association has the obligation to comply with their elders' request, its members also have rights as laborers. The tontigi has the right to demand the participation of all young people in the village in the communal farming activity. In principle, when the youth association leader calls the kamalen ton into session, no elder can refuse to let a member of his household participate in these activities.

When requesting the association's labor, lineage elders make a formal request to the village chief, who then calls in the tontigi. The tontigi relays the request to the association as a whole. Although it is highly improbable and some say impossible that the ton would choose to refuse the request of their elders, association members defined this process as one that admits at least the possibility of the ton choosing this latter option.

In any activity performed by the group, the tontigi and his officers take full responsibility for the organization of the work groups requested and for the labor activities. Today, the kamalen ton in many villages, including Kirango, asserts its right to payment for labor in the agricultural sector. Each household pays the association a customary amount in millet or goats. Goods or monies received by the ton for their labor are held collectively by the membership. Each year the association reinvests its accumulated wealth back into the community through the Sogo bò festivals and other dry-season entertainments.

The Kamalen Ton and the Sogo bò: The Production of Meaning in Performance

During kamalen ton festivals, the everyday social order is inverted and young people become the primary actors while the elders are recast as the audience. Youth's fadenya challenge to the elders rises to the surface and the community manages the potential danger that is exposed in this inversion of the social order through the use of several definitional and behavioral strategies.

The youth association always recognizes the authority of the elders by formally asking permission from the dugutigi, the village chief, to stage the festival. In Kirango the tensions between elders and youth are also mediated by the custom of granting the final authority for setting the masquerade program to the age-set that has most recently moved out of the youth association into their new status as elders.[21] Finally, the association recognizes its responsibilities to its community by reinvesting its wealth back into the village during these festivals. This redistribution of wealth takes the form of providing the festival food and drink and financing the theatre itself.

The elders, for their part, state that the purpose of the Sogo bò festivals is to promote unity within the village. As baptisms, weddings, and funerals draw individuals back into the sphere of their patrilineage, so the association festivals bring absent members back into the community. Through participation in these performances people reestablish their identity as members of the village and confirm their responsibilities to their balima, kin. Elders offset any direct challenge to their authority by symbolically reclassifying everyday social relationships within the context of the festival. They state that during the festival, *Bèe be kelen*, everyone is equal. In this way they temporarily deny their superior status over their juniors, and of men over women, thus allowing younger men and women to "speak" with impunity in the public arena.

The community defines these association festivals as *tonko*, the affairs of the youth association. In Kirango and surrounding villages, tonko stands in contrast to *cèko*, affairs of the men. In these communities cèko refers to those activities and events controlled by elders and that are considered serious and powerful affairs. Conversely, they define tonko festivals, organized by the youth, as entertainments and amusements. This characterization of cèko and tonko is consistent with the characterization of elders and youth within the everyday world of social experience. By defining the youth association events as social contexts clearly set apart from the mundane world, but ones which are defined as play, young men and women can act powerful without threatening elders' authority outside the festivals.

This careful framing of the event as play is also a protective device. People believe that speech transcends time and place and can have serious consequences for the society. The following Bamana proverb makes this point quite emphatically: If you put your foot or arm into something, you can remove it, but if you put your tongue into it, you cannot take it away.[22]

The repercussions of speech acts can follow an individual throughout his life and extend into the lives of his descendants. Managing one's speech is a moral responsibility and one which the elders feel that neither young men nor women have mastered. The expressive arts used in the theatre, including masquerade dancing, song, and drumming, are forms of speech that are understood to be powerful because of their mythic bush origins and their validation by the ancestors. In the theatrical context the definition of the event as amusement and play circumvents the energy released through these multiple expressive forms. The play frame protects both the performers and their audience from the nyama, life force or energy, which is released.

During the festival young people themselves also take on roles intended to obscure their fadenya challenge to the elders. In the New Year festival, for example, the first public event is a procession of ton members to greet each household head in the village. In Kirango, the procession is led by the Gòn masquerader. Gòn, the Baboon, stands as the antithesis of hòrònya, but at each household in the quarter the masker respectfully drops to one knee to make his greetings to the elders. In this phase of the festival, the ton concedes the elders' superiority and publicly acknowledges the association's commitment to the community.

During the masquerade performances, some young men and women take on the theatrical role of kòrèdugaw, clowns, and in these roles their identities are not obscured. Their impolite dancing is well beyond the boundaries of hòrònya, but because it is framed as ludic, it is expressly intended to be interpreted as play and not to be taken seriously. Their roles as clowns simultaneously empower and protect these performers.

Drinking alcohol is associated with casting aside social constraints and freeing the emotional self to act. In the oral traditions, the name given to the precolonial tribute to the state was *dinònò*, honey, a reference to its use in making a type of mead. In the epics, dancing and drinking among hunters and warriors is part of their heroic ethos (Dumestre 1979, 15). In those villages like Kirango that still brew millet beer for the festival, young men often pretend to an exaggerated drunkenness. During the 1979 performance in Kirango when Lynn Forsdale and I were down among the young men filming the masquerade, we were getting buffeted back and forth by the mass of unruly and "drunken" young men. We spotted a young man from our family in the crowd of revelers and called out to him. Instantly he dropped his drunken pose and he, along with several age-mates, helped us extricate the equipment and move to safer ground. As soon as we were resettled, off they went into the fray, stumbling and acting drunk and out of control. While in certain cases some of these young men may indeed have been inebriated, for others exaggerated drunkenness is a successful strategy that allows them to cast off social constraint and to act outside the boundaries of hòrònya.

The masquerades themselves protect the performers from the creative energy released during the performance. Everyone knows that young men dance the masks and masquerades, but this is never publicly acknowledged during the performance. Performers employ several strategies to obscure and deny any human agency in the masquerade performance. For example, during the afternoon performances, the large animal masquerades are often surrounded by a group of attendants, who encircle the character while holding up mats that hide the dancer's feet. At night when masqueraders perform the shape-shifting dances of the grass masquerades, they perform in total darkness. While the use of mats and control of the illumination of the dance area are both dramatic strategies that heighten the effect and wonder of these masquerades, they also effectively obscure any view of the dancers and free them from the consequences of their actions by shifting responsibility directly to the masquerades.

The Sogo bò Performances: Exploring the Nature of Unity and Rivalry

Much of the dramatic content of the youth theatre is concerned with exploring the interplay between unity and competition, between the collective and the individual, and between tradition and change. In the contemporary period, the prologue dances set the badenya and fadenya interpretative frame for the masquerade event that follows.

In Kirango, circle dances and acrobatic dance competitions, the Bònjalan, precede the masquerade performances. Both men and women in the ton participate in the circle dances, and the performance ideal, which is choreographic unity, promotes the experience of "dancing (as one body)" (Jackson 1983, 340). These circle dances are the kinesthetic expression of badenya sentiments of unity and solidarity. This visual expression of unity achieved through the dance is reinforced by the songs which accompany them. In these songs the lead singer praises friendship and cooperation, linking the verbal messages to the experiential oneness the dancers experience.

The second dance segment consists of individual acrobatic competitions between young men. In these dances young men from the same age-set compete with one another. A high value is given to individual skill and athletic prowess in these dances. The drummers generally start each sequence with a slow rhythm and move quickly to a much faster tempo. The dancers must display their dance/acrobatic skills within the limits set by the drummers. Young girls praise their favorites by bestowing on them scarves as tokens of their admiration, and the women sing of bravery and heroes. A young dancer's age-mates often enter the ring and with gestures of support, such as pulling firmly on the dancer's arms, they celebrate and encourage him. The focus of this segment is clearly fadenya. Young men not only compete with their peers, they challenge both the past accomplishments of older men in the audience and the future accomplishments of young boys who watch from the sidelines. Young girls actively participate in fostering this rivalry among men, who are in theory their potential husbands, by bestowing on them their favors and by singing an individual's praises.

The badenya/fadenya themes that orchestrate these dance performances are carried forward into the puppet drama. The bush animal masquerades, which are associated with the original Binsogo bò performances that were held during kawula in October or November, are considered to be explicitly oriented toward fadenya themes. The tile fè sogow, the daytime masquerades, which were formerly part of the original rainy season festival in May, celebrate unity and solidarity.

In the epics and heroic poetry still performed in this region, it is the hunters and warriors who perform extraordinary deeds and are society's heroes. Taking a life is the most nyama-laden act. A hunter or warrior must have the necessary store of nyama in order to kill and the necessary force to control the energy released by the animal or person at death (McNaughton 1988, 16). Hunters are the masters of the bush. Through long apprenticeship they learn the science of the trees, *jiridòn*. They study animals and their behavior and they forge relationships with bush spirits. Through this process they acquire the means to control the life force or energy released in their encounters with the inhabitants of the bush[23] (Bird 1974; Bird and Kendall 1980; Cashion 1982; Cisse 1964). Oral traditions also suggest that hunters played a central role in the armies of the preco-lonial state (Cashion 1982, I: 108; Meillassoux 1963). In myths and epics, hunters and warriors are completely oriented to the fadenya axis.[24]

In one performance of the heroic poem *Manden Mori*, the hunter's bard, Seydou Camara, sang of the power of the true hunter and the threat he poses to society:

> I greatly fear tangling with a hunter.
>> Put it in my hand, put the tail in my hand.
> If you offend a hunter,
> Don't trouble yourself plowing your fields,
> For your seeds will never flower.
>> Put it in my hand, put the tail in my hand.
> If you offend a hunter,
> Don't bother to marry,
> For your woman will never become pregnant, much less give birth.
>> Put it in my hand, put the tail in my hand.[25]
> (Cashion 1982, II: appendix II, lines 476–482, pp. 49–50)

In this song the hunter's fadenya orientation and the power he controls are captured in the image of the animal's tail, which is the hunter's trophy. The threat that the hunter poses to society from his accumulated nyama stands in sharp contrast to the images of continuity and the maintenance of society encapsulated in the images of farming and human reproduction.

There are certain parallels between the hunters' association and the youth association in these communities. The hunters' association also draws it members from every segment of society, without regard to social class or status. It is the ethos of hunters, whom society defines as men of action and means and as heroes, that the kamalen choose to emulate in many Sogo bò masquerades, songs, and dances.

In the evening segment of the performances, which was the original Binsogo bò, the majority of characters are bush animals. The opening verse of many of these characters' songs establishes the link between the kamalen performers and hunters/warriors. For example, in many performances of Sigi, the Buffalo, the masquerade appears as a solitary figure of enormous size and large horns [Figure 6.1]. The lead verse of his song reads:

Korondon sigi dankelen
Korondon i be cèw bolo

Bellow lone buffalo
Bellow for you are in the hands of men [hunters].

According to hunters' lore, the condition of *dankelen*, being alone, refers to old bulls, either buffalo or elephants, who leave the herd and move independently through the bush. *Korondon*, bellow, evokes the size and power of these animals. Hunters describe

6.1. A Bamana performance of Sigicè, the male Buffalo. 1980. Segou region, Mali. *Photograph by Lynn Forsdale.*

these beasts as nyama-laden animals, who are dangerous and difficult to bring down. The song praises the power of the master hunter who has both the force and the means to make the kill and to control the energy released by his action. The phrase *i be X bolo*, to have something in one's hand, is a standard form of stating ownership. Some people interpreted this song line as the expression of the essential fadenya relationship between men and animals in the bush. Other people extended this interpretation to state that Sigi represents the power of tradition [associated with cèkòròw, elders] and the forces that plot one's destiny. The hunter [here associated with the kamalen] represents the power to overcome tradition and to gain one's *tògò*, one's name or reputation. There are variations in Sigi's performance. In some villages the male buffalo first appears with his female companions. This joint appearance lends itself to a somewhat different interpretation, which will be discussed below.

In other masquerades it is the animal character itself which forges the link to hunters and hunting. For example, Duga, the Vulture, is a metaphor for the master hunter. A well-known proverb collected by Cashion and applied to master hunters reads:

> *Duga-mansa be jigi fen kan*
> *fen te jigi duga-mansa-kòrò kan*
>
> King Vulture may set upon anything
> but nothing sets upon old King Vulture.
> (Cashion 1982, I: 245)

In the youth theatre the masquerade song for the character Duga plays upon this association and the sentiments encapsulated in the proverb that describes the attributes of the master hunter. One version of a Sogo bò song reads:

> *Duga, mansa kòrò k'i be taa min*
> *a ko n'be taa n'yaala*
> *n'be taa n'yaala ka hèrè nyini*
> *e koni bi taa hèrè nyini*
> *E be jigin fèn kan fèn te jigin e koni kan*
>
> Vulture, old king where are you going
> He says I am wandering
> I am wandering in search of good fortune
> You find only good fortune
> You land on something, but nothing lands on you.

Many other versions of the song sung for the vulture masquerade that I collected also refer directly to this proverb. In the song cited above, *yaala*, wandering, may be a reference to the *dalimasigi*, the hunter's adventure. This is the long voyage that hunter's periodically embark upon during their lives. In myths throughout south central Mali, the fact that hunters are often remembered as the founders of villages might reflect this long tradition of hunters' voyages. Today people also regard long distance labor migrations as part of this tradition of heroic voyages (Cashion 1982, I: 111–112).

Other animal masquerades, such as Baninkònò, the Stork [Figure 3.3], and Waraba, the Lion [Figure 1.15], are equally potent symbols for master hunters. Cashion notes that because the lion is itself a hunter, when a hunter killed a lion he was required to first ask its forgiveness before he made the kill (Cashion 1982, I: 315). Hunters classify an animal as either a *sogofin*, dark or powerful animal, or a *sogojè*, clear or less nyama-laden animal. Among the Bamana all of the carnivores, the lion, the hyena, the wildcats, which are themselves hunters, are sogofinw. Large mammals like the buffalo and the elephant also fall within this category. Among the Boso and Sòmonò the crocodile, the hippo, and the manatee, which is protected by the water spirits, are the most powerful animals and the most dangerous animals. It is by bagging one of these powerful animals that hunters make their reputations. At hunters' funerals or during ceremonies that take place to com-memorate a hunter's death, several dances are reserved for special classes of hunters. Only men who have faced death can dance the *maransa*. These hunters have killed animals after having survived being wounded by them. Only men who have killed the elephant can dance the *nyin-tege-foli*. Hunters who have killed lions, wildcats, hyenas, or buffalo dance the *donso ta natananin* and the *nyangalan* (Cashion 1982, I: 220).

Several species of antelopes, which are protected by bush genies, are classified as nyama-laden animals. Dajè, the Roan Antelope, is considered to be a sogofin [Figure 3.19]. The women sing the following song for its performance:

Dajè sarama yoo ee
ee sogo makari be n'na ee
Dajè sarama yoo ee
ee sogo makari be n'na ee

Dajè the well loved yoo ee
ee the animal makes me feel pity
Dajè the well loved yoo ee
ee the animal makes me feel pity.

Both men and women describe the song as a lament for the animal. They cite both the slow, sonorous tempo and phrasing of its entry and the use of the word *makiri*, pity, in the song as evidence for this interpretation. People explained that the roan antelope is an exquisitely beautiful animal. Beauty was given to Dajè by the bush genies and it serves as the animal's protective cloak. Dajè's extraordinary beauty can paralyze the hunter. Thus, the hunter must have the necessary means to overcome the animal's paralyzing beauty and to make the kill. He must also have the ability to protect himself from the wrath of the bush spirits, who protect the roan antelope. The song in essence expresses pity for the animal. This expression of pity for the death of a beautiful animal is intended to pacify the animal's protective genie and to disperse and ward off the nyama which is released when the animal is killed.

Other characters within the theatre, many of whom are defined as a *k'a ye*, an imaginary character, are interpreted in terms of the sentiments that underlie badenya or fadenya. While these two terms are rarely explicitly invoked in the theatre, they are frequently implied and regularly emerge in people's postperformance exegesis of the masquerades. I did record one song in Kirango sung by Mei Diarra, the lead singer for the Sogo bò theatre, that directly expressed the sentiment of badenya. She did not perform this song as part of the theatre in 1979, but sang this song for a group of women who were involved in processing karitè butter, a labor-intensive and arduous task. In the song she exhorts the women to unite because only through collective action will they succeed in the task at hand.

> *Balimaw yooo*
> *Badenya ka di*
> > *A ye to an ka jè*
> > *ka badenya ke*
> > *badenya ka di*
> My kin yooo
> *Badenya* is good
> > Let us unite
> > to attain *badenya*
> > *Badenya* is good.

This same focus on unity and collective action underlies the interpretation given to Dugu-duman-yiri-bi-wooyo, The Good Village's Tree Cheers, a masquerade performed by one of Kirango's neighbors. The masquerade appeared as an antelope head with a small puppet of a mother and her child riding on its back. Its performance was accompanied by multiple repetitions of this lead verse:

> *Aw ka wooyo den n'a ba la*
> *Dugu duman yiri bi wooyo*
>
> Cheer the child and his mother
> The good village's tree cheers.

In this instance both the visual image and the verbal metaphors in the song worked in tandem to express the theme of unity. During post-theatre interviews several members of the troupe explained that the image of the mother and child was the visual metaphor for the qualities of unity and solidarity which underlie the ideal relationship between a mother and her children, baden. The masquerade's song reinforced this visual message by focusing the audience's attention on the correspondence between the sentiments that characterize the relationship between the mother and child and the badenya orientation of a good (prosperous) village, *dugu duman*. A group of men offered the following exegesis of the masquerade. They said that the puppet and its song refer not only to unity among a mother and her child, but to cooperation and amicability between young and old, men and women, the village and its neighbors, and Bamana and other ethnic groups. The key verbal image in the masquerade song is the cheering tree, *yiri bi wooyo*. They explained that every village has a large shade tree under which people regularly gather in the heat of the day to talk and exchange news. When you enter a village that is unified, the first thing you hear are the sounds of chatter and laughter coming from this gathering place. However, when you enter a village that is being pulled apart by fadenya (the actual term the young men used), what you are greeted with is silence. During the performance of this masquerade, as the lead singer repeated the verse the young women's chorus inserted the names of neighboring villages in each repetition, thus elaborating and extending the theme of solidarity and kinship beyond their immediate village.

Later in the same performance the troupe played the puppet masquerade Cèw-ye-kelen-ye, All Men Are Equal, which focused attention on the inevitability of rivalry and competition in social life [Figure 6.2]. This masquerade, classified as k'a ye, appeared as an antelope. Its song provided the key to its interpretation.

Cèw ye kelen ye
Cèw ye kelen ye de
nka konin kelen ye
Cèw bo nyògòn na

All men are equal
All men are equal
but in fact one thing
makes the difference among men.

The same group of men who had interpreted the Dugu-duman-yiri-bi-wooyo song as a celebration of unity described this puppet's song as a *fadenya donkili*, a song of rivalry. In interpreting the masquerade, they agreed that although people recognize that everyone is a human being, *Adama den* (literally, child of Adam), each person is an individual and has at least one trait—intelligence, luck, or charisma—that makes him different from everyone else and that shapes his destiny. These differences among people contribute to the inevitable condition of fadenya. For these men, fadenya was an integral part of the human condition. The song continued in this vein by praising the hero/young man who overcomes his rivals, both his peers and his patrilineage. Only the hero possesses those extra qualities that will win him his tògò, his reputation.

Bamana derive one dimension of their identity from their patrilineal clan, and from one of three social strata: hòròn, nyamakala, or jòn. In addition a person's gender and social age—child, young adult, or elder—contribute to this identity. Bamana also recognize a second dimension of identity, which is based on individual innate qualities such as *hakili*, intelligence, *hèrè*, luck, and *dawula*, charisma. These qualities are uninheritable and are unequally distributed throughout the society. These two dimensions of identity are inherently unrelated. Thus it does not automatically

6.2. A Bamana performance of Cèw-ye-kelen-ye, All Men Are Equal. 1979. Segou region, Mali. *Photograph by Lynn Forsdale.*

follow that a person who has inherited a superior status position based on lineage and birth order within the lineage would also necessarily have superior intelligence or charisma. A person who has great charisma, luck, or intelligence may have a low status position. Jackson noted that the discrepancy between the two dimensions, inheritable or ascribed status and individual traits, is considered one of the central dilemmas in social life (Jackson 1977, 149–151). The masquerade Cèw-ye-kelen-ye speaks eloquently to the nature of this dilemma by focusing attention on the differences among individuals in their capacities and potential.

Another character, Son-min-te-maa-na, which was played by Kirango's neighbors in 1978–80 and performed in Kirango in 1989, also appears as an antelope. This character's song speaks more directly to the destructive nature of uncontrolled fadenya.

> *U b'a fe, Son min te maa na*
> *I jugu y'o da i la*
> *Son min te maa la*
> *faden jugu y'o da i la*

> The character that a person does not have
> Your rivals will attribute to you
> The character that a person does not have
> Your rivals will attribute to you.

In this masquerade song, the term faden openly refers to jealousy and rivalry as a social fact. This masquerade character reinforces people's belief that nobody is without rivals. It is one's rivals who will try to malign and destroy a person's good name. In all the interviews I conducted, both men and women generally agreed that the interplay between badenya and fadenya as manifested in the relationship between elder and junior men and in terms of an individual's relationships to the group was an important theme in these performances. The competing forces, which underlie the relationships between kamalen and cèkòrò and between the individual action and the collective will, organize the dramatic action and become the subject of much of the dramatic discourse.

Cè and Muso: Exploring Relationships between Men and Women in the Sogo bò

Women play as important a role in the production of the Sogo bò theatre as do the young men. As the singers for these events, women are the Sogo bò's verbal artists. They are the voices of the masquerades. While men determine the masquerade program it is the lead singer who determines what songs will be sung and what issues and themes will be addressed in the musical interludes between masquerades. While men and women may speak with one voice in the theatre, they do not always do so. During the performance of particular masquerades and at different points in the musical interludes, the relationships between men and women and between women are brought forward and highlighted in the theatre. The relationship between men and women is also interwoven into the more dominant theme of the competition between kamalen and cèkòrò.

Women foster the rivalry between young men and their elders through their praise songs for the kamalen. During the 1979 performance in Kirango the women's chorus participated in asserting the young men's challenge to the elders by acknowledging the young men as the sogotigi, the owners of the masquerades.

> *Sogow bi na, wari danbe*
> *Kamalen sogow bi na, sanu danbe*
> > *Sogow bi na, wari danbe*
> > *Kamalen sogow bi na, sanu danbe*

> The animals are coming, silver honors
> The young men's animals are coming,
> golden honors
> > The animals are coming, silver honors
> > The young men's animals are coming,
> > golden honors.

Yet, while these masquerades associate young men with heroic behavior and challenge the social order of the village through the rivalry between elders and junior men, they also intensify the separation between men and women (Grosz-Ngate 1989, 177). As the owners of the theatre, men prepare the masquerades. These preparations take place, symbolically if not actually, outside the village, and women and uncircumcised boys are barred from participation in these activities. Women's praises of men as the owners of the masquerades in these songs implicitly support men's claims to authority over the bush, over animals, and, by extension, over land, over households, and over women.

Yet despite the fact that women regularly praise young men as the owners of the masquerades in these performances, they also occasionally challenge men's authority over women when they sing their own praises and claim the status of *nganaw*, heroines, for themselves. In one song recorded in 1979, the women sang with great enthusiasm:

> *ee nganaw y'an ye*
> *cèw y'a don nganaw y'an ye*

> ee We are the heroines
> Men know that we are the heroines.

In another 1979 performance, the song for Ngongo, the Land Turtle masquerade, served as an occasion for men and women to hurl friendly insults at each other. When the young men brought the masquerade into the dance arena they sang:

> *eee ngongo yo*
> *suma derele*
> *musow ka ngongonin*
> *suma derele*

> Eee turtle yo
> Terrible odor

Women's little turtle
Terrible odor

The women's chorus then picked up the refrain and returned the insult by substituting the word men for the word women in the verse.

eee ngongo yo
suma derele
cèw ka ngongonin
suma derele

Eee ngongo yo
Terrible odor
Men's little turtle
Terrible odor

This exchange of insults and reference to the terrible odor provoked much laughter. In postperformance interviews both men and women explained that the reference to the turtle's terrible odor was a reference to the fact that the other group (whether men or women) were like turtles. In order to get them to act you would have to light a fire in their ass, thus resulting in the terrible odor.

While animal masquerades still dominate the repertoire in most villages today, masquerades and puppets representing women in the multiplicity of their social and symbolic roles have gradually become more prominent in many communities' theatres. In Kirango, for example, seven of the masquerades played in the 1979 and 1980 performances were female characters. In these performances a number of the songs sung in the interludes addressed the nature of the relationship between men and women.

Women are jural minors, and the fact that they depend on their husbands and his affines to achieve full personhood through marriage does not escape either men or women. The marriage ritual emphasizes the bride's identity as an outsider in her husband's household. Her outsider status as a musomisèn, married woman, is continually re-created through a variety of everyday practices until as a musokòrò she is redefined as an insider in her husband's lineage.[26]

While woman retain de jure membership in their kin group even after marriage, they have no decision-making powers, and no control over any of their husband's or their own lineage's agricultural products. While women as wives are essential to domestic and agricultural production, they labor for their husband's lineage. Farming is under the control of men and it is the head of the lineage who makes all of the decisions in this regard, from planting to the daily distribution of stored grain. It is only after menopause, when a woman retires from communal agricultural labor, that she may be assigned her own field to cultivate (Grosz-Ngate 1989, 176).[27]

Certain productive activities are clearly gendered. Spinning cotton, winnowing and pounding grain, and collecting and processing karité butter nuts are considered to be women's activities. These gendered activities are represented in the puppet theatre through small rod and string puppets. These puppets reinforce through artistic imagery what people accept as the appropriate division of labor between the sexes. Small puppets of men wielding hoes appear alongside those of women working [Figures Pref.3 and 3.9]. The *daba*, hoe, remains the dominant symbol of farming, although the plough has now widely replaced the hoe for preparing the fields in many communities. While both men and women still use hoes in different phases of the farming process, I have only seen small male puppets carrying hoes. Clearly this potent metaphor for Bamana identification with farming also reinforces men's claim to ownership and authority over land and over the agricultural process. In all my discussions with people, I found that the interpretation of puppets representing gendered activities drawn from domestic life were never contested by men or women. Gendered activities are so sanctioned by tradition and have become naturalized over time that men and women speak with one voice about these characters. This voice reinforces the values associated with gendered identity as it is manifested in everyday life.

Visual and verbal images of the mother and child are as widespread in the youth theatre as they are in other contexts in these societies. These images appear as female puppets, of a woman carrying her child on her back or of a woman nursing her child. From a woman's perspective, children are the symbol of her successful life. The many references to maternity in the theatre extol the process through which a woman attains full personhood in her old age through her children. Infertility is a cause for anxiety for women as well as for men. It is not only a private source of anguish, but a public one because it threatens alliances forged between lineages at marriage (Ezra 1986, 37–38).

From both men's and women's perspectives, the nursing mother is a profound symbol, not only of maternity but of personhood. Among the Bamana a child receives his/her father's blood via the father's semen and his/her mother's blood through the mother's breast milk. As Katherine Dettwyler noted:

> Analogous to the belief that children of one father share the same blood by virtue of inheritance, children who nurse from the same woman are said to share the same blood through her milk. In fact, children of the same woman are related to each other on the maternal side not because they were all born from her body, but because they all nursed from her breast. . . . Two children who nurse from the same woman are related through the process itself and cannot marry, whether they are "genetically" related or not. . . . This belief is reflected in the kinship terminology: a man may refer to his full brother as *shin-ji* (literally "breast-milk"). (Dettwyler 1988, 179–180)

Puppets representing women nursing their children not only symbolize nurturing and psychological bonding in a Western sense, they allude to the Bamana belief that breast milk, as transformed blood, and the process of breast feeding are fundamental to the production of a child as a human being, maa or mògò.

From a male perspective, the mother and child image is equally powerful because it involves cultural beliefs about destiny. A man inherits his patrilineal affiliation and ascribed status from his father, but his destiny comes from his mother. A man's destiny is said to be determined by his mother's own successful socio-moral career. Thus, the image of the mother as a *muso nyuman*, the morally good woman, symbolizes her son's access to the means to achieve, to gain reputation, and to succeed. This belief is clearly articulated in the hunter's proverb *Bèe i ba'bolo*, Everyone is in his mother's hands (Cashion 1982, I: 244n24), and in the line from the epic of Famori, "*Môgô barakayila, o i ba-la di*. A man's power comes from his mother" (Cashion 1982, II, appendix 1, lines 675–678 pp. 79–80).

There are many female masquerade characters currently performed in the youth theatre that are interpreted as representing muso nyuman, morally good women. One popular character since the 1960s in western Segou villages is Yayoroba, the Beautiful Woman [Figure Pref.4]. In Kirango and in several neighboring villages, this body puppet has firm jutting breasts, rounded buttocks, and a slender waist. She is elaborately costumed and coiffed. Her image is that of a young married woman. Although she does not appear with a child, her role as the good mother is implied in people's interpretations of this character. She is said to represent a woman of exemplary character. She demonstrates respect for her elders and her husband's kin, thus assuring her sons' destiny. Her appearances in Kirango always highlight these qualities, as she begins her performance by modestly bowing first to the elders, then to the lead singers, and finally to the assembled audience. When she dances around the arena, slowly swaying her hips to the right and left, it is with grace and dignity. People said that a person's character is revealed through the body and is made visible in the way a person walks, sits, and stands. Yayoroba's characterization as a muso nyuman is clearly communicated through both her sculptural form and her dance and is further reinforced in her signature song:

E Yayoroba
Ala min i balo la

E Yayoroba
May God give you long life.

Additional verses of the Yayoroba song describe her physical attributes. They celebrate her soft skin, her ample size, and her pleasing pear-shaped proportions. While aspects of physical beauty are featured in these verses, most older men and women drew a direct relationship between physical beauty and a woman's moral worth. However, in a neighboring village Yayoroba's character had undergone a transformation, at least among the younger set. Because of her exceptional physical beauty these young men recast her in the role of a *sungurunba*, a term they currently used for a lover. After listening to their interpretation of the Yayoroba character, the village chief, who was present at this discussion, took umbrage. He launched into a tirade, berating the young men for thinking only of physical beauty and for not valuing a woman's moral character above all when seeking a wife. A lively discussion ensued in a spirit of good-natured disagreement that was peppered with a bawdy repartee.

The difference in men's attitudes toward women, especially those they expressed about their mothers and their female kin and those they hold about women who are not kin, is marked in Bamana society. Jackson comments upon men's attitudes toward women who are kin and those who are not as these attitudes are commonly expressed in folklore among the Kuranko, a Mande-speaking group that is culturally related to the Bamana. He states:

> The former is characteristically an attitude of reciprocal trust and affection while the latter is often modulated by a sense of distrust and potential threat. In several Kuranko folktales, it is a man's mother who rescues him from the clutches of a malevolent spirit who manifests itself in the form of a beautiful and alluring woman. (Jackson 1977, 91)

Among both the Kuranko and the Bamana there is this same distrust of women's sexuality and this distrust often translates to attitudes that define women as basically promiscuous, untrustworthy, and morally weak. The power and danger associated with female sexuality are frequent subthemes in Bamana stories and legends, epics and heroic poetry, and contain a paradox. Many epics feature episodes in which a woman through her sexual charms is able to discover the secret of the antagonist's power. For example, it is Sunjata's sister who betrays her husband, Sumangaro Kante, by giving the secret of his power to her brother. This knowledge affords Sunjata the means to vanquish his opponent. In these epics it is often the hero's female kin who gives him the secret to his opponent's power and the antagonist's wife or lover who betrays him (Kesteloot 1972, 38).

In the youth theatre allusions to women's sexuality are equally complex. *Musomisènw*, married women of child-bearing age, are identified as *dunanw*, strangers, in their husband's household, a social identity that is constructed during the marriage ritual and reinforced in practice on a daily basis (Grosz-Ngate 1989, 175–177). The theme of woman as stranger and ambivalence toward women's sexuality find frequent expression in the youth theatre. These themes organize the interpretations of Mèrèn and Jinè-Faro.

Mèrèn, a puppet representing a beautiful young woman, was widely popular in the Segou region in the first half of this century. In some Bamana villages people said she represented a Fulani maiden, alluring but unobtainable as a wife. One song I collected that supports this interpretation reads:

N'i y'a file kojugu
N'i ye Mèrèn file kojugu
Fuladen Mèrènin file kojugu
I na ba duru bo

If you look too long
If you look at the little Mèrèn
If you look at the little Fulani maiden
You will have to pay 5000 francs.

In several other villages people cast this character as a genie in the guise of a beautiful woman. In one village they sang this song:

Kolo te Mèrèn na
Fosi te
Kolo te n'na
Bu te n'na

There are no bones in the Mèrèn
Nothing
I do not have bones
I do not have flesh.

People believe that genies regularly appear to men in the guise of beautiful women. There are countless stories of men having been placed in mortal danger by their encounter with a female genie. These encounters generally take place in the bush, and today the bush may refer to Abidjan or some other city where men go on labor migration.

A character currently played in Kirango is Jinè-Faro, Faro the female water genie [Figure 3.28]. People explained that this character was inspired by a local legend of a beautiful and powerful female genie who lived in the Niger River. When men passed her by she would lower her hands and if they looked directly at her beautiful face they were struck down and died. During her performance, this puppet figure raises and lowers her hands in front of her face and her gestures recall the local legend. In the 1979 performance in Kirango Mei Diarra sang:

> *Fatulen*
> *Jinè fatulen*
> *eee maanu jinè fatulen*
> *Tontigi Musa, yo jinè fatulen*

> She is dead
> The genie is dead
> eee people the genie is dead
> Tontigi Musa, yo the genie is dead.

The song refers to a well-known story where a man tricked a genie and killed her. In each verse of the song Mei Diarra inserted the name of a former tontigi, starting with Moussa Coulibaly, who was the leader of the association when the masquerade was first played in 1960. Her performance links these leaders to the hunter/hero in this story, who defeated the powerful genie.

Women recognize the power of their sexuality and sometimes celebrate it. In a song the women sang during the Kirango performance in 1979 they laughingly mocked marriage.

> *ee Mariya eee, kanun wulajanba la*
> *kanun ka di furu ye*
> > *ee Mariya eee, kanun wulajanba la*
> > *kanun ka di furu ye*

> ee Mariya eee, flirting from a distance
> Flirting is better than marriage
> > ee Mariya eee, flirting from a distance
> > Flirting is better than marriage.

Another theme that explores the ambiguity in relationships between men and women and between women is encapsulated in the character Barabara, the Favorite Wife. This character focuses attention on the problems of domestic relations. Although the ideal behavior between co-wives stresses harmony and cooperation, the sources for women's discontent in polygamous households are manifold. Besides the hierarchy between men and women that regulates behavior, there is a hierarchy among wives based on the number of years a woman has been married into the household. Women in polygamous households often find themselves competing with each other for scarce resources for their children. This competition can be destructive and can contribute to a woman's anxieties for her own welfare and for that of her children. On a more personal and individual level, co-wives living in the same compound may not even like each other.

Conflict among co-wives is a popular theme in many stories and popular entertainments, and the source of conflict often revolves around women's sexuality (Jackson 1982, 246–254; Brink 1980, 158–159). This is certainly the case for Barabara, the Favorite Wife character in the youth theatre. Men praised her as a *muso nyuman*, a woman who fostered unity in the household. In contrast they derided the *galomuso*, the bad wife, as the cause of fadenya. The masquerade song draws out this contrast quite clearly:

Cè ni bara ma na kèlè
K'o ye don kèlènke ye
nka n'a ni galomuso kèlèla
k'a be kalo wòorò k'o da la

When a man fights with his favorite wife
There is only one day of fighting
But if he fights with his least favorite wife
Then it will last for six months.

Women, however, were not as generous toward the character of Barabara as were men. Many woman associated her with the new bride, the *kònyò muso*, who they referred to sarcastically as the wife whose mosquito net has no holes. This image of the new mosquito net referred obliquely to sexual politics where the new bride often exerts undue influence over her husband through her sexual favors. Because of her standing as the favorite wife, she is often arrogant to her senior wives and openly defies their authority, causing dissent in the household. From these women's perspective it is the power of the favorite wife's sexuality that is seen as the root cause of fadenya in the household where the favorite wife gains an advantage for herself and her children over the other wives and their children.

In one masquerade performed in 1979 in Kirango, not only did men and women construct different interpretations of a female character outside the theatre, but their conflicting voices were sometimes played out in the performance. This was the case with the masquerade Taasi Dòoni, Reflect a Little [Figure 1.18]. Women sang a song for this masquerade that was a veiled plea by young women to their elders to think and have compassion for them when negotiating their marriages. They asked not to be engaged in marriages which do not please them. They pleaded not to be given as gifts to close relatives or forced into marriages, but to be allowed to marry for love.

The masquerade and its performance, which was created by the young men, subverted the mood and message of these women's song. The dancer wearing a mask representing a woman appeared with amply padded derriere and bust and when he performed he punctuated his movements with exaggerated pelvic and hip thrusts. Young men sitting on the sidelines jumped into the ring and fell down before the character as if overwhelmed by lust and desire. Women's and men's intentions expressed through song and masked performance in this case seemed poles apart.[28]

A character currently played in a neighboring village, Furusa Tilè, Divorce Today, also elicited quite different responses from men and from women. These differences arose in the dissonance between the interpretation of the masquerade imagery and its song. This grass masquerade appears as a creature with three heads. During its performance it darted erratically around the dance arena, not knowing which of its heads to follow. Men said quite emphatically that this masquerade spoke to the destructive aspects of divorce. Like the masked performance, divorce disrupts alliances and pulls the household apart, leading to chaos. Women, on the other hand, based their interpretations of the masquerade on its song. They said equally emphatically that the masquerade song actually celebrated the first woman from the area who obtained a legal divorce after Independence. Talking with women who had divorced during that period, I heard several chilling stories of husbands who had beat and humiliated these women beyond any acceptable standards. Family efforts at mediation were unsuccessful and these women remembered having felt hopelessly trapped. The change in marriage and family law following Independence empowered these women to seek divorces (Dicko 1965, 476–486). This feeling of newfound empowerment is what women celebrate in this masquerade's performance.

Men define themselves as working for the collective while they define women as oriented more toward self-interest. The paradox embedded in these definitions of men's and women's behavior and intentions was exposed through the masquerade Pari that was performed in a village near Kirango in 1979. Pari appears as an antelope, but it is the name for small-scale revolving savings and credit associations generally organized by and among women in this area [Figure 3.34]. Each woman who becomes a member puts a small sum of money into the "bank" at designated intervals. Each member in her turn can draw upon this accumulated capital as venture capital to invest in goods that she will sell at the local market. In Kirango, as well as in many other villages in the area, many women are involved in this kind of small-scale trade in foodstuffs, beads, cloth, and other goods. They carry out these activities to accumulate small amounts of expendable cash to use for themselves and to provide for their children's needs and their daughters' wedding goods. Both men and women celebrated the masquerade Pari during its performance. Herein lies the irony. While men on one hand criticize women for their orientation toward accumulation of wealth and see this as a node of conflict within the household, they conversely say that a woman who is too dependent on her husband is lazy or worthless, sometimes likening her to a slave (Grosz-Ngate 1989, 178). A woman's successful participation in small enterprise activities contributes to her gaining a *tògò*, reputation or good name. As Grosz-Ngate noted, men's definition of women as motivated toward self-interest "glosses over the fact that it may actually be the tensions between men of the kin group which lead women to place special emphasis on personal wealth, since such wealth becomes crucial in the event of fission" (Grosz-Ngate 1989, 179).

The ultimate statement of women's destructive power and the potential danger that women pose to the society is expressed through the character Sumusonin, the Sorceress [Figure 1.12]. The sorceress or the witch is the antithesis of the dutiful mother, the muso nyuman. According to Jackson it is the witch that embodies "the worst fears of men, namely that women may actively intervene in the processes of destiny" (Jackson 1982, 247). It is no mere coincidence that men, who are the creators of these masquerades, represent this destructive power as female. Her song reads:

> Sumusonin yo t'i bugu de
> cèko ye bana ye
> nyagba musonin yo t'i bugu de
> cèko de ye bana ye

> Little sorceress, go lay down
> the affairs of men are a sickness
> little sorceress, go lay down
> the affairs of men are a sickness.

While blacksmiths, practicing griots, and hunters may be praised as *soma*, sorcerers, the attitude toward this masquerade character was not celebratory. The sentiments expressed here by both men and women were ones of resignation about the indeterminate nature of social life, the "sickness" of society, and the destructive power of fadenya out of control.

Imagining a Moral Universe through Animals

A few animal characters that appear in particular communities' theatre performances are closely linked to specific tales, legends, and narratives, and the masquerade songs generally provide the audience with the link to the story or legend. But many animals are more loosely drawn, allowing for a greater flexibility in their interpretation from village to village and from individual to individual. People negotiate and play with the meanings ascribed to these animal characters. Animals and their attributes are often the focal point around which people build their discussion of moral values and judge behaviors. For example, one hunter said that a *Sinè mògò*, a gazelle-person, was someone who spent an inordinate amount of time on his or her personal appearance. A *Son mògò*, kob antelope-person, was a reflective person that people respected. However, one man said this was a bad quality in a wife, because it might undermine the authority of her husband in his household.

It was clear that particular animal tales had been the inspiration for theatrical masquerades in at least two cases I documented. In a village near Kirango, the song for Sonsan, the Hare masquerade, related it directly to a well-known animal tale.

> Sonsannin ko ne malola
> Sonsannin e ko i ka keku
> Sonsannin e malola
> O ye k'a yelen do yan

> Little hare, I have known shame
> Little hare, you say you are clever

Little hare, you have known shame
You were seen here and we went on and left you.

In discussing the masquerade, a group of young men from the village invoked the following folktale. The hare constantly boasted that he was so much more clever than all the other animals. One day while wandering in the bush, hare was startled by something and hid himself behind a bush. Long after any danger had past, he remained in hiding. When the other animals happened to stroll by they spied the hare cowering in his hiding place, but they could clearly see that he was in no danger. As they passed by his hiding place, the crane broke into a mocking song. At this point in their story, the young men broke into the song sung for the hare during the youth theatre. They then used the discussion of the hare masquerade and the original animal tale to create a moral commentary. They said both the tale and the masquerade stand as a warning to people to remember that a person can never win his reputation by singing his own praises. Others must sing them for him.

Later, the discussion of the performance of the masquerade Kònòsogonin, the Ostrich, invoked a second animal tale. In this case the ostrich's behavior was the inverse of that of the hare. One day all the animals came together for a festival. Although each animal danced, no one could equal the dance of the ostrich. When the ostrich's turn came to dance, all of the other animals judged him to be the most adept and joined together to sing his praises.

i yalo Kònòsogonin
i yalo danan kèrè fè

Leap little ostrich
Leap in time with the bell.

The young men related the story of the animal festival in the tale directly to their own performances, saying that to come forth and dance with mastery in the puppet theatre gains a young man his reputation and makes him a hero. Whereas the ostrich hero wins his song from his baden, the other animals, so it is for young men, whose peers are the only ones who can bestow his praise song upon him.

A masquerade song often focuses on a single attribute of an animal, as is the case with Kalakadane [Figure 3.20].

Kalakadane yoo sogo binye kelen
Kalakadane sogo kelen, binye kelen

Kalakadane yoo animal with one horn
Kalakadane the only animal with one horn.

The village that performed this masquerade interpreted its song in much the same way that others had interpreted the masquerade Cèw-ye-kelen-ye, All Men Are Equal. The single horn that makes this animal unique among all animals was seen as a reference to the individual traits that separate people from one another. This animal masquerade throws into high relief the ambiguity engendered between inheritable and ascribed status and individual qualities.

In working with different troupes within the region, I was struck by the stress that certain communities placed upon the tension between community and individual in their interpretations of their masquerades. In the last thirty years these villages have created many imaginary characters that speak forcefully to these social tensions. While these same troupes also perform many of the standard bush animals, they have created such characters as Cèw-ye-kelen-ye, All Men Are Equal, Son-min-te-maa-na, The Character That a Person Doesn't Have, Dugu-duman-yiri-bi-wooyo, The Good Village's Tree Cheers, and Furusa Tilè, Divorce Today. People's interpretations of masquerades such as the hare, the ostrich, and the one-horned antelope also highlight critical dimensions of social relationships.

It is not unusual in daily conversations for people to talk of their lives as hard, *ka gèlèn*. Life is indeed hard in Mali. In rural areas people have a well-founded anxiety based on their experience of drought and poverty in the recent past. They worry about whether the rains will come or not, whether the harvest will be good, where they will find the cash to pay their taxes. In towns as in the country people are very aware of the unequal access to opportunity and wealth that they see all around them. While young men who work outside the agricultural sector are supporting more and more of the needs of their extended families, they do not have an equal share in making decisions in the family. This is a growing node of tension in many households. These tensions and concerns are not unique to any single community and are expressed in daily conversations among men and women in villages and towns throughout Mali. What is noteworthy is that some villages have translated their concerns into new masquerade characters that directly address what people in these communities see as the changing circumstances of their lives. While cast as universal and timeless themes, many of these new masquerades seem to have been created as a direct response to local situations. Sometimes these characters are adopted by other villages and become popular throughout the region, but many of them emerge and fade within a generation and within a single locale.

Often the same masquerade character is presented somewhat differently from village to village, and the different emphases can evoke a variety of alternative interpretations. This is true for Sigi, the Buffalo, which is widely popular in the region. In some villages troupes play only Sigicè, the male Buffalo [Figure 6.1]. In other villages, the Sigicè is accompanied by one or more female buffalo masquerades [Figures 6.3 and 3.26]. In still other villages the bull appears alone but carries a whole array of small puppets on its back [Figure 6.4].

Hunters often described the buffalo as a *Sogo Mansa*, a King of Animals, because of its great physical bulk and its great store of nyama, life force or energy. This interpretation of Sigi as a dangerous and powerful animal is emphasized above all other interpretations when the buffalo appears as a solitary masquerade. The word *dankelen*, to walk alone, the key image both in the masquerade's performance and in its song, is a reference to sorcery.[29]

When both the male and the female buffalo masquerades are played, the male always enters the arena first and is then followed by its mate(s). People interpreted this as asserting the proper order of the world, both in the community of animals and in that of men. When both the male and female versions of Sigi are performed, it is the bull

6.3. A Bamana performance of Sigicè, the male Buffalo. Sigicè appeared with his mate, Sigimuso [see 3.26]. 1979. Segou region, Mali. *Photograph by Lynn Forsdale.*

which first takes center stage to perform solo. During this solo performance the image of the solitary buffalo, the powerful and dangerous animal, is highlighted over other interpretations.

The image of Sigi as the lone bull buffalo symbolizes the elders. When Sigi performs with an array of small rod puppets on its back, the character reads as a microcosm of the village, past and present. The cluster of small puppets carried on Sigi's back feature people and animals drawn from domestic life and highlight particular occupations and gendered activities—for example, the farmer, women pounding millet, the sheep, and the chicken. Other characters represent different social strata and different ethnic groups: the jeli musician, the hòròn drummer, the Fulani herder, and the Boso fisherman. Characters are also drawn from different historical periods: the precolonial warrior, the colonial administrator or military officer, and the president of the Republic of Mali. Sigi, here, stands as the symbol of cultural continuity and as the guardian of tradition. This version of the bush buffalo supports the commonly held beliefs which associate moral authority with the ancestors and with past time.

Many other animal characters are equally rich in cultural associations, and one of the most complex of these characters, and one that appeared without fail in every youth theatre repertoire I surveyed, is the hyena. In some cases people described the hyena as a thief that preys upon their livestock. He also appears in a large body of animal folktales and in many of these tales the hyena is often pitted against the hare. In the hare/hyena tales, hyena is associated with cèkòròw, elders, and the hare with dògòw, juniors. These tales often address problems of reciprocity and justice. As Jackson noted, hyena stands for "inflexible virtue and the blind voice of custom" while hare embodies "cleverness, guile, insight, and intellectual subtlety" (Jackson 1982, 90).

In contrast to the interpretation of hyena that emerges in the hyena/hare folktales, Charles Bird points out that when, in the heroic songs for the hunter Kambili, the bard sings "Kambili is a hyena," it (hyena) is a praise name that links the power and intelligence of the hyena to the hunter/hero (Bird 1976, 96). Only those hunters who have killed carnivores like lions and hyenas can participate in key dances at hunters' funerals and commemorative ceremonies (Cashion 1982, I: 220).

Hyena is also an important animal in the symbolic universe of the Kòrè men's association. According to Zahan, *surukuw*, the hyenas, is the name given to one of the eight groups within the association. In its multiple manifestations within Kòrè, the hyena not only alludes to gaucherie, naivete, and self-complacency, but to thought, intuition, knowledge, wisdom, and power (Zahan 1960, 183–193). McNaughton reports that in the Kòmò men's association the hyena symbolizes intelligence and great power and is said to devour sorcerers (McNaughton 1988, 137).

In Kirango, not one but four different hyena masquerades appeared in the 1979 Binsogo bò performance. Nama, a grass masquerade [Figure 2.13], Suruku Nama, a rod puppet masquerade [Figure 1.11], Suruku Malobali, a cloth masquerade [Figure 2.17], and Jado Nama, a rod puppet masquerade. Nama, the grass masquerade, is one of the oldest characters in the Kirango theatre and its longevity and age contribute to its association with tradition and the elders. Its shape-shifting performance and its signature song emphasize the power of the hyena. This grass masquerade is sometimes called Nama Kòrò, the Old Hyena, and it opens the su fè sogo in Kirango and in many other villages. Similar interpretations are given for the newer rod puppet version of the hyena, Suruku Nama. In Kirango, for example, Suruku Nama was regularly substituted for the grass masquerade version during the spring festival and it opened the evening segment of the masquerade event. In Kirango's Jado Nama character, the important role that the hyena plays in traditional medicine is featured in its narrative song.

Suruku Malobali, the Shameless Hyena, a character that was first introduced into Kirango in the 1950s, presents the audience with yet another set of complex associations.

The Suruku Malobali song reads:

Malobali nana
Surukunin Malobali nana
o taara
   Malobali nana
   Surukunin Malobali nana
   o taara

The shameless one has come
Little hyena without shame has come
and gone
   The shameless one has come
   Little hyena without shame has come
   and gone

The association of *malobali*, shamelessness, with the hyena in his song is further emphasized in its performance, where the hyena runs into the arena flapping its enormous mouth, and suddenly exits with no warning. Its performance violates all cultural expectations for the sogo masquerades. People described the character as impolite and gauche and Suruku Malobali's performance was likened to that of Gòn, the Baboon, and to the dances of the kòrèdugaw, the clowns, and to the young men who are drunk during the festival. This hyena is a comic character, and its ludic aspect arises from the fact that Suruku Malobali is the very antithesis of hòrònya, the attitudes and behaviors expected of the hòròn class. Children who misbehave are often rebuked by being called malobali, shameless, and malobali was formerly a slave name. In the traditional Bara dance event, the dance of the jòn, slave, was described as wild and impolite and it stood in marked contrast to the more restrained hòròn dances that open and close the event (Meillassoux 1968, 103–104). Yet casting off malo, shame and social constraint, in order to act is the special accomplishment of great hunters and warriors. They are society's heroes, and during the Sogo bò young men and women strongly identify with this heroic behavior.

Who, then, is this Suruku Malobali and what is its relationship to the other hyena characters played in the event? Is he merely the stupid, gauche character who is reviled for his behavior and associated with thieves who steal in and out so quickly? Does he represent the inversion of hòrònya? Does he allude to the hierarchy of groups, ages, and gender? Or does he symbolize the heroes and heroines whom young men and women praise so lavishly in the theatre? Does his large gaping mouth, the symbol of his lack of malo, represent his tremendous nyama, life force, and his ability to devour sorcerers? Could his quick entrance and exit also be a reference to hunter's beliefs that the hyena has the ability to render himself invisible in the bush? He symbolizes all of these attitudes, beliefs, and values and more.

The Shameless Hyena resonates with every other hyena masquerade performed in the theatre and with the attributes and characters assigned to all powerful bush animals. The possibility for intertextual resonance exists not only between any single masquerade and its song, dance, and drum rhythm, but between Suruku Malobali and the other hyena masquerades and between Suruku Malobali and all other bush animals played in the event. Suruku Malobali also resonates with the values, beliefs, and attitudes that surround the hyena in other expressive contexts, whether in songs, in folktales, in hunter's lore, in proverbs and adages, or in men's associations' esoteric beliefs and practices. How any individual interprets Nama, Suruku Nama, Jado Nama, or Suruku Malobali certainly depends on the person's social status, age, and gender, and his or her personal predilections. Many adults in the audience are aware of the multiplicity of meanings associated with the hyena in various settings, but which of these interpretations they will choose to privilege differs greatly from individual to individual. To limit the potential interpretations of the hyena or any other masquerade character to a single set of symbolic associations impoverishes the experience of the theatre. The project of the fictional world of youth theatre is to open up the universe of possible meanings through the massing of visual and verbal images that continually play off one another and are intensified through the aesthetic experience.

Kuma man nyi,
Kumabaliya fana man nyi

"Talk is dangerous, but refusal to talk is equally dangerous" (Hoffman 1990, 136). Talk, *kuma*, is the lubricant of social life in Mande communities, as Hoffman, Jackson, and most outsiders who have lived and studied in Malian communities have come to understand (Hoffman 1990; Jackson 1982). Talk provokes and ameliorates tensions; its tone and tenor can be seemingly benign or aggressively combative. Withholding speech can be deemed culturally appropriate or inappropriate depending on the situation and upon the players. In the world of Mande speech, Segou's youth puppet masquerade is a specialized and highly valued genre of kuma; more than a narrative constructed only from words, it is a dialogue that arises through the interrelationship of sculpture, song, drumming, and dance. While the tenor of these masquerades is playful, the topics are profoundly serious.

I have argued that form and content merge in these performances and that the dramatic context takes its shape from the convergence of past and present and from the intersection of culture and nature. Each individual Sogo bò performance is a site for the production of meaning. Yet, the theatre is linked to its own performance history over time and, in specific ways identified in this study, to the larger history of artistic forms and performance in Mande communities. Participants discuss these performances as singular events situated in time and place and as an artistic form that takes account of and emerges from its past.

The fictional world of the Sogo bò is also thoroughly connected with the everyday world of experience, from which it draws the inspiration for its content. It is in this resonance between fiction and ordinary life that people query morality and create their interpretations of the universal themes played out through these masquerades. The messages communicated within the theatre are a commentary about a Mande world located simultaneously in the past and in the present where artistry and the moral order are inseparable and central to people's lives.

Art is selective and the messages communicated within the youth theatre draw from the universe of experience and the realm of appropriate cultural expressions of that experience. Artistic expression is patterned, identifiable, and reproducible in ways that open it to evaluations not of its essence, its nyi or goodness, but of its practice, its di or tastiness. Youth association masquerades have a long history both as a highly valued artistic form and as a cogent commentary on Mande life.

Bateson has argued that for the attainment of grace in artistic expression "the reasons of the heart must be integrated with the reasons of the reason" (Bateson 1973, 235). I believe that the Mande fundamentally share this view. In the context of youth theatre, the reasons of the heart (and liver), primary loci of Mande character and passion (Cisse 1973, 156–157), must be integrated with the reasons of reason, the *hakili*, intelligence, and *miiri*, reflection, located in the head (Cisse 1973, 147). The reasons of the heart give the arts their tastiness, the reasons of reason their cultural form, their goodness. What is communicated within the youth puppet theatre is about "both itself internally patterned and itself a part of a larger patterned universe—the culture or part of it" (Bateson 1973, 237). It is the dialectic between heart and mind, between tastiness and goodness that is made manifest through performers' expressive skills, conscious and embodied, that underlies the performances of the Sogo bò. It is this dialectic between heart and mind that links this theatre to all other Mande arts.

People in Segou define what the Sogo bò is and what it is not by siting the genre within the larger group of performance traditions that are now played or were formerly performed by communities in Segou. All of the troupes, whether they are Bamana, Boso, Sòmonò, or Maraka, locate the youth association puppet masquerades within the category of play and entertainment. Puppetry's definition as play sets it apart from powerful men's associations' performances (Kòmò, Kònò, and Jara) owned by elders and from the nyama-laden specialized speech and performance of professional bards and diviners. Moreover, its particular myth of origin and its history within the Segou region sets this masquerade theatre apart from all other forms of play within these communities.

The play frame that contains and defines these performances manages the tensions and the energy released through performative action. The shared definition of the event relays the message to the participants to interpret what is said and done within these performances as nonserious and instructs people to act and react to the masquerades accordingly. By consistently relating the action to its definition as entertainment, young men and women create an environment that allows them to explore the inconsistencies and ambiguities of their daily lives without endangering themselves or their audiences. While the primary metamessage of rituals is "let us believe" (Handleman 1977, 187), the metamessage of Sogo bò, "let us play," opens up the dialogue about the past and present, exposing it to scrutiny and commentary. It masks any one group's competing claims about authenticity, power, and knowledge.

Knowledge of the past is powerful in Mande communities, and in many contexts the invocation of history is carefully controlled. It is not surprising, then, that many studies of Mande culture and society focus on history encoded in mythic charters, genealogies, epics, and heroic stories. This emphasis in Mande scholarship is not misplaced. It reflects Mande people's own emphasis on history and the active role it plays in the negotiations of their daily lives. Puppet performances are a public context in which people invoke the authenticating voice of history to affirm their collective identity and explore their relationships with their neighbors. Shared idioms among these different groups are drawn from a common experience of the environment and from shared ideologies and political and social experiences built up over at least three centuries or more of interaction. These idioms give the puppet theatre its identity as a regional and multiethnic art form. Yet, communities or segments of communities also make competing historical claims. The process of making historical claims through the vehicle of drama is analogous to that which takes place in myth. In puppet drama, groups make use of different historical moments realized through different artistic styles and different dramatic personae to assert their rights and identities against a backdrop of common regional experiences. The different historical claims that emerge in these performances and the potential disorder that may arise are carefully managed by framing these events as play. While the production of historicity, in theatre as well as in contexts not defined as play, is labile and not monolithic, the "non-seriousness" ascribed to these performances allows the participants an outspokenness that is not possible in other contexts where the invoking of history can have real and lasting consequences within a community and between communities.

The Mande concepts of badenya, mother-childness, and fadenya, father-childness, find direct and indirect expression in the very definition of the social identity of the actors, in the organization of the event, and in interpretations people construct of the theatre and its dramatic content. Over the many hours of these performances, the emphasis constantly shifts from one axis to the other. The stress that is placed on collective responsibility and on individual artistry at different moments in the production of theatre energizes these performances. The dialectic interplay between the maintenance of the social order and its subversion is accomplished through characters and songs. These arts assert the shared or competing viewpoints of either elders and youth or men and women. It is the cacophony of different viewpoints and different voices, intensified through artistic expression, that is the special kuma, speech, of youth association theatre. It sustains each performance, relates it to its past, and moves the theatre forward from generation to generation.

Theatre is appropriate to the kamalen waati, the time of youth. In these performances, young people learn through praxis the skills necessary to become socially competent adults in their society. Learning to manage the tensions between tradition and change, between unity and rivalry, and between collective and individual purpose and action is essential for negotiating the range of social relationships outside the theatre. Youth association provides young people with a legitimate public context within which they can begin to develop these skills. Yet, even as everyday roles are inverted, the definition of puppetry as play protects these neophytes and their audiences from the consequences of these actions.

The individual and collective patterns of responses are the affective and inchoate aspects of performances and are the means through which people constitute the experience of these events as emotionally satisfying, satiating, and fun. Actors offer up to their audiences a wide range of possible interpretations about the ambiguities of their everyday lives, which they not only think about but which they feel. No one would deny that life in these communities is hard and that rancor and anxiety are as much a part of daily life as are feelings of goodwill toward others. In the puppet performances, troupes proceed with a seriousness of purpose to examine the nature of their world and their lives. They realize the expression of their joys and of their sorrows with grace and style and oftentimes with great wit and humor.

Preface

1. The official 1987 census lists the population of Markala as 19,500. This figure includes residents from both the villages of Djamarabougou and Kirango as well as those families living in the administrative complex. The census bureau collected no separate figures for the village of Kirango itself, although I estimate that its population is about a third of the total figure for Markala (La République du Mali 1990, vol. 0: 186).

2. Kirango is located only a few kilometers from the administrative complex of Markala. This complex houses the office of the Chef d'Arrondissement, offices and related facilities for the Office du Niger, a military camp, the post office, the hospital, the high school, and elementary schools. A certain number of residences are also reserved for the chef d'arrondissement and members of his staff and for personnel from the Office du Niger, the hospital, and the schools. Nationally Kirango's identity is regularly subsumed under that of Markala, as the official census figures demonstrate.

3. During my two years in the Peace Corps, I served as co-director of a Social Center in Tivaouane, Senegal. In this capacity, I was the official sponsor of the Center's theatrical troupe, whose actors were local young men and women in their late teens and early twenties. My primary role in the Center's theatre was as a mentor, smoothing the way between the troupe and both the government and the town's Islamic hierarchy. The production of the plays and the choice of dramatic content were wholly in the hands of the troupe itself and were based on plays performed by the National Theatre in Senegal. As the official sponsor I attended the many organizational meetings and the weeks of rehearsals and from this experience gained a certain insight into performance processes, negotiations, and the final theatrical realization. During those two years in Senegal I also participated in a variety of other performance events, which took place during festivals, weddings, baptisms, and the like.

1. A Bamana Tonko Festival, Kirango, June 1979

1. Several different species of wildcats were once common in this area, including serval, caracal, lion, leopard, and cheetah. Outside of the very specific characterization of the lion in the masquerade theatre, people in Kirango were not able to make specific species identifications for the other wildcats, including the characters Jarawara, Njona, and Waraba Caco.

2. Mali Kònò was often identified as Baninkònò, the Abdim's Stork. However, certain features of the Mali Kònò rod puppet, which include the feather tuft on the crown, the hooked downward curving beak, and the striped markings on the beak, are closer to those of the cormorant, a fishing bird that frequents lakes, rivers, and marshes throughout this area. I was never able to satisfactorily resolve the species identification of the Mali Kònò puppet head.

2. The Definition and History of the Segou Puppet Masquerade Theatre

1. Pâques's ethnography of the Bambara, commissioned by the International African Institute in London, followed a standardized format. It addressed the topics of demography and ethnicity, linguistics, economics, history, and traditions of origins, social organization, and cultural practices. The arts and performance were included under the heading of "cultural aspects" and were briefly discussed

by type in a scant four pages immediately before the conclusion. Not surprisingly, the youth association masquerade theatre was not mentioned (Pâques 1954).

2. In interviews with Budagari Coulibaly and Vadama Traore, fishermen's bards, both singers associated the heroic songs with the hunter/hero Fadama from Dia. In the Boso youth association performances, the singing of the panegyric for Fadama establishes a link among all Boso communities who trace their origins from Dia through the line of master Boso hunters beginning with Fadama. The panegyric ends with the names of hunter ancestors from the community holding the performance.

3. Pageard's suggestion that the theatre evolved from rituals may have resulted from his unwitting conflation of the term Do bò, the name fishermen regularly give to their youth association masquerades, with the term Do, the name of a men's initiation association. Do is an association found to the south and west of the Segou region. The term Jo is also used for men's initiation associations, including Kòmò and Nama. In and around present-day Bougouni, however, Jo refers specifically to one particular men's initiation association still extant in that area (Ezra 1983; Meurillon 1992). Contrary to Pageard's assertion, in the Segou region people always stated that the Do bò theatre and the Do and Jo men's associations had quite different origins and histories.

4. Most ethnographic research up until quite recently regarded the men's initiation associations as the most important site for the production and transfer of knowledge in Bamana society. Zahan, however, recognized, if only in a footnote in his study of the Ntomo and Kòrè men's associations, that people's access to knowledge in Bamana communities had never been restricted to participation in the men's secret societies. Zahan specifically cites the kamalen ton and its masquerades, the sogow, as an important context for the production of knowledge (Zahan 1960, 12n3). Recent work by Grosz-Ngate among the Bamana in the Segou region also clearly demonstrates how important notions of personhood and gender are maintained and manifested not only in rituals but in activities of everyday life (Grosz-Ngate 1989).

5. McNaughton noted in his study of Kòmò that early ethnographers like Henry recognized an important distinction among the various men's associations and the production of their masquerade performances that was often overlooked in later studies. The masquerades and objects associated with Kòmò, Nama, Nya, and Kònò were considered to be boliw, while those associated with Ntomo and Kòrè were not power objects (McNaughton 1979, 5). Many observers have reported that the Ntomo and Kòrè masquerades and the masquerades used in the Jo initiation society in Bougouni, south of Segou, like those used in the youth puppet theatre, were displayed publicly and their performances were designated as nyènajèw (Henry 1910; Monteil 1976 (1924); Zahan 1960; Ezra 1983). Despite the inclusion of *nyènajè fènw*, amusing things, within the public ceremonies of these men's associations' rites, it is the sacrifices that took place away from public view that link Ntomo, Kòrè, and Jo to other men's associations like Kòmò and Kònò and that separates them from the youth association events.

6. Although my own research was not directed to the study of boliw or to men's initiation associations, I found that when the topic came up in conversation people generally lowered their voices, their body attitudes changed, and they often appeared nervous and often changed the subject. On one occasion I showed a photograph of a Kòmò mask to a male friend in the village. He recoiled and asked how I knew of these things. I quickly changed the subject. Later, while walking with him to a neighboring village, we were conversing in normal tones when he hesitated slightly and then quietly informed me that we were passing a Kòmò shrine. He cautioned me several times not to look openly in the shrine's direction.

Later, in 1987 I stopped to ask directions at a village off the main road. I noticed that no women or children were about and that a group of elder men were gathered around a mask. I stayed my distance while my Bamana male colleague approached the group. When we were driving away, he told me that the men had been preparing a Nama mask for the annual performance of the association in this village.

7. The Manyan masquerade in Kirango was described as a horse and rider figure. Père Bailleul defines the term *manyan* as a type of boli or power object (Bailleul 1981, 137).

8. In a community near Kirango, a bird masquerade known as Kirina Kònò was a boli and like Manyan it had been played every seven years during the annual puppet festival until the 1970s. Its dalilu was said to have been originally obtained from a blacksmith living in the Mande heartland to the south. A consortium of seven men comprised of a blacksmith and the village chief along with five of their descendants were the owners of the masquerade and its secret. According to one surviving member of this group, the original puppet dated from between 1920 and 1930. Kirina Kònò is no longer played in this

village today. The reason given for its demise was that four of the original members of the group who had controlled the secret were now deceased and the remaining three members were scattered. They have chosen not to initiate any of their descendants into the masquerade's secrets.

9. Soleillet's late nineteenth century account describes the entry of the bird masquerade into the village by boat. This is a common convention in fishermen's performances, although in a few instances farmers living along the river team up with their fishermen neighbors to bring the masquerades to the village by boat. Because of the early date of Soleillet's account, he was most probably witnessing a fishermen's rather than a farmers' performance.

10. Secrecy surrounds most esoteric knowledge and activities within Segou communities. During my research people often expressed concern that I wanted to discover their secrets. However, when I assured them that I was not at all interested in the content of secrets, people were not reluctant to talk about secrecy as a concept and they frequently made distinctions between orders of secrets. There is secret knowledge that is the exclusive purview of individuals and of groups of men or women. There are whole bodies of technological and esoteric knowledge that belong to particular professional groups, e.g., blacksmiths, bards, and fishermen. The association of knowledge with secrecy, and by extension the implication for understanding notions of power and the transmission of knowledge from past to present, has been the topic of many studies throughout Africa. In the case of puppet theatre, secrecy, as I came to understand it, concerned the rights sanctioned by tradition over the ownership of the theatre, sometimes expressed in ownership rights over the theatre's material repertoire. In the context of youth association puppet theatre, current and former male members of the association own the actual masquerades. They store, prepare, and perform them. Even though men recognize that women are essential members of the performance team, women along with children and strangers do not have a claim on the masks and masquerades nor do they have the right to recite the masquerade history.

11. The term *Cèko* for the youth theatre has been in use in the eastern portion of the Segou region since at least the mid 1930s. In 1934–35 F. H. Lem collected examples of theatrical sculptures in the eastern portion of the region and noted that they were used in the annual ceremonies of the "Ntieko" (Lem 1949, 39).

12. In Liger's ethnography he uses the term Sorko as the global designation for fishermen living along the Niger from south of Segou to Lake Debo. It is interesting that his only account of a masquerade performance was from the Segou region (Ligers 1964, I: 134–135). In 1979 when I discussed the Segou Boso's claim with Bernhard Gardi, a Swiss ethnographer who has worked extensively in the Mopti region, he confirmed that the puppet masquerade was not performed by fishermen in and around Mopti.

13. The generally accepted dates given by historians for the rise of the Coulibaly dynasty fall within the first half of the eighteenth century not the seventeenth century. See *Grandes Dates du Mali*, which lists Biton Coulibaly's reign as 1712–1755 (Konare and Konare 1983, 230).

14. The dates given for Da Monzon Diarra's reign are taken from *Grandes Dates du Mali* (Konare and Konare 1983, 231).

15. *Rapport Politique Annuel Soudan*, 1940. National Archives of Senegal. 2G 40, 10.

16. According to interviews I conducted in Nienou in 1987, most Bobo communities in the eastern zone did not embrace the theatre until after Malian independence from the French in 1960.

17. Siriman Fane dated the carving of his first puppet to the birth of his older brother's son, Moussa. During the interview he showed me Moussa's carte d'identite listing Moussa's date of birth as 1925.

18. Moussa Traore was the President of Mali from 1968 to 1991. He was overthrown by the military as a result of a popular uprising in 1991.

19. I have avoided using the English kinship terms uncle and nephew where they do not accurately express Bamana kinship relations. I have chosen instead the somewhat awkward phrase elder brother's sons when speaking of the relationships between Siriman and Bafing, Saliya, and Moussa, and sister's son when speaking of Siriman's relationship with Manyan Kumare. Bafing, Saliya, and Moussa, who are related to Siriman through the male line, addressed him as *fa*. This term translates as father in English. Manyan, who is Siriman's sister's son, addressed Siriman as his *benke*, a term that translates as uncle in English.

20. Some of the earliest Bamana pieces to arrive in Europe were Ntomo masks, Ciwara headdresses, twin figures, and other figurative statues (Paudrat 1984 I: 128). Manyan Kumare recalled that he had also carved a Ciwara crest mask for a colonial administrator.

21. The smiths at Nienou provided the following list (from eldest to most junior) of the principal blacksmiths in each generation who had been or are presently active in the production of puppet sculp-

ture for both Nienou's theatre and for neighboring communities. There are two quarters in the village and the blacksmiths were resident in both quarters. Sculptors include 1) Marou Diarra; 2) Nuomana Ballo and Komassa Konate; 3) Zuomana Soni; 4) Youssouf Diarra; 5) Ali Diarra; 6) Numu Jon Diarra; 7) Beni Koni. Several of these sculptors were active at the same time. In 1978 when I interviewed Youssouf Diarra many of his sculptures were still extant in the theatre, although he claimed to have quit carving by 1965. In 1978 Numu Jon Diarra was considered the premier sculptor in his quarter. When I revisited Nienou in 1987 Numu Jon Diarra and Beni Kone were actively carving. Another sculptor, Tenbaba Konate, was also producing sculptures.

22. Interviews at Ngarababougou, Tiebala, Shianro, and Berta in 1980. Interview with Numu Jon Diarra at Nienou, 1987.

23. Interview with Ishaka Coumare, son of Bina Fatouma Coumare. Koulikoro, 1987.

24. It was clear in talking with Siriman Fane and with Numu Jon Diarra that access to certain categories of sculptures that are constituted as boliw was still highly restricted. Whether access to the carving of theatrical sculptures was as open in the past as it clearly is today was never adequately addressed in my conversations with smiths. I can only state that by the late 1970s there were no restrictions on women or children watching any of the smiths carving the theatrical sculptures. In fact, Numu Jon said that he had been invited in the 1980s to set up his atelier at the National Museum in Bamako to demonstrate his artistry.

25. When I commissioned a set of Numu Jon Diarra's puppets for the Smithsonian in 1987, he expressed only one concern about their future exhibition. He asked that when they were exhibited they remain fully costumed, so that the public could not see their operating mechanisms.

26. Official government-sponsored arts and sports festivals began in 1962 and took place annually until 1967 (Hopkins 1965). After the coup d'etat that overthrew Modibo Keita, Moussa Traore's government instituted a biennial arts and sports competition under the direction of the reorganized Ministry of Arts, Sports, Youth, and Culture. These competitions were held through 1988. The 1990 festival was not held because of widespread political unrest. The Traore government was ousted in 1991, but it is not yet clear if these festivals will be resumed.

27. Several films have been made over the last decade of the youth association masquerades. The National Museum in Mali produced a film of a performance near Koulikoro entitled *Manifestations du Dò de Jarabugu*. Another film entitled *Sogow* was made by the anthropologist/filmmaker Jean Colleyn. This film includes sequences from several performances in and around Kirango. The National Museum of African Art, Smithsonian Institution, included footage of a youth association masquerade performance from Nienou in its film *Toguna and Cèko*.

28. Personal communication. Barbara Hoffman, 1990.

29. The official history of the Kirango Bamana theatre was given to me by Moussa Nakamissa Coulibaly. Coulibaly was designated by the youth association as its official historian. I did extensive interviews with him in 1980 and again in 1987. According to his accounts, the first promoter of the masquerade in the quarter was from his family. He himself was the ton leader around the period of Independence in 1960. This official history was not wholly uncontested by younger men who attended the interviews. They privately disagreed with Coulibaly about when certain masquerades had been introduced, especially those introduced after Moussa Coulibaly had retired from the association. The reconstruction of the masquerade list takes into account the younger men's information about post-1960 masquerades.

30. In one Boso community the elders said the character Falakani was not a bush animal at all, but was an imaginary masquerade that was intended to represent an old dance once performed by young men among these fishermen. They took special delight in the fact that their farming neighbors did not understand what this masquerade represented.

31. For an in-depth discussion of the integration of Sama and surrounding villages into a cash economy and the resulting shifts in social practices see Grosz-Ngate 1986, 72–111.

32. Interviews in Kirango with Manyan Kumare and Dunamari Kumare in June 1987.

33. The Kirango troupe identified the puppet head used on the Karankaw masquerade as a representation of a giraffe. Out of the back of this giraffe, small rod and string puppets emerge. These small figures include the farmer with his hoe, women pounding millet, the colonial officer on horseback, and the water genie, among others. This masquerade is always performed during the afternoon and another giraffe rod puppet is used during the evening performances.

3. The Sogo bò's Expressive Forms

1. McNaughton published two articles that examined the distribution of the horizontal mask type in West and Central Africa. He presented a wealth of visual evidence regarding these masks and extensive ethnographic documentation concerning the historical interactions among various groups within this larger zone. His work suggests the strong possibility of a complex art history for this mask form across both time and space (McNaughton 1991, 1992).

2. Up until the kawule performances were abandoned sometime in the early to mid 1980s, the four original grass masquerades were never played in the spring festival. Other masks and rod puppet characters that were defined as binsogo, however, were regularly played in both seasons. I noticed in the 1987 spring festival, and again in 1992, that the four original grass masquerades were now being played in the evening segment of the spring theatre. Their inclusion in the spring festival marks a change from the theatrical practices that had been current in 1978 when I first began my research in Kirango.

3. While this distinction still holds for Kirango, it is not universal throughout Segou. In several neighboring villages, cloth masquerades representing people and grass masquerades representing bush animals regularly appear together in evening performances.

4. The word maa is the word for person among Bamana speakers in the Segou dialect, although today it is often used interchangeably with the Bamana word mògò, used in the Bamako dialect. The Bamako dialect has become the standard for the Bamana language and is used on the radio, on television, and in literacy programs.

5. Brink noted that in Kotèba youth theatre in the Beledougou, troupes were restricted from using boliw in their performances although the actual skits could allude to their existence as part of the universe of power and knowledge in the Bamana world. Similarly in the Kirango Boso performances I attended, power objects were not used in the reenactments of the hunting scene, but clear and direct allusions to hunters' manipulation of power objects as part of their universe of knowledge and skill were made.

6. Although I never saw Mèrèn performed in a village Sogo bò, I did attend a performance of a Mèrèn body puppet in 1979 that was sponsored by the Malian government. This performance was part of a cultural exchange between local Sogo bò troupes and a visiting French puppet troupe. The performance was held at the government reception center in Markala. The puppet was carved with the traditional sagittal crest hairdo and was painted black.

7. Identifications of the animals were provided by hunters and other people in the community and correlated when possible with information from the following published sources: Père Charles Bailleul, Petit Dictionnaire Bambara-Français, Français-Bambara, 1981; Moussa Travélé, Petit Dictionnaire Français-Bambara et Bambara-Français, 1954; D. C. D. Happold, Large Mammals of West Africa, 1973; A. H. Booth, Small Mammals of West Africa 1960; and W. Serle, G. J. Morel, W. Hartwig, A Field Guide to the Birds of West Africa, 1980.

8. There are a few documented cases of voiced masquerades. Around Kita in the Bamako region puppets are reported to speak during the performances. According to these accounts the puppeteer uses a voice modifier to distort the character's voice and an interpreter accompanies its performance and translates its speech for the audience (Darkowska-Nidzgorska and N'Diaye 1977, 15). However, in Segou I did not find any troupes using these voice modifiers with the masquerades.

9. Personal Communication from Barbara Hoffman, 1987.

10. Besides the various local power masquerades that I documented in and around Kirango, Youssouf Cisse published a study of a masquerade in Sansanding known as Ba kara. According to Cisse, there are male and female versions of the mask in the form of bovine. These bovine are the mounts for the "Esprit divin" (Cisse 1987, 49). According to a Boso man I interviewed in 1980 in Sansanding, Ba kara was an old masquerade in their quarter, but from my own survey of villages in the surrounding area, the character was not part of any other village's repertoires. People in other villages knew of this character and did recognize it as an old and powerful masquerade. It had until 1979 been performed during the Sogo bò theatre during kawule. It was not considered the property of the kamalen ton, and the mask remained under the control of the elders. I was told in 1979 that the sculpture had been stolen the previous year from Sansanding.

11. Père Bailleul translates Bònjalan as the name for both the young men's acrobatic dance and its drum rhythm (Bailleul 1981, 21).

12. In McNaughton's study of Mande blacksmiths he summarizes the various interpretations that have been given to the concept of nyama, including definitions by Henry, Monteil, Cisse, and Bird, among others. While these various definitions differ in whether they include both living beings as well as inorganic substances as having nyama, they all essentially define nyama as life force or energy (McNaughton 1988, 17).

13. In Kirango in June 1987, both the Dajè puppet and the Ciwara crests were performed in the festival.

14. Because there is very little puppet sculpture extant from the early part of this century, it is not clear if these two different approaches to the representations of animals have always existed parallel to one another and if they were conditioned by their distinctive contexts. While some youth association sculptures do combine these animal and human features, it was rare in the villages where I worked [Figure 3.33; also see Arnoldi 1977, illustrations 35 and 37].

4. Time, Timing, and the Performance Process

1. The expansion of the spring festival in the mid 1950s coincides with the period when the quarter abandoned its men's initiation associations, both Ntomo and Kòmò. The demise of the men's associations may have been the catalyst for the expansion of the youth association festivals; however, no one ever made a causal link between these two events.

2. Elders stated that in the past the all-night vigil took place in the compound of the Bamana village chief. Formerly, it was attended by the entire quarter. As the population increased, this was no longer practical. Today the youth association stages and participates in the all-night musical event.

3. A number of film crews, both national and international, have negotiated with individual villages to perform the theatre outside of its customary time. The Center for African Art in New York has for several years conducted art study tours to Mali and they have regularly arranged for a performance with a village near Koulikoro in January or February. A film team from the National Museum of African Art in conjunction with the National Museum of Mali arranged to film the Cèko in Nienou in 1988. The filming took place in early May. This is somewhat earlier than the regular performance period. Other villages who had been approached declined, partially because they were still heavily engaged in farming activities.

In February of 1979, the French Cultural Center in Bamako arranged a performance exchange between French puppeteers and youth association troupes from around Markala. The performances were given at the government reception center in Markala and I attended with a number of ton members from Kirango. None of them considered these performances to be real theatre.

4. In 1992 the government agencies adopted a new standard work week. People now work only from Monday through Friday. Prior to 1992, people worked a full day from Monday through Thursday and a half day on Friday and Saturday mornings.

5. Unlike Kirango, more rural villages often face a different and more serious dilemma. In those villages whose residents do not regularly enjoy access to local wage labor opportunities, young men are becoming increasingly involved in long-distance labor migrations. These migrations now take them out of the village for longer and longer periods of time. Colonial archival records and many personal narratives make clear that seasonal labor migration is hardly a new phenomenon in the Segou region. Large numbers of men have participated in dry season labor migration throughout the past century. However, unlike today's migrants, who regularly stay away for years at a time, men formerly did not leave their villages until after the harvest and they returned well before the rainy season in time to prepare the fields and participate in the new agricultural season. Thus, the necessary contingent of young men was regularly on hand in the transitional seasons to organize and perform the masquerade theatre. Today, many villages, whose young men are migrating for extended periods of time, are finding it difficult to mount their annual Sogo bò theatre.

Not only is increased labor migration affecting the theatre, but, as Grosz-Ngate noted, it has also begun to alter the timing of other important social events, such as weddings. Formerly, most weddings took place during the dry season, but increasingly they are being planned for the rainy season, when more of the groom's age-mates will have returned to the village from labor migrations (Grosz-Ngate 1986, 208).

6. Training through direct bodily manipulation is analogous to that described by Bateson and Mead for Balinese children (Bateson and Mead 1942).

7. Kris Hardin describes an altercation between two young Kono girls, who were then ridiculed by older women because of their lack of emotional control (Hardin 1987, 186–187).

8. The attainment of personhood is progressive in an individual's life. Maria Grosz-Ngate discusses how personhood is manifest in different mortuary rituals and in the times set aside for condolences for infants, adolescents, and adults (Grosz-Ngate 1989, 172–173). Babies and young children have yet to be incorporated into society and therefore the time of public condolences is extremely short, lasting only the morning of the burial.

9. Both young men and women can play the role of clown at these performances, and these roles are not restricted to particular classes in the society. In the 1979, 1980, and 1987 performances I attended in the Kirango Bamana quarter, several young men and women played this role. At the 1992 spring performance in Kirango, there was a group of women who were dressed in tattered clothes with empty tin cans and assorted other objects attached to their costumes. They carried rattles and other small homemade percussive instruments. They congregated in front of the women's section and periodically they would jump into the dance arena and surround the drum team and dance enthusiastically, often breaking into ribald and bawdy dances. They were called kòrèdugaw, clowns. The obligation to perform as clowns passes through specific families from every strata of society. Playing the clown can fall to either men or women in the family. What if any historical relationship there is between the men and women who take the role of kòrèdugaw in the masquerade performance and the kòrèdugaw adherents that Zahan discusses in his study of the Kòrè men's society is not clear (Zahan 1960).

10. Both Bafing Kane's grandson and Numu Jon Diarra's son showed me small masks which they had carved themselves and which they used to play at masquerade theatre.

5. Bringing the Past into the Present in Masquerade Theatre

1. H. Bazin translated the word si as peuple, race, generation. (H. Bazin 1914, 530). Père Bailleul translates si as race, espece, nature, sens, descendance (Bailleul 1981, 185). I have often heard people use the term siya to refer to the abstract concept of group or ethnic identity.

The anthropological literature on ethnicity is now so vast that it is impossible to cite it fully here. While there are theoretical disagreements about the approach to the study of ethnicity, most scholars agree that ethnic identity is situationally constructed. In this study of ethnicity and puppet performances I am using Anya Royce's definitions of ethnic group and ethnicity. According to Royce, "An 'ethnic group' is a reference group invoked by people who share a common historical style (which may be only assumed), based on overt features and values, and who, through the process of interaction with others, identify themselves as sharing that style. . . . 'Ethnicity' is simply ethnic based action" (Royce 1982, 18).

2. One of the best recent discussions of these processes for Mali is Jean Bazin's essay on the "Bamana." In this essay he outlines the history of the nomenclature Bamana and Bambara, the variation in meanings through time, and the often contradictory feelings and values associated with the nomenclature held by both Malians and outsiders. He demonstrates how this term was and is still used by a variety of actors in different spaces and contexts as a means of marking themselves as part of this group or to distinguish those they call the Bamana or Bambara as the "Other." He provides a variety of examples which demonstrate that the nomenclature Bamana or Bambara is a relative and not absolute category and that it provides actors with a body of practical knowledge which allows them to organize their action within a social space—a social space that exists in time (J. Bazin 1985).

The final section of his essay details the reconstruction of the invention of "the Bamana" as an absolute entity fixed in time and space by ethnologists working under the auspices of the colonial administration. He identifies Maurice Delafosse's work in the first decades of this century as the "founding text" for all the "bambarologie" to come (J. Bazin 1985, 114). The nomenclature "the Bamana" (later modified to "the Bambara" by Tauxier and consistently used as the preferred term in ethnology until recently when the term "the Bamana" again took precedence) and the spatial delimitation of the group became part of the existing ethnological taxonomy and have generally been uncritically repeated in most ethnographies well into the present. See also Maria Grosz-Ngate's study for an excellent analysis of the ethnographic construction of the Bamana (Grosz-Ngate 1986, 1–26).

3. For further information on the precolonial era in the Western Sudan see the following sources: Al-Sa'di 1964 (1900); Ba and Daget 1962; Brown 1969; Hunwick 1972; Levtzion 1963, 1972; Levtzion and Hopkins 1981; Mahmud K't Ibn al-Mutawakkil K't 1964 (1913–1914); Marty 1927; Mauny 1954, 1961; Monteil 1929, 1953, 1971 (1932), 1976 (1924); Niane 1965; Pageard 1961a, 1961b, 1964; Park 1799; Roberts 1978, 1980, 1988; Tauxier 1930a, 1930b, 1942; Willis 1972.

4. According to some Boso groups in Segou, fishermen living from Segou to Myeru on the Niger River are called Kelenko Boso, while those from Konkuru north to Lake Debo are referred to as Jibala Boso. The Jibala Boso, or Jila Boso (on the water Boso), refers to fishing groups known in the north as the Sorko. Sorko are seminomadic fishermen who live in temporary fishing camps along the Niger. These seminomadic fishermen are sometimes called Bosofin by Boso groups living in Segou. All agree that the Bosofin are the great hunters of the crocodile, the hippopotamus, and the sea cow. Segou Boso also distinguish between the Jila Boso and the Gerenkan Boso (on the high ground Boso). The latter are Boso groups who live in permanent settlements and who now practice some farming as well as fishing.

Segou Boso distinguished four dialects of Boso. From Segou to Kokri fishermen speak a dialect known as Kelenkokan; from Ke-Macina to Myeru they speak Fenonkokan; and from Djenne to Gao they speak Djennekan. Djennekan is said to be a mixture of Songhay, Soninke, and Boso, and the dialect reflects the particular social history of this area. Djennekan is spoken by both Boso and Sòmonò, and people said it was the Boso dialect most often heard on contemporary Radio Mali broadcasts. To the west, in and around the area of Dia and Diafarabe, fishermen speak Diakakan, which they claimed was the authentic Boso language. Such claims were made by Boso who traced their origins to the area around Diafarabe. Interestingly, the term Boso, according to folk etymologies, is a Bamana term, and Segou Boso construction of the nomenclature for the Boso dialects combines geographical location with the Bamana word *kan*, language (Interviews with Banankoro Boso in 1980).

5. These Boso's claim to descent from Wagadu is expressed in terms of a protohistorical kinship relationship with the Soninke and is encapsulated in a classic elder brother–younger brother myth. According to one recounting, the Boso and the Soninke were once of the same family, but following a dispute between two brothers, they split. The eldest brother and his descendants, the present-day Boso, retained their original occupation as fishermen, while the younger brother and his descendants, the Soninke, became the rulers of Wagadu and long-distance traders throughout the area. The retelling of this tradition bolsters the Boso's assertion of primacy by virtue of their birth position as elder brothers to the Soninke, their belief that fishing is the original occupation of all mankind, and their claim to a certain symbolic cache through their historical relationship to the Soninke rulers of the great medieval state.

6. In one version, it was the Keita rulers of Mali who gave the Boso from Ke-Macina to Lake Debo the title of *jitigi*, owner of the water (Dieterlen 1957, 135). Another legend, which I collected in a Boso community in Segou, recalls how their ancestors living around Dia received their family names. During the reign of Tarawele Mansa, who is said to have ruled sometime prior to the foundation of the Segou state in the early eighteenth century, groups of fishermen were regularly called to fish for the state. One day, in the process of hauling in the catch, they landed a *faroden*, a child of Faro, the water genie. They took their prize to the Tarawele court, and the ruler demanded to know who had caught the genie. Since the fishermen had no family names, the Mansa decreed that whatever part of the genie each of the fishermen had hauled into the boat, this part would from that day forward become his family name. Thus the Boso lineages became known as Serata, the foot, Centa, the trunk, Konta, the neck, Tomata and Farota, the head. Tarawele Mansa then asked who had led the fishing party, and to this man he gave the surname Karabenta. In many Boso communities living along the Niger River in the Segou region, it is a member of the Karabenta lineage who still holds the title of jitigi, owner of the water (Interview with Budagari Coulibaly, Banankoro, 1980).

7. In Kare Tammoura's recitation of the history of the Segou state, recorded and published by Monteil, the bard related that during the reign of Da Monzon Diarra the ruler placed two hundred heads of Boso families between Konkonkuru and Djenne and resettled the Boso living from Dina to Kangaba in and around Mopti (Monteil 1976 [1924], 96).

8. Richard Roberts noted that while French colonial laws outlawed slavery, French administrators rarely actively engaged in abolishing the practice. It was only in the first decades of the twentieth cen-

tury that slaves themselves began the exodus from their masters in ever-increasing numbers. Those that remained renegotiated their relationships with their former masters (Roberts 1988, 282–307).

9. Gomitogo was the village cited in the Boso legend about the origin of puppet masquerades and Shianro is still called the sogo jamani, the country of the masquerades.

10. One etymology of the term Sòmonò given by a group of elders states: *An sommina monnike in na sa an te se ka far'a la*, We have understood the importance of fishing and we cannot abandon it. Boso fishermen, however, say of these Sòmonò, *Jirikuran ti ke bama ye*, A log in the river does not become a crocodile. According to the Boso, a person must be born a Boso to be Boso, but anyone can become a Sòmonò. Thus both Boso and Sòmonò recognize that the continual assimilation of outsiders into Sòmonò ranks through their adoption of fishing as their primary activity is an explicit process of Sòmonò group formation (Interviews with Boso and Sòmonò elders in the Segou region, 1980).

11. In the history of the Segou Bamana state, bards often open their accounts with the lines *Segu dugu naani ani maraka dugu konoto, o ye Segu ye*, Four Segou villages and nine Maraka villages, this is Segou (Dumestre 1979, 62–63). Much of the history of the formation and consolidation of the Bamana Segou contained in the epic deals with efforts to bring the Maraka commercial communities under the Coulibaly and Diarra dynasties' control. Once this was accomplished, the Segou warrior state and the commercial cities became mutually interdependent. Imports of firearms and taxes on commercial activities provided the state with the means and revenue for maintaining and reproducing itself. The state through warfare and raiding provided the commercial interests with slaves both for export and for labor in the production of cloth and grain, which were important Maraka commercial products, and the state established a certain stability throughout the areas they controlled and provided security for the movement of goods and people along the commercial routes (Roberts 1978, 22–64). In the war between El Hadji Oumar Tall and the Segou State in 1861, it was the Maraka city of Sansanding [Sinzani] that betrayed Segou and offered the Toucouleur armies a base of operation for their invasion of Segou.

12. According to the seventeenth-century chronicle from Timbuctou, the *Tarikh es-Soudan*, the Traores were already established as chiefs in the Segou region during the period of Mali's suzerainty over the area (Pageard 1961a, 78). For example, the Traore family has governed in Shianro since at least the early eighteenth century and it traces its descent from a hunter who migrated from the Manden (Interview in Shianro, 1980). In the epics of Mali, the Traores have always played an important role. They were the rulers of the chiefdoms of Kiri which predated the consolidation of the Mali empire by Sunjata Keita. Within the Segou region, Traore chiefs in the villages of Kamia, Fara, Niaro, Sibila, and Sokolo claim descent from Touran Maghan Traore, one of Sunjata's most able and loyal military commanders.

13. In several villages around Kirango, Bamanan troupes have "borrowed" the Boso character Koon. A number of these troupes defined the character as *k'a ye*, an imaginary animal, rather than as *sogo*, a real animal. The Boso, however, identify Koon specifically as a roan antelope, although most of the Bamana troupes did not identify it with the roan antelope character Dajè, which they play regularly in their theatres.

14. I conducted a series of interviews in this community in 1978–80 and again in 1987 and in 1989. Participants in these interviews included both farmers and fishermen. The village youth association cuts across the ethnic divisions, yet in the production of the theatre a shared community identity is played against the backdrop of these ethnic differences. Unlike Kirango, where farmers' and fishermen's performances are completely separate, this village suggested that a positive value is given to ethnic rivalry within their theatre and it is based on the performers' perceptions of ethnic competition as critical to the maintenance of a desirable aesthetic edge.

15. According to this popular legend, after a young man killed the sacred python, the Ghana empire was destroyed and its people were dispersed throughout the Western Sudan.

16. The three founding Sòmonò lineages in Kirango are memorialized in the names of the three Sòmonò quarters: Thierola, Konela, and Danbelela. Among the Sòmonò the Thiero retain the title of jitigi, owner of the water.

17. In 1987 and in 1992 when I attended the June performances in Kirango, several men in the youth association performed a lengthy song more in the style of the Boso bards than in the style of the Bamana women's chorus. While it has always been true that the attendants for a particular masquerade sing its song as they lead it into the plaza, between 1978 and 1980 as soon as the women's chorus began singing the men relinquished the song to them. In the 1992 performance, rather than relinquishing the song to the women the men approached the microphones and continued to perform for an extensive period. When the women's chorus did finally take over the song, the chorus increased the

tempo of the singing to mesh more closely with the tempo the drummers had already established for the masquerade performance. People explained that in the past it was not uncommon for a talented male singer to perform during the event. It is noteworthy that the male singers in the 1987 and 1992 performances I attended were not griots.

18. The dog is the most common sacrificial animal used in Kòmò rites. One of the men told me that the goat had been substituted for the dog out of respect for the sensibilities of the majority of people in the quarter, who are practicing Muslims.

19. Ligers recorded a number of adages that express the Boso's strong association with fishing and its central role in their group identity. They include: The Sorko exist for fish; The duty of Sorko men is fishing; the duty of Sorko women is to prepare the fish; and The Sorko cannot live without water (Ligers 1964, II: xi; my translations).

20. Modibo Keita was removed from office in a coup d'etat in 1968. Moussa Traore, then a young officer, took control and remained the head of state until 1991, when he was deposed by the military following a series of popular uprisings.

21. Both D'Azevedo and Appadurai discuss various formal constraints on the manipulation of history in the present. Appadurai notes that while anthropologists generally accept that discourse about the past involves competition, opposition, and debate, he is concerned with how that debate is culturally organized. While norms that regulate the debates about the past certainly vary from culture to culture, he has suggested that at the most general level all cultures must reach a consensus in terms of at least four minimal formal criteria: authority, continuity, depth, and interdependence (Appadurai 1981, 202–203). These constraints are certainly evident in Mande approaches to history where ownership of certain pasts is held by different segments of society and issues of authority, continuity, depth, and interdependence do regulate the production of these histories in different social settings.

6. The Production of Meaning and the Play of Interpretations

1. I am limiting my remarks in this section to the Bamana for several reasons. First, I worked extensively in the Bamana quarter of Kirango and with other Bamana and Maraka communities who share a similar notion of personhood and of social relationships. My data on Sòmonò and Boso communities are less complete, although according to the literature and from my own field work these communities do not include an equivalent nyamakala group. In all these communities public discussions of slave descent are considered inappropriate and are generally carefully avoided except in certain ritual contexts. What all of these groups do share, however, are similar beliefs about the roles and capacities of different age groups and of different genders.

2. The problem of translation emerges in discussions of hòròn and nyamakala. Hòròn has been regularly translated as nobles although there is no corresponding group of people that are commoners. In the context of the political epics of Western Sudanic states, hòròn lineages were the ruling class, and in most villages in the Segou region today only hòròn can assume the role of dugutigi, literally owner of the village or village chief. Nyamakala have been regularly described as casted groups and most accounts identify three separate subgroups within the nyamakala strata: jeli (griot or bard), numu (blacksmith), and garange (leatherworker). Garangew, while they are sometimes included in local categories of Bamana nyamakala, regularly associate themselves with Soninke, not Bamana (Frank 1988).

Viviana Pâques identified the Sòmonò as a casted group, but few people I interviewed in the Segou region considered the Sòmonò to be nyamakala, although they were seen as a different si from Bamana, Boso, and Maraka, for example. Kule, whose men carve domestic wares such as wooden bowls and plates, but who are best known for fashioning planks for making canoes, and whose women repair calabashes, have sometimes been included in the nyamakala group (McNaughton 1988, 5). While Kule are clearly defined as having a lower status than hòròn, most people I interviewed did not consider them to be nyamakala. Acquisition of a Sòmonò identity is tied to the occupation of fishing, and the diverse origins of Sòmonò are a recognized feature of this group.

3. Wright, following Abadoulaye-Bara Diop, distinguishes between two different systems in operation in Wolof society: one of castes and one of political orders. That there were also two different systems among the Bamana seems to gain credence if we examine social practices. In the system of castes the Wolof geer is analogous to the Mande hòròn. The Wolof ñeño is analogous to the Mande nya-

makala. Within the system of political orders the Wolof geer is analogous to the Mande hòròn and the Wolof jam is analogous to the Mande jòn (Wright 1989, 55n4). Although Bird suggested that caste and the condition of servitude were ideal jural distinctions, caste affiliation seems to have been more fixed than the condition of servitude. Strong marriage prohibitions still exist between hòròn and nyamakala castes, and people still declare their caste affiliation openly. Although slavery was legally abolished in the early twentieth century, even today the public discussion of an individual's or a lineage's slave origins rarely occurs, except in certain ritual contexts, and is considered unseemly. There is, however, anecdotal evidence that in the past both jòn women and jòn men passed out of servitude into either the hòròn or nyamakala castes. If a hòròn man took a slave wife, her children were considered to be hòròn. Bird and Kendall note that one avenue for accession of slaves into nyamakala status has always been through smithing or bardship (Bird and Kendall 1980, 25n4).

4. While early ethnographers often described nyamakala as a despised class, this characterization echoes the ambivalence that hòròn regularly express about nyamakala. More recently a number of scholars have worked extensively with nyamakala groups and have analyzed the relationship between hòròn and nyamakala from a nyamakala perspective (Hoffman 1990; Kendall 1982; McNaughton 1988; Wright 1989).

5. Jeli remain important public voices for the transmission of news and announcements, the official spokesmen for parties involved in negotiations, mediators in disputes, witnesses at every important life ritual, and society's premier verbal and musical artists. They recite genealogies, sing praises, compose and perform poetry and stories, and provide specialized musical and dance entertainment during public celebrations. The recitation or singing of genealogies and praises of heroic deeds is considered one of the most potent and nyama-laden of their specialized activities.

Numu men and women are Bamana society's technological specialists and its premier material artists. Numu men are smelters, smiths, and wood carvers and numu women are potters. Numu men and women play a critical role in circumcision and excision, nyama-laden activities by which children are transformed from androgynous beings into fully male or female persons. Numu men are also the leaders of the powerful Kòmò men's association.

6. Certain Boso and Sòmonò masquerade performances stand in sharp contrast to those of the Bamana. During Boso and Sòmonò performances a male bard can be invited to sing lineage praises for past heroic deeds. These songs are sung for a small category of lineage-owned masquerades. Although these singers are recognized as exceptional, they, unlike the Bamana jeli, are not members of any particular segment in Boso or Sòmonò society.

7. Hòròn often describe nyamakala as somaw, sorcerers. McNaughton writes that "*Somaw* often aspire to greatness; they wish to become heroes, *nganaw*, so that their names and deeds will be remembered by the bards and become part of Mande history" (McNaughton 1988, 49). As Kòmòtigi, leaders of the Kòmò men's association, blacksmiths are always considered to be sorcerers (McNaughton 1988, 46). Hoffman writes that "To attain renown as a sorcerer is, for the Mande griot the pinnacle of achievement: *ngara-soma* (master bard-sorcerer) is the highest compliment one can pay a practicing griot" (Hoffman 1989, 6). Nyama-laden activities that require knowledge of secret things, including rainmaking, divining, doctoring, amulet making, etc., are not limited to nyamakala. However, most people believe that nyamakala tend toward these activities by virtue of their birth and their inherited dalilu and by the fact that they can augment this dalilu through professional training (McNaughton 1988, 41–64).

8. After circumcision, a boy moves out of his mother's house and into a room with other boys in the family of relatively the same age. Only when a cèmisèn becomes a kamalen in his later teenage years does he gain the right to build his own house. In the past in non-Islamic communities, boys were generally not circumcised until about the age of fourteen or fifteen. However, today, because most communities now practice Islam, boys are circumcised much earlier than in the past, generally about the age of five to seven. Once a boy is circumcised today, he is no longer referred to as a bilakoro. But even though circumcision is still seen as transforming a boy into a fully male person, he is not properly addressed as a cè, man or kamalen, young man, until he enters the youth association at age fourteen or fifteen.

9. Men's circumcision was performed within the context of initiation rites in the Ntomo. Today, boys are still circumcised, but they undergo the operation at a much earlier age and it is tied into their early Islamic training.

10. Formerly people said that a man's status from kamalen to kòrò changed at the initiation of his first son. In Kirango, between 1978 and 1980 the senior age-set in the kamalen ton were beginning to see their first sons enter the association's junior sets and these senior men began to express their desire to pass out of the kamalen ton. This senior age-set passed out of the association in 1981.

11. Women who were born and married in this quarter participated in the dance, but those married women who were born outside the quarter generally refrained from dancing on this occasion. Women who marry into the quarter can choose to become active participants as singers in the Sogo bò or they can choose not to attend at all. One of my friends, who is a Bamana woman from Bougouni who married into the village, never attended the Sogo bò. One day I asked her why she did not participate in the festival and she stated flatly that these were not her masquerades, songs, or dances. She clearly acted upon her status as dunan, stranger, in the most radical way, by not attending the performances at all.

12. One context where older men who are hunters regularly dance is during the funeral celebrations for other hunters (Cashion 1982, I: 218–220).

13. In discussions of marriage patterns and preferences, for example, one village will refer to neighboring villages with whom they regularly exchange wives as their baden or balima and they describe these marriage exchanges as taking place along balima siraw, kin roads (Grosz-Ngate 1986, 213).

14. The number of years defining each age-set varies from one village to another in the Segou region. In a number of communities it has undergone one or more modifications over the past century.

15. Men in the same age-set come together outside the kamalen ton to create a *furu ton*, a marriage association. Members of this group play various roles in the marriage process, sometimes providing agricultural labor for the bride's family, arranging and participating in the dance entertainment at the marriage celebrations.

16. Although I documented a number of other village associations besides Kirango's who have adopted age-set costumes for their theatre, this is still not a common practice throughout the region. People in Kirango considered this practice to be an expression of their modernity.

17. In the Kirango Bamana ton, a unique restriction can influence the choice of tontigi. In this quarter, no lineal descendant from the Diarra ruling dynasty can be chosen as tontigi even though he may be the oldest member of his age-set. People defined state and village leadership differently and in Kirango they pointed out that no one can be the faama (ruler of the state) and the dugutigi (village chief) at the same time. Although descendants of the tonjòn military class often became the chefs de canton and chefs d'arrondissement under the French colonial regime, they are rarely village chiefs. Tonjòn do not claim to have been founders of villages, only their conquerors. Dugutigi, owners of the village, however, generally trace their descent from the founding lineage. Although the Kirango ton claims a historical relationship with the state, the present association was reconstituted as a village organization after the French occupation. The military class was disbanded and people's orientation shifted away from military and state concerns toward farming and local village affairs. The organizational model for this reconstituted ton was therefore based on the political and jural model for the village, not that of the state. People explained that in order for the descendants of the Diarra dynasty to claim their birthright as rulers of the state, they would have to transcend any single village identity or loyalty. This eliminates them from consideration for the office of leader of the ton.

18. In Lewis's analysis of the Segou data he concluded that the historical importance of these organizations rested with the fact that the ton brought together both precolonial savanna defense requirements and technical and production needs. While the demand for slaves and the conditions of warfare that slaving produced no longer prevail, the demand for young men as migrant laborers is seen as an analogous sort of threat to village security and productivity. Today the Segou ton function through peer pressure to help keep youth in the village as labor rather than encouraging them to seek wage labor abroad (Lewis 1980, 17–18). Although the past and present pressures of environmental constraints, labor needs, and village security requirements explain in part elders' past tolerance of the ton and its persistence in Segou, Grosz-Ngate, myself, and others have observed that in the late twentieth century the increasing demands of a cash economy have weakened the effect of peer pressure to keep young men and young women in the village, especially in smaller rural areas with no easy access to local wage-labor opportunities.

19. While these percentages are based on the age distribution fourteen through forty-four as representative of the social category of kamalen, young men, this interval represents the broadest age spread for inclusion in this category (La République du Mali 1990, 4: 7–9). Thus, the ratio of kamalenw, young men, to cèkòròw, elder men, can change significantly from locale to locale. In Kirango, for instance, the eldest age group included men who were in their early forties. In many other villages, however, the most senior age-set in the youth association consisted of men between the ages of thirty and thirty-four. According to statistical information collected about marriage in this census, men begin to marry in significant numbers between the ages of twenty-five and thirty-five (La République du Mali 1990, 4: 187).

20. In the kamalen ton of the Bamana quarter of Kirango these rights to autonomy of organization and control over activities are explicitly associated with the history of the Segou state. Part of the unique identity of this quarter's kamalen ton arises out of the association's claim to a historical origin within the tonjòn military class. According to oral traditions, Biton Coulibaly, the founder of the empire, organized the original tonjòn, who swore allegiance to the state. Its membership has always been said to have cut across ethnic and social categories. The tonjòn's relationship to the state as described in the traditions was always volatile, and these histories record several periods in which revolts resulted in the deposition of leaders and the rise of new state leaders out of the ranks of the military class. Young men in Kirango invoked this potential for political upheaval that existed in the tonjòn's relationship to state authority when they discussed their rights and their obligations to the elders in the quarter.

Although the jural structure of the ton reproduces that of the village and lineage organization, the Kirango ton's historical claims to tonjòn rights are made explicit in the association's retention of Segou court titles for its officers. In Kirango, the association leader is known as the *faama*, the title of the head of the precolonial Segou state, rather than as the tontigi, the title that is more common throughout the region. The faama is assisted by five officers from the senior age-set who also take court titles: *mabere kanou, moricè, nieni maguele ndjie, yereladi,* and *mbeseri*.

According to people in Kirango, the mabere kanou, the second in command, was a title reserved for the military commander of the jònba, the foot soldiers, who was second to the war chief who headed the sofa, the cavalry. The moricè was a chief advisor of the faama and in the Kirango ton he acts as principal spokesman for the faama on formal occasions. The nieni maguele ndjie acts as an advisor to the faama. The yereladi today functions as the sergeant at arms during formal meetings and assigns various members to specific work details and activity groups, while the mbeseri oversees the youngest age-sets.

21. In Kirango, this age-set takes this role for a period of three years. To what extent this practice is formalized in other communities throughout the region is not exactly clear, although in many villages where I attended performances and conducted interviews, men who enjoyed the status of junior elders did actively participate in the discussions about the organization of the theatre, the history and development of the masquerade repertoire, and the interpretations of the characters, and they were a presence at the performances.

22. In Bamana the proverb reads: *N'i sen wala i bolo y'i bila ko la, i be se ka b'a la. N'ka n'i nen y'i bila ko la, i te se ka bò a la.*

23. Several scholars have suggested that hunters were central to the formation of the warrior classes in the various precolonial states that held sway over this larger region. Oral traditions state that the founders of these empires were themselves hunters and that the military wings of the state were made up of hunters (Bird 1974; Johnson 1978; Meillassoux 1963). Hunters and warriors share a similar ethos that places a high value on assertiveness that is the antithesis of hòrònya. Their domain of action is the bush and not the village and these men are all considered to have acquired extraordinary nya, means.

24. Charles Bird explains: "The Maninka hero ngana is a person totally oriented along the fa-den-ya axis. He considers the social conventions for accommodation, conciliation and expression of respect as barriers to the quest for his true destiny. . . . The hero is asocial, capable of unrestricted cruelty and destructiveness, whose presence is always a threat to the stability of the collectivity. He is, however, perhaps the only member associated with the group who is capable of swift and conclusive action. Through his actions, the hero can enhance the collective reputation of the group and perhaps bring riches to it, even though his motivation is unqualifiedly selfish" (Bird 1974, vii).

25. *Ne sirannin donso-kèlè nye kojugun*
    A don n bolo la, ku don n bolo la
  E bara bila donsokè la
  E kin'i tòrò sènèkè-daba tala
  I ya sènèkè suman tè fèrèn na
    A don n bolo la, ku don n bolo la
  I bara bila donsokè la
  I kin'i tòrò muso furala
  E muso tana kònò ta sanko ka den wolo
    A don n bolo la, ku don n bolo la
(Cashion 1982, II: appendix 2, lines 476–482, pp. 49–50)

In a version of the heroic epic of Famori sung by Seydou Camara, the following verse also attests to the nature of hunters as extraordinary beings (Cashion: 1982, II: appendix 1, lines 80–84, pp. 79–80):

> *Môgô tè se kè donso di boli t'i bolo*
> *I tè kèla donso di lônko t'i la*
> > *Namu . . .*
> *I tè se kè donso di yèlèma t'i la*
> > *Namu . . .*
> *I ta donsoya bara kè lolan di*
> > *Namu . . .*

> He who controls no juju does not become a hunter
> He who has not occult knowledge does not become a hunter
> > Namu . . .
> He who has no changing power does not become a hunter
> > Namu . . .
> Such hunting would not be true hunting
> > Namu . . .

26. During the phase of the marriage ritual when a bride arrives at her husband's household, two women, the bride and an elder woman who is resident in that household, play the principal symbolic roles. When the young bride arrives at the threshold of her husband's compound she symbolizes the outsider. She is dressed in a man's tunic, wears a man's hat, and carries a walking stick, the dress associated with a traveler. The elder woman, who greets her in the vestibule and conducts the welcoming rituals, is the insider. Because of the years that she has labored for her husband's kin group, borne them children, and grown old in this household she symbolizes the culmination of a woman's ideal moral career (Grosz-Ngate 1986, 208).

27. Several practices re-create the outsider status of the musomisèn, young married woman. First, young men who are aligned with the collective efforts of their household and lineage receive no compensation for their agricultural labor. However, musomisènw receive a portion of grain from the harvest as payment for their participation in winnowing, and this is designated as their personal property. This payment continually reproduces their identity as dunanw, strangers. Secondly, Grosz-Ngate observed that young married women also participate in enacting their status as outsider when they "steal" grain from the household harvest after winnowing, while musokòròw, whose interests have merged with the lineage, no longer "steal" grain. Whether or not older women or men disagree with the practice, they are powerless to stop it (Grosz-Ngate 1986, 135).

28. In a neighboring village, the Taasi Dòoni masquerade appeared as a graceful antelope and the message of the song and the masquerade performance did not subvert one another.

29. I was also told that the term mògò dankalen is sometimes used to refer to a sorcerer. McNaughton notes that dankalen can be a praise name for people who have gained a certain renown in sorcery and art (McNaughton 1988, 135, 154).

Adama den   literally, child of Adam; human being

Allah ka jòn   literally, slave of Allah; Muslim

baden   literally, mother's child; full sibling

badenya   solidarity, unity, cooperation

balafon   type of xylophone

balima   kin, relative

balima sira   kin road; alliance based on kinship relations

balimali   recited or sung lineage genealogy

bamada   Bamana men's cap with two points worn front to back

Bamana (Bambara)   ethnic group in south central Mali

Bamanaya   literally, Bamana-ness; Bamana ethnicity

Bara   Bamana dance event

barabara   favorite wife

barika   grace, power or moral force

bee   all, everyone

benke   mother's brother

bilakoro   uncircumcised male

binsogo   grass masquerade

Binsogo bò   name for the Sogo bò performed at the beginning of the dry season

bògòlanfini   Bamana handpainted mud-dyed cotton cloth

boli   power object

boloko fènw   literally, excision things; part of groom's family's marriage payment to bride's family

Bònjalan   Bamana dance event

bònkolo   Bamana drum type

Boso (Bozo)   ethnic group in south central Mali

Bosoya   literally, Boso-ness; Boso ethnicity

buru   animal horn trumpet

cè   man, husband

cèko   literally, affairs of men; in western Segou a general term for men's initiation associations

Cèko   in eastern Segou a name for the youth association puppet masquerade theatre

cèkòrò   elder man

cèkòròba   very elderly man

cèmisèn   young man

cikèla   farmer

cikènumu   blacksmith attached to a farming village

Ciwara   Bamana men's initiation association

cogo   way, manner, method

da   mouth

daba   hoe

Daba bila nyènajè   literally, lay down the hoe entertainment; name for the Sogo bò performed at the beginning of the dry season

Daba taa nyènajè   literally, take up the hoe entertainment; name for the Sogo bò performed to mark the beginning of the rainy season

dalilu   motive, cause, manner of doing something

dalimasigi   hunter's journey of adventure

dankelen   solitary bush animal, e.g., bull elephant or buffalo

Dawòorò   public celebration for young women following excision

dawula   charisma

dembaya   relative living in same household

dembayatigi   head of the household

di   good, sweet, tasty

dibi   dark, obscure

dibikan   specialized speech of diviners

dinònò   honey; formerly part of precolonial tribute

diya   goodness, tastiness

do [gundo]   secret

Do   name of men's initiation society in southern Mali

Do bò   literally, the secret comes forth; fishermen's name for the Sogo bò

Do Mansa   King of Puppets

dògò   junior

dòlò   locally brewed millet beer

dòn   dance

dòn kè   to dance

Dònkan   ceremony that recalls warriors' fealty oaths to the ruler of the precolonial Segou state

dònkili   song
dònkili da   to sing
dònkili da cogo   literally, the way the song is sung; the melody and phrasing of the song
dònsen   dance step
dònsen cogo   literally, the way the dance steps are done; the structure and patterning of a dance
donso ta natananin   hunters' dance
donsokè   hunter
dubatigi   head of the household
dugutigi   village chief or headman
dunan   stranger
dunun   drum
dunun fò   literally, drum speech; to play the drum
dunun fò cogo   literally, the way the drum is played; the structure and patterning of the drumming
dununba   large wooden kettledrum
fa   father, father's brother
faama   leader of precolonial Segou state; in Kirango the term is currently a title for the head of the youth association
faden   literally, father's child; half sibling
fadenya   rivalry, competition
fasa   praise sung or recited by griots
fèrè   public plaza
fini   cloth
Fini tigè nyènajè   literally, fonio cutting entertainment; the name for the Sogo bò performed at the beginning of the dry season
finisogo   cloth masquerade
Fula   an ethnic group throughout West Africa; known variously as Peul or Fulani
furu   to marry
furu sira   marriage road, alliance based on marriage relations
furu ton   marriage association
furusa   divorce
galomuso   bad or unloved wife
garange   also garanke; leatherworker
gèlèn   hard, difficult
gundo [do]   secret
hakili   intelligence
hèrè   luck
hòròn   free person
hòrònya   literally, hòròn-ness; attitudes and behaviors associated with hòròn
jako   embellishments
jalan   dried
jama   crowd, assembly
jamani (jamana)   country
Jara   Boso men's initiation association

jatigi   host
jayan   structure, form
jè   unity, clarity, light
jeli   bard, griot
jelicè   male bard
jelikan   specialized speech of bards
jelimuso   female bard
jeliya   literally, jeli-ness; attitudes and behaviors associated with jeli
jiri (yiri)   tree, wood
jiridòn   the science of trees
jirikun (yirikun)   wooden mask or rod puppet head
jitigi   owner of the water; ritual title
Jo   Bamana men's initiation association
jòn   slave, descendant of slaves
jònba   precolonial infantry
k'a ye   phrase applied to imaginary characters in the Sogo bò
kafo   precolonial term for a military division
kamalen   young man
kamalen ton   literally, young men's association; youth association
kamalen waati   the time of youth
kawule   transitional period between rainy and dry seasons
kèlèko nyènajè   warrior dance
kelen   one
kènèya   suppleness
kènkònò   poison administered in food or drink
kolo   kernel, nut, bone, nucleus
kòlò susu   to process karité nuts in oil
Kòmò   Bamana men's initiation association
Kòmòtigi   leader of the Kòmò association
Kònò   Bamana men's initiation association
kònyò muso   bride
Kòrè   Bamana men's initiation association
kòrèduga   clown
kòrò   old
kòrò waati   literally, the time of elders; old age
Kotèba   satiric theatre
kuma   talk, speech
kuma jè   direct, clear speech
kumatigi   owner of speech; title given to bards
kunanfa   type of cylindrical drum
kura   new
laada   custom, tradition
laansara   Muslim prayer time, about 5:00 P.M.
lenburuji   lemon ginger beverage
maa (mògò)   person
maa sèbè   serious person, title given to elder men and women

maani literally, little person; name for small rod and string puppet representing a person, or a spirit in anthropomorphic form

mabere kanou in precolonial Segou a title for the commander of the infantry; currently a title used in the Kirango Bamana youth association

makiri pity

malo social constraint, shame

malobali without social constraint or shame

mansa ruler, king

Maraka ethnic group in south central Mali

Marakaya literally, Maraka-ness; Maraka ethnicity

maransa hunters' dance

masiri embellishment, decoration

mbeseri court title in precolonial Segou; currently a title used in the Kirango Bamana youth association

miiri reflect, contemplate

mògò (maa) person

mògò dankalen sorcerer

mòni kè to fish

mònikèla fisherman

moricè Islamic advisor to the precolonial Segou court; currently a title used in the Kirango Bamana youth association

murukalatigi owner of the knife handle, ritual title

muso woman, wife

muso nyuman morally good woman

musokòrò elder woman

musokòròba very elderly woman

musomisèn young married woman

Nama Bamana men's initiation association

ngana hero, heroine

nganga small handheld drum

Ngolosi descendants of Ngolo Diarra

nieni maguerle ndjie title in the precolonial Segou court; currently a title used in the Kirango Bamana youth association

npogotigi excised young woman

npogotigi kuntigi leader of the female wing of the youth association

ntinenin species of African tetra

Ntomo (Ndomo) Bamana boys' initiation association

numu blacksmith

numucè male blacksmith

numumuso female blacksmith

nya the means

Nya Bamana men's initiation association

nyama life force, energy

nyamakala Bamana craft specialist; includes the blacksmith, the bard, and the leatherworker

nyan (nyene) literally, before the power object; ceremonies involving power objects

nyangalan hunters' dance

nyè la jako pleasing to the eye

nyènajè entertainment, amusement

nyènajè cogo literally, the way the nyènajè is done; the structure and organization of the entertainment

nyènajè fèn plaything, reference to the youth association masquerades

nyènajè nyana a good or successful entertainment

nyi good

nyin tege foli hunters' dance

nyò susu to pound millet using a mortar and pestle

nyuman good, morally good

pari credit association

saafo Muslim prayer time, about 8:00 P.M.

samiyè rainy season

samiyè daminè beginning of the rainy season

san year

san yèlèma literally, the year turns over; new year

sèbè serious

Segoukaw people who claim descent from the precolonial Segou state

selifana Muslim prayer time, about 2:00 P.M.

si ethnic group

Sinè mògò literally, a gazelle-person; a person who spends excessive amounts of time on his or her appearance

siya ethnicity

sofa precolonial cavalry

sogo antelope and, by extension, animal; Sogo bò masquerade

Sogo bò literally, the animal comes forth; farmers' name for the youth association puppet masquerade theatre

sogo jamani country of the masquerades; reference to Shianro in the eastern portion of the Segou region

Sogo Mansa King of Animals

sogo nyana a successful masquerade performance

sogoba complete masquerade, including the mask or rod puppet and its costume

sogoden literally, child of the animal; term used for the small rod and string puppets, and for actors in the masquerade theatre

sogofin literally, dark animal; dangerous and powerful animal

sogojè literally, white animal; an animal without great stores of life force or energy

sogokòrò   literally, old animal; term used for the most traditional masquerades in the Sogo bò repertoire

sogokun   mask or a rod puppet head used in the Sogo bò

sogotigi   owner of the masquerade

soma   sorcerer

Sòmonò   an ethnic group in south central Mali

Sòmonòya   literally, Sòmonò-ness, Sòmonò ethnicity

Son mògò   literally, kob antelope–person; a reflective person

Sorko   fishermen living north of Segou region, Mali

sòròdasi   African colonial soldiers

su   night

su fè   evening

su fè sogo   evening masquerade

subaga   sorcerer, witch

sungurun   young girl

sungurunba   female lover

tèrèmèli   to bargain; performance term used to describe revisions and innovations off of a form

tigè   to cut; performance term used to describe revisions and innovations off of a form

tigi   owner

tile   day

tile fè sogo   daytime masquerade

tilema   dry season

tògò   name; good name or good reputation

tògòma   namesake

ton   any association; shortened form of youth association

tonjòn   precolonial warrior class

tonko   affairs of the youth association

Tonko nyènajè   name for Sogo bò performed to mark the beginning of the rainy season

tonso   youth association meetinghouse

tontigi   leader of the youth association

tulon   play

tulonko fèn   plaything; term for youth association masquerade

tuma   time

waati   time

wòkulò   bush genie

Wolof   ethnic group in Senegal

woloma   Bamana women's ritual at marriage

woron   to husk, shuck

yaala   wander

yèrè   real, authentic

yereladi   title in the precolonial Segou court; currently a title used in the Kirango Bamana youth association

yiri (jiri)   tree, wood

yirikun (jirikun)   wooden mask or rod puppet head

MASQUERADE LIST

Bamana Name	English Name	Figure #
Avion	Airplane	2.11
Bakòrò	Ram	no illustration
Bala	Porcupine	2.16
Balakònònin	Crocodile Bird	no illustration
Balanin Fola	Balafon Musician	Pref.3
Bama	Crocodile	3.18
Baninkònò	Abdim's Stork	3.3, 5.2
Barabara	Favorite Wife	no illustration
Bèn ka di	Unity Is Good	no illustration
Bilanjan	generic bush animal	2.15
Bilisi	Bilisi, a genie	3.27
Bodakolon kolon	Twirling Beast	no illustration
Cèkòròba	Elder	3.12
Cèw-ye-kelen-ye	All Men Are Equal	6.2
Cikèla	Farmer	Pref.3
Ciwara	Ciwara association mask	3.1, 3.35
Conpe	Wanderer	no illustration
Dajè	Roan Antelope	2.7, 2.24, 2.25, 3.19
Dankalankule	Oryx	no illustration
Dasiri Sogo	Dasiri Antelope	2.26
Donsocè	Hunter	3.31
Duga	Vulture	no illustration
Dugu-duman-yiri-bi-wooyo	The Good Village's Tree Cheers	no illustration
Duguma Sa	Ground Snake	3.24
Falakani	generic bush animal/Boso Dance	2.14
Fali	Donkey	no illustration
Fulacè	Fulani Horseman	no illustration
Furusa Tilè	Divorce Today	no illustration
Gòn	Baboon	1.4, 1.10, 3.7
Jado Nama	Nama of Minjado	no illustration
Jarawara	Wildcat	1.3, 2.28, 2.29
Jinè	Genie	2.10
Jinè-Faro	Water Genie	3.28
Jinèjan	Tall Genie	3.29
Jobali	Boso Woman	1.16
Juguni	Hedgehog	no illustration
Kalaka Sogo	Ensemble of small puppets	no illustration
Kalakadane	Antelope (no ID)	3.20
Kamalen Sogo	Young Man's Antelope	3.14
Kankari Kònò	Bird (no ID)	no illustration

Karankaw	People of Karan	2.4
Kirina Kònò	Bird (no ID)	no illustration
Kolanjan	Pelican (?)	no illustration
Kòmò	Kòmò procession; Kòmò helmet mask	1.14, 3.2
Kònkòrò	Reedbuck	no illustration
Kònò Jolenjo	Bird (no ID)	no illustration
Kònò Meguetan	Bird (performed in Koulikoro)	3.4
Kònòsogonin	Ostrich	no illustration
Koon	Roan Antelope	3.21
Koorishena-muso	Woman Cottoncarder	no illustration
Kuruntigi	Boatman	3.15
Ma	Manatee	no illustration
Madame Sarata	Mrs. Sarata	1.20
Maisa	Umu Assita, a woman	no illustration
Mali	Hippopotamus	3.22
Mali Bonyè	Celebrate Mali	3.33
Mali Kònò	Bird of Mali	Pref.1, 1.17, 2.20, 2.21
Mankalan	Crowned Duiker	no illustration
Manyan	Manyan	no illustration
Mèrèn	Mèrèn	no illustration
Minan	Bushbuck	no illustration
Misi	Cow	1.2
Mobili	Automobile	no illustration
Mònikèla	Fisherman	no illustration
Moriba	Marabout	no illustration
Moussa Traore	President Traore	2.4
Nafèlu	Policeman	no illustration
Nama	Hyena	2.13, 4.4, 4.5
Ngongo	Land Turtle	no illustration
Njona	Wildcat	2.9
Nkoloni	Oribi	no illustration
Nkuman	Crowned Crane	no illustration
Nteke-dalen-be-Naje-kun	Naje, a woman	no illustration
Ntilen	Giraffe	Pref.2, 3.23
Ntomo	Ntomo association mask and puppet	1.13, 3.36
Nyò-surulan-musow	Women Winnowing Grain	no illustration
Nyò-susu-musow	Women Pounding Millet	3.9
Pari	Credit Association	3.34
Saalen	Nile Perch	3.25
Saga	Sheep	2.23
Sama	Elephant	3.11
Sanfè Sa	Tree Snake	3.6
Sanin Kojan	Heron	no illustration
Sensen	Waterbuck	no illustration
Sigi	Buffalo	2.19, 2.27, 3.26, 6.1, 6.3, 6.4
Sinè	Gazelle	3.5
Soden Mali la	Malian Horsemen	2.1, 5.4
Sogofin	Antelope (no ID)	no illustration
Sogoni Kelen	Antelope (no ID)	2.22

Son	Kob	no illustration
Son-min-te-maa-na	The Character a Person Doesn't Have	no illustration
Sonsan	Hare	no illustration
Sotigi	Horseman	3.10, 3.32
Sumusonin	Sorceress	1.12
Suruku Malobali	Shameless Hyena	2.17
Suruku Nama	Hyena	1.11
Taasi Dòoni	Reflect a Little	1.18, 2.18
Tankon	Hartebeest	no illustration
Taw	Water Turtle	no illustration
Tubabu	European	2.8, 3.16, 3.17
Wagadu Sa	Snake of Wagadu	5.1
Walè	Action	no illustration
Waraba	Lion	1.15, 3.38
Waraba Caco	Striped Wildcat	1.19
Waraninkalan	Leopard	no illustration
Wòkulò	Bush Genie	3.8, 3.30
Wonto	Chimpanzee	no illustration
Yan Ka Di	This Place Is Good	3.13
Yayoroba	Beautiful Woman	Pref.4

Al-Sa'di, Abd Al-Rahman Ibn Abd Allah
 1964 *Tarikh es-Soudan.* Ed. and trans. by O. Houdas. Rpt. of 1898 to 1900 edition. Paris:
        A. Maisonneuve.
Appadurai, Arjun
 1981 The past as a scarce resource. *Man* (N.S.) 16: 201–219.
Arens, William, and Karp, Ivan
 1989 Introduction. In *Creativity of Power: Cosmology and Action in African Societies*, eds. W. Arens
        and I. Karp, pp. xi–xxix. Washington, D.C.: Smithsonian Institution Press.
Arnoldi, Mary Jo
 1977 *Bamana and Bozo Puppetry from the Segou Youth Association.* West Lafayette, Ind.: Department
        of Creative Arts, Purdue University.
 1981 Regional Puppet Theatre in Segu, Mali. *The Puppetry Journal* 32(4): 14–19.
 1983 Puppet Theatre in the Segu Region in Mali. Ph.D. dissertation, Indiana University.
 1986 Puppet Theatre: Form and Ideology in Bamana Performances. *Empirical Studies of the Arts*
        4(2): 131–150.
 1988a Performance, Style and the Assertion of Identity in Malian Puppet Drama. *Journal of Folklore
        Research* 25(1–2): 87–100.
 1988b Playing the Puppets: Innovation and Rivalry in Bamana Youth Theatre of Mali. *TDR* 32(2):
        65–82.
 1989 Reconstructing the History and Development of Puppetry in the Segou Region, Mali. In *Man
        Does Not Go Naked: Textilen und Handwerk aus Afrikanischen und Anderen Landern*, eds. B.
        Engelbrecht and B. Gardi, pp. 221–234. Basel: Universität Basel und Museum für
        Volkerkunde.
Arnoldi, Mary Jo, and Ezra, Kate
 1993 *Samaba* the Elephant in Bamana Art. In *The Elephant and Its Ivory in African Art*, pp. 99–111.
        Los Angeles: Fowler Museum of Cultural History.
Ba, A. H., and Daget, Jacques
 1962 *L'Empire Peul du Macina 1818–1853 I.* Paris: Mouton.
Bailleul, Père Charles
 1981 *Petit Dictionnaire Bambara-Français, Français-Bambara.* Amersham, England: Avebury.
Bakhtin, Mikhail
 1981 *The Dialogic Imagination.* Trans. Caryl Emerson. Ed. Michael Holquist. Austin: University of
        Texas Press.
 1984 *Rabelais and His World.* Trans. Helene Iswolsky. Rpt. of 1968 edition published by MIT Press.
        Bloomington: Indiana University Press.
Bateson, Gregory
 1972 A Theory of Play and Fantasy. In *Steps to an Ecology of Mind*, pp. 177–193. New York:
        Ballantine Books.
 1973 Style, Grace and Information in Primitive Art. In *Primitive Art and Society*, ed. Anthony Forge,
        pp. 235–255. London: Oxford University Press.
Bateson, Gregory, and Mead, Margaret
 1942 *Balinese Character: A Photographic Analysis.* Special publication no. 2. New York: New York
        Academy of Sciences.
Bauman, Richard
 1977 *Verbal Art as Performance.* Rowley, Mass.: Newbury House Publishers.
 1986 *Story, Performance and Event.* Cambridge: Cambridge University Press.

Bazin, Hippolyte
  1965 *Dictionnaire Bambara/Français*. Rpt. of 1914 edition. Ridgewood, N.J.: Gregg Press Inc.
Bazin, Jean
  1974 War and Servitude in Segou. *Economy and Society* 3(2): 107–145.
  1985 A chacun son Bambara. In *Au coeur de l'ethnie: ethnies, tribalisme et état en Afrique*,
         pp. 87–127. Paris: Editions la Découverte.
Beidelman, T. O.
  1986 *Moral Imagination in Kaguru Modes of Thought*. Bloomington: Indiana University Press.
Bird, Charles
  1974 *The Songs of Seydou Camara. Kambili*. 2 vols. Bloomington: African Studies Program, Indiana
         University.
  1976 Poetry in the Mande: Its Form and Meaning. *Poetics* 5: 89–100.
Bird, Charles, and Kendall, Martha
  1980 The Mande Hero. In *Explorations in African Systems of Thought*, eds. I. Karp and C. Bird,
         pp. 13–26. Bloomington: Indiana University Press.
Bloch, Maurice
  1977 The past and the present in the present. *Man* (N.S.) 12: 278–292.
Booth, A. H.
  1960 *Small Mammals of West Africa*. West African Nature Handbook series, ed. H. J. Savory.
         London: Longman.
Bourdieu, Pierre
  1977 *Outline of a Theory of Practice*. Trans. by Richard Nice. Cambridge: Cambridge University
         Press.
Bravmann, Rene
  1973 *Open Frontiers: The Mobility of Art in Black Africa*. Seattle: University of Washington Press.
Brett-Smith, Sarah
  1984 Speech Made Visible: The Irregular as a System of Meaning. *Empirical Studies of the Arts* 2(2):
         127–147.
Brink, James
  1978 Communicating Ideology in Bamana Rural Theater Performance. *Research in African
         Literatures* 9(3): 382–394.
  1980 Organizing Satirical Comedy in Kote-tlon: Drama as a Communication Strategy among the
         Bamana of Mali. Ph.D. dissertation, Indiana University.
  1981 Dialectics of Aesthetic Form in Bamana Art: An Introduction. Unpublished paper. Presented
         at the University of Wisconsin, Milwaukee.
  1982a Time Consciousness and Growing Up in Bamana Folk Drama. *Journal of American Folklore*
         95(378): 415–434.
  1982b Speech, Play and Blasphemy: Managing Power and Shame in Bamana Theatre.
         Anthropological Linguistics 24(4): 423–431.
Brown, William A.
  1969 The Caliphate of Hamdullahi ca. 1818–1864: A Study in African History and Tradition. Ph.D.
         dissertation, University of Wisconsin.
Cashion, Gerald
  1982 Hunters of the Mande: A Behavioral Code and Worldview Derived from the Study of Their
         Folklore. Ph.D. dissertation, Indiana University.
Chenais, Jacques
  1947 *Histoire générale des marionnettes*. Paris: Bordas.
Cisse, Youssouf
  1964 Notes sur les sociétés de chasseurs Malinké. *Journal de la Société des Africanistes* 34(2):
         175–226.
  1973 Signes graphiques, représentations, concepts et tests relatifs à la personne chez les Malinké
         et les Bambara du Mali. In *La Notion de personne en Afrique Noire*, ed. Germaine Dieterlen,
         pp. 133–179. Paris: Centre National de la Recherche Scientifique.
  1987 Signes graphiques, masque et mythe. In *Ethnologiques: Hommages à Marcel Griaule*, eds.
         Solange de Ganay, Annie and Jean-Paul Lebeuf, and Dominique Zahan, pp. 49–65. Paris:
         Hermann.

el Dabh, Halim
    1979   Puppetry and Masked Dance Traditions of the Republic of Guinea. A Report of field findings
            submitted to the Smithsonian Institution Foreign Currency Program. Smithsonian Institution
            Folklife Program and The Puppeteers of America. Washington, D.C.
Daget, Jacques
    1949   La Pêche dans le Delta Central du Niger. *Journal de la Société des Africanistes* 19: 1–73.
Dalby, David
    1971   Introduction: Distribution and Nomenclature of the Manding People and Their Language. In
            Papers on the Manding, ed. Carleton Hodge. African Series, volume 3, pp. 1–14. Bloomington:
            Indiana University.
Darkowska-Nidzgorska, Olenka
    1980   *Théâtre Populaire de Marionnettes en Afrique sud-saharienne*. Serie II, volume 60. Bandundu,
            Zaire: Centre d'études ethnologiques.
Darkowska-Nidzgorska, Olenka, and N'Diaye, Francine
    1977   Marionnettes et Marottes d'Afrique Noire. *UNIMA-France* 58: 9–20.
d'Azevedo, Warren
    1958   A Structural Approach to Esthetics: Toward a Definition of Art in Anthropology. *American
            Anthropologist* 60: 702–714.
    1962   Uses of the Past in Gola Discourse. *Journal of African History* 3(1): 11–34.
Delafosse, Maurice
    1972   *Haut-Sénégal-Niger*. 3 volumes. Rpt. of 1912 edition. Paris: G. P. Maisonneuve et Larose.
Dettwyler, Katherine A.
    1988   More Than Nutrition: Breastfeeding in Urban Mali. *Medical Anthropology Quarterly* (N.S.)
            2(2): 172–183.
Dicko, Ousmane B.
    1965   Le mariage et le divorce au Mali. *Recueil Penant* 75: 319–329, 471–486.
Dieterlen, Germaine
    1951   *Essai sur la Religion Bambara*. Paris: Presses Universitaires de France.
    1957   The Mande Creation Myth. *Africa* 27(2): 124–137.
Dieterlen, Germaine, and Cisse, Youssouf
    1972   *Les Fondements de la société d'initiation du Komo*. Paris: Mouton.
Drewal, Margaret Thompson
    1989   Performers, Play and Agency: Yoruba Ritual Process. Ph.D. dissertation, New York University.
    1991   The State of Research on Performance in Africa. *African Studies Review* 34(3): 1–64.
    1992   *Yoruba Ritual: Performers, Play, Agency*. Bloomington: Indiana University Press.
Dumestre, Gerard
    1979   *La Geste de Segou*. Paris: Armand Colin.
Ezra, Kate
    1983   Figure Sculpture of the Bamana of Mali. Ph.D. dissertation, Northwestern University.
    1986   *A Human Ideal in African Art: Bamana Figurative Sculpture*. Washington, D.C.: National
            Museum of African Art.
Fabian, Johannes
    1983   *Time and the Other: How Anthropology Makes Its Object*. New York: Columbia University Press.
    1990   *Power and Performance. Ethnographic Explorations through Proverbial Wisdom and Theatre in
            Shaba, Zaire*. Madison: University of Wisconsin Press.
Frank, Barbara
    1988   Mande Leatherworkers: A Study of Style, Technology and Identity. Ph.D. dissertation, Indiana
            University.
Gallais, Jean
    1967   *Le Delta interieur du Niger: étude de géographie régionale I*. Dakar: IFAN.
Ganay, Solange de
    1960   Les Communauté d'entr'aide chez les Bambara du Soudan français. In *Men and Cultures*, ed.
            A. F. C. Wallace, pp. 424–429. Philadelphia: University of Pennsylvania Press.
Giddens, Anthony
    1979   *Central Problems in Social Theory: Action, Structure and Contradictions in Social Analysis*.
            Berkeley: University of California Press.

Goffman, Erving
  1974   *Frame Analysis*. New York: Harper and Row.
Goldwater, Robert
  1960   *Bambara Sculpture from the Western Sudan*. New York: Museum of Primitive Art.
Grosz-Ngate, Maria
  1986   Bambara Men and Women and the Reproduction of Social Life in Sana Province, Mali. Ph.D. dissertation, Michigan State University.
  1989   Hidden Meanings: Explorations into a Bamana Construction of Gender. *Ethnology* 28(2): 167–183.
Handelman, Don
  1977   Play and Ritual: Complementary Frames of Metacommunication. In *It's a Funny T'ing, Humour*, eds. A. Chapman and H. Fort, pp. 185–192. London: Pergamon Press.
Happold, D. C. D.
  1973   *Large Mammals of West Africa*. West African Nature Handbooks series. London: Longman.
Hardin, Kris
  1987   The Aesthetics of Action: Production and Re–Production in a West African Town. Ph.D. dissertation, Indiana University.
  1988   Aesthetics and the Cultural Whole: A Study of Kono Dance Occasions. *Empirical Studies of the Arts* 6(1): 35–58.
  1993   *The Aesthetics of Action: Continuity and Change in a West African Town*. Washington, D.C.: Smithsonian Institution Press.
Henry, Joseph
  1910   *L'âme d'un peuple africain: les Bambara, leur vie psychique, éthique, sociale, religieuse*. I(2). Münster: Aschendorff.
Hoffman, Barbara
  1989   Mande Jeliw and the Structuring of Power. Unpublished manuscript.
  1990   The Power of Speech: Language and Social Status Among Mande Griots and Nobles. Ph.D. dissertation, Indiana University.
Hopkins, Nicholas
  1965   Modern Theatre in Mali. *Présence africaine* 25(53): 159–193.
Huizinga, Johan
  1938   *Homo Ludens*. Boston: Beacon Press.
Hunwick, John
  1972   Songhay, Bornu, and Hausaland in the Sixteenth Century. In *History of West Africa*, volume 1, eds. J. F. A. Ajayi and M. Crowder, pp. 202–239. New York: Columbia University Press.
Ibn Battuta
  1984   *Travels in Asia and Africa*. Trans. and selected by H. A. R. Gibb. Rpt. from 1929 edition. London: Routledge and Kegan Paul.
Imperato, Pascal J.
  1972   Contemporary Masked Dances and Masquerades of the Bamana Age Sets from the Cercle of Bamako, Mali. Paper presented at the Conference of Manding Studies. School of Oriental and African Studies, London.
  1980   Bambara and Malinke Ton Masquerades. *African Arts* 13(4): 47–55, 82–85, notes 87.
  1981   The Yayoroba Puppet Tradition in Mali. *Puppetry Journal* 32(4): 20–26.
Jackson, Michael
  1977   *The Kuranko Dimensions of Social Reality in a West African Tribe*. New York: St. Martins Press.
  1982   *Allegories of the Wilderness: Ethics and Ambiguity in Kuranko Narratives*. Bloomington: Indiana University Press.
  1983   Knowledge of the Body. *Man* (N.S.) 18(2): 327–345.
Johnson, John W.
  1978   The Epic of Sun-Jata: An Attempt to Define the Model for African Epic Poetry. Ph.D. dissertation, Indiana University.
  1986   *The Epic of Son-Jara: A West African Tradition*. Bloomington: Indiana University Press.
Kaeppler, Adrienne
  1978   Melody, Drone and Decoration: Underlying Structures and Surface Manifestations in Tongan

Art and Society. In *Art and Society*, eds. Michael Greenhalgh and Vincent Megaw. London: Duckworth.

1986   Art, Aesthetics, Values and Thought. In *Aesthetics: Evaluative Ways of Thinking*. Unpublished Una Lectures in the Humanities presented at the University of California at Berkeley.

Karp, Ivan
1987   Laughter at Marriage: Subversion in Performance. In *Transformations of African Marriage*, eds. David Parkin and David Nyamwaya, pp. 137–154. Manchester: Manchester University Press.

Kasfir, Sidney
1984   One Tribe, One Style? Paradigms in the Historiography of African Art. *History in Africa* 2: 163–193.

Kendall, Martha
1982   Getting to Know You. In *Semantic Anthropology*, ed. David Parkin, pp. 197–209. ASA Monograph 22. London: Academic Press.

Kesteloot Lilyan
1972   Acteurs et valeurs dans l'épopée bambara de Segou. *Canadian Journal of African Studies* 6(1): 29–41.

Kesteloot, Lilyan, and Ba, A. H.
1972   *Da Monzon de Segou*. 4 volumes. Paris: Ferand Nathan.

Konare, Alpha Oumar, and Konare, Adam Ba
1983   *Grandes Dates du Mali*. Bamako: Editions Imprimeries du Mali.

Labouret, Henri
1941   *Paysans d'Afrique Occidentale*. Paris: Gallimard.

Labouret, Henri, and Travélé, Moussa
1928   Le Théâtre Mandingue (Soudan Français). *Africa* (London) I: 73–97.

Leiris, Michael
1934   *L'Afrique Fantôme*. Paris: Librarie Gallimard.

Lem, F. H.
1949   *Sudanese Sculpture*. Paris: Arts et Metiers Graphiques.

Levtzion, Nehemia
1963   The Thirteenth and Fourteenth Century Kings of Mali. *Journal of African History* 4(3): 341–353.

1972   The Early States of the Western Sudan to 1500. In *The History of West Africa*, Volume 1, eds. J. F. A. Ajayi and M. Crowder, pp. 120–157. New York: Columbia University Press.

Levtzion, Nehemia, and Hopkins, J. F. P., eds.
1981   *Corpus of Early Arabic Sources for West Africa*. London: Cambridge University Press.

Lewis, John V. D.
1979   Descendants and Crops: Two Poles of Production in a Malian Peasant Village. Ph.D. dissertation, Yale University.

1980   Village-Level Restraints on the Exodus from Rural Mali. Paper presented at the African Studies Association Annual Meetings, Philadelphia.

Leynaud, Emile
1966   Fraternités d'âge et sociétés de culture dans la Haute Vallée du Niger. *Cahiers d'Etudes Africaines* 6: 41–68.

Ligers, Ziedonis
1964   *Les Sorko (Bozo) Maîtres du Niger*. 3 volumes. Paris: Librarie des Cinq Continents.

McNaughton, Patrick
1978   The Bamana Blacksmiths: A Study of Their Sculptors and Their Art. Ph.D. dissertation, Yale University.

1979   *Secret Sculpture of Komo: Art and Power in Bamana (Bambara) Initiation Associations*. Working Papers in the Traditional Arts, no.4. Philadelphia: ISHI.

1982   Language, Art, Secrecy and Power: The Semantics of *Dalilu*. *Anthropological Linguistics* 24(4): 487–505.

1987   Nyamakalaw: The Mande bards and blacksmiths. *Word and Image: A Journal of Verbal/Visual Enquiry* 3(3): 271–288.

1988   *The Mande Blacksmiths: Knowledge, Power, and Art in West Africa*. Bloomington: Indiana University Press.

1991   Is There History in Horizontal Masks? A Preliminary Response to the Dilemma of Form. *African Arts* 24(2): 40–53, notes 88.

1992   From Mande Komo to Jukun Akuma: Approaching the Difficult Question of History. *African Arts* 25(2): 76–85 notes 99–100.

Magasa, Amadu

1978   *Papa–Commandant a jeté un grand filet devant nous: les exploits des rives du Niger 1900–1962.* Paris: François Maspero.

Mahmud K't Ibn al-Mutawakkil K't

1964   *Tarikh el-Fettach.* Trans. O. Houdas and M. Delafosse, Rpt. of 1913–14 edition. Paris: A. Maisonneuve.

Mali, République du

1990   *Recensement général de la population et de l'habitat 1987: Ensemble du Pays, Repertoire de Village.* Vol 0(2). Bamako: Ministère du Plan.

1990   *Recensement général de la population et de l'habitat 1987: Segou.* Vol 4. Bamako: Ministère du Plan.

Mara, Cheik Omar

1980   Yayoroba. *Sunjata* 21: 35–37.

Marty, Paul, trans.

1927   *Les Chroniques de Oulata et de Nema.* Paris: Librarie orientaliste Paul Geuthner.

Mauny, R. A.

1954   The Question of Ghana. *Africa* 24: 200–213.

1961   *Tableau géographique de l'ouest africain au moyen âge.* Memoires de l'IFAN, 61. Dakar: IFAN.

Mauss, Marcel

1979   The Notion of Body Techniques. In *Sociology and Psychology Essays*, pp. 97–105. London: Routledge and Kegan Paul.

Meillassoux, Claude

1963   Histoire et institutions du Kafo de Bamako d'aprés la tradition des Niaré. *Cahiers d'Etudes Africaines* 38: 173–183.

1964   The 'Koteba' of Bamako. *Présence Africaine* 24(52): 28–62.

1968   *Urbanization of an African Community: Voluntary Associations in Bamako.* Seattle: University of Washington Press.

Meurillon, Georges

1992   *Initiations septiennales et institution du Jo bamanan du Baninko (Mali).* Memoire Ecole Pratique des Hautes Etudes. Paris: Sorbonne.

Monteil, Charles

1929   Les Empires du Mali: Etudes d'histoire et de sociologie soudanais. *Bulletin de la Comité d'Etudes historiques et scientifiques de l'AOF.* 291–447.

1953   La legende du Wagadou et l'origine des Soninke. *Melanges Ethnologiques Memoires de l'IFAN*, 23: 349–408.

1971   *Une Cité Soudanaise Djenne.* Rpt. from 1932 edition Paris: Editions anthropos.

1976   *Les Bambara du Segou et du Kaarta.* Rpt from 1924 edition. Paris: Maisonneuve et Larose.

N'Diaye, Bokar

1970   *Groupes Ethniques au Mali.* Bamako: Edition populaires.

N'Diaye, Francine

1992   *Marionnettes et Marottes de l'Afrique Noire.* Paris: Musée de l'Homme.

Niane, D. T.

1965   *Sundiata: An Epic of Old Mali.* Trans. G. D. Pickett. London: Longman.

Ottenberg, Simon

1975   *Masked Rituals of Afikpo, the Context of an African Art.* Seattle: University of Washington Press.

1989   *Boyhood Rituals in an African Society, an Interpretation.* Seattle: University of Washington Press.

Pageard, Robert

1961a   La Marche orientale du Mali (Segou–Djenne) en 1644 d'après le Tarikh es–Soudan. *Journal de la Société des Africanistes* 31(1): 73–81.

1961b   Note sur le peuplement de l'est du pays de Segou. *Journal de la Société des Africanistes* 31(1): 83–90.

1961c   Note sur les Somono. *Notes Africaines* 89: 17–18.

1962   Travestis et marionnettes de la région de Segou. *Notes Africaines* 93:17–20.
1964   Une Tradition Musulmane relative à l'histoire de Segou. *Notes Africaines* 101: 24–25.
Pâques, Viviana
1954   *Les Bambara*. Paris: Presses Universitaires de France.
Park, Mungo
1799   *Travels in the Interior Districts of Africa: Performed under the Direction and Patronage of the African Association in the Years 1795, 1796, and 1797*. 3d edition. London: G. and W. Nicol.
Paudrat, Jean-Louis
1984   From Africa. In *Primitivism in 20th Century Art*, Vol.1, ed. William Rubin, pp. 125–175. New York: The Museum of Modern Art.
Paulme, Denise, ed.
1969   *Classes et associations d'âge en Afrique de l'Ouest*. Paris: Librarie Plon.
Peel, J. D. Y.
1984   Making History: The Past in the Ijesha Present. *Man* (N.S.) 19(1): 111–132.
Proschan, Frank
1980   The Puppetry Traditions of Sub–Saharan Africa: Descriptions and Definitions. Honors B.A. thesis, Anthropology, University of Texas, Austin.
Roberts, Richard
1978   The Maraka and the Economy of the Middle Niger Valley 1790–1908. Ph.D. dissertation, University of Toronto.
1980   Long distance trade and production: Sinsani in the nineteenth century. *Journal of African History* 21(2): 169–188.
1987   *Warriors, Slaves and Merchants: The State and the Economy in the Middle Niger Valley, c. 1712–1914*. Stanford: Stanford University Press.
1988   The End of Slavery in the French Soudan, 1905–1914. In *The End of Slavery in Africa*, eds. S. Meiers and R. Roberts, pp. 282–307. Madison: University of Wisconsin Press.
Royce, Anya Peterson
1982   *Ethnic Identity: Strategies of Diversity*. Bloomington: Indiana University Press.
Schechner, Richard
1977   *Essays on Performance Theory 1970–1976*. New York: Drama Book Specialists.
1985   *Between Theatre and Anthropology*. Philadelphia: University of Pennsylvania Press.
Serle, William, Morel, Gerard J., and Hartwig, Wolfgang
1980   *A Field Guide to the Birds of West Africa*. Rpt of 1977 edition. London: Wm. Collins and Sons, Ltd.
Soleillet, Paul
1886   *Voyages et Decouvertes de Paul Soleillet*. Paris: Gros.
Tauxier, Louis
1930a Chronologie des Rois Bambaras (1er article). *Outre Mer* part 2, III and IV: 120–130.
1930b Chronologie des Rois Bambaras (2e article). *Outre Mer* part 2, III and IV: 254–266.
1942   *Histoire des Bambara*. Paris: Librarie orientaliste Paul Geuthner.
Travélé, Moussa
1954   *Petit Dictionnaire Français-Bambara et Bambara-Français*. Paris: Librarie orientaliste Paul Geuthner.
Turner, Victor
1969   *The Ritual Process*. Chicago: Aldine.
1974   *Dramas, Fields, and Metaphors*. Ithaca, New York: Cornell University Press.
1986   *The Anthropology of Performance*. New York: PAJ (Performing Arts Journal) Publications.
Willis, John R.
1972   The Western Sudan from the Moroccan Invasion (1591) to the Death of al-Mukhtar al-Kunti (1811). In *History of West Africa*, Vol. 1, eds. J. F. A. Ajayi and M. Crowder, pp. 441–484. New York: Columbia University Press.
Wright, Bonnie L.
1989   The Power of Articulation. In *Creativity of Power: Cosmology and Action in African Societies*, eds. W. Arens and I. Karp, pp. 39–57. Washington, D.C.: Smithsonian Institution Press.
Zahan, Dominique
1960   *Sociétés Initiation de Bambara, le Ntomo, le Komo*. La Hague: Mouton.

1963   *La Dialectique du verbe chez les Bambara.* Paris: Mouton.
1972   Modèle et "objet d'Art" chez les Bambara (Mali). Paper presented at the Conference of Manding Studies. School of Oriental and African Studies, London. 1–14.
1974   *The Bambara.* Institute of Religious Iconography, State University of Groningen, Iconography of Religions VII, 2. Leiden: E. J. Brill.
1980   *Antilopes du Soleil: arts et rites agraires d'Afrique noire.* Vienna: Editions Schendl.

Acrobatic dance competition (*Bònjalan*): in 1979 Bamana Tonko festival, 7–8; as dance event in youth association puppet masquerade, 90; as exploration of unity and rivalry, 163

Age: and costume in 1979 Bamana Tonko festival, 6–7; and development of youth association puppet masquerade, 35–37; and social relationships in youth association puppet masquerade, 149–56, 203n.21

Animal characters, in youth association puppet masquerade, 77. *See also* specific characters

Appadurai, Arjun, 200n.21

Art: Malian theatrical masks and puppets as, xi–xii; Shianro blacksmiths and carving of wooden masks and puppets, 30–35. *See also* Sculpture

Audience, timing and production of youth association masquerade events, 120–30

Avion, the Airplane (masquerade character), 39

Badenya (sibling relationship): as theme in Sogo bò performances, 156–57, 163–70; Mande concept of and social identity of puppet masquerade actors, 188

Bailleul, Père Charles, xxi, 192n.7, 196n.11, 197n.1

Ba kara (masquerade character), 195n.10

Bakhtin, Mikhail, xv

Bakòrò, the Ram (masquerade character), 11, 46

Bala, the Porcupine (masquerade character), 45, 46, 90

Ballo, Ahmadu, 94–95

Ballo, Kari (from Ngarababougou), 51

Ballo, Sidi, 90

Bama, the Crocodile (masquerade character), 76

Bamako region, puppet masquerade theatre in, 34–35, 195n.8

Bamana: and ethnicity in Kirango, xii–xiii; and youth associations in Kirango, xiii; note on orthography, xxi; description of 1979 Tonko festival in, 1–17; and history of Segou puppet masquerade, 25; history of youth association puppet masquerade in Kirango, 41–57, 203n.20; precolonial history and ethnic identity of, 132, 133–34, 199n.11; historicity, ethnicity, and style in masquerade performances, 138–48; use of Bamako dialect, 195n.4; ethnological taxonomy and, 197–98n.2; role of Numu in society of, 201n.5. *See also* Kirango; Sogo bò; Youth association puppet masquerade

Baninkònò, the Stork (masquerade character), 61, 144, 167

Barabara, the Favorite Wife (masquerade character), 176–77

Bateson, Gregory, 115, 187

Battuta, Ibn, 60–61

Bazin, Jean, 134, 197n.1, 197n.2

Beledougou region, Kotèba drama in, 22–23, 27, 195n.5

Bilanjan (generic bush animal masquerade), 45, 46, 119

Bilisi, the Genie (masquerade character), 83, 96, 144

Binsogo (grass masquerade), 63–64, 195n.2

Bird, Charles, 94, 151, 157, 159, 183, 201n.3, 203n.24

Birds, as characters in youth association puppet masquerade, 82. *See also* Mali Kònò; specific characters

Blacksmiths: and development of youth masquerade theatre, 29–35; and history of masquerade repertoire in Bamana quarter of Kirango, 50–52, 54–55; list of principal at Nienou, 193–94n.21. *See also* Numu; Nyamakala

Boli. *See* Power objects

Bònjalan (acrobatic dance competition): description of in 1979 Bamana Tonko festival, 7–8; as dance event in youth association puppet masquerade, 90; as exploration of unity and rivalry, 163

Boso: ethnicity in Kirango, xii–xiii; youth associations in Kirango, xiii; Jobali maskers in Bamana puppet theatre, 14–15; history of Segou puppet masquerade, 25, 26, 28, 199n.9; antelope rod puppets and men's associations, 69; precolonial history and ethnic identity of, 132, 134–36, 198n.5; historicity, ethnicity, and style in masquerade performances, 138–48; panegyric for hunter/hero Fadama in youth association performances, 192n.2; ethnic identity and dialects of, 198n.4; myths concerning family names, 198n.5; fishing and group identity of, 200n.19. *See also* Jara men's association

Boure, Fatimata, 39

Bravmann, Rene, 19

Brink, James, 22–23, 27, 150, 155, 195n.5

Calendars, Islamic and Gregorian in Mali, 108

Camara, Seydou, 204n.25

Cashion, Gerald, 166, 167

Cèko (puppet theatre in Segou region): use of term, 25–26; and definition of youth association puppet masquerade, 161

Cèkòrò (elder men), 152, 153, 202n.19

Cèkòròba, the Elder (masquerade character), 70, 71, 89

Cèmisèn (male youth), 152, 201n.8

Center for African Arts (New York), 196n.3

Cèw-ye-kelen-ye, All Men Are Equal (masquerade character), 169, 170, 180

Characters, masquerade: sculptural forms in youth association puppet theatre, 68–88; list of Bamana and English names for, 209–11. *See also* specific characters

Children: process of becoming performers in puppet masquerade, xiv, 114–16, 117–20; and 1979 Bamana Tonko festival, 5

Circle dances: as dance event within youth association puppet masquerade, 90; as expression of unity in youth association puppet masquerade, 163

Cisse, Youssouf, 195n.10

Ciwara men's association, 62, 69, 104

Class. *See Hòròn; Jòn; Tònjòn*

Clowns. *See Kòrèdugaw*

Cogo (manner, way, or style), 102, 103

Colonialism: and history of Segou puppet masquerade, 27, 29, 42; impact of on group identity in Mali, 131; representations of in puppet masquerade performances, 146–47

Community: puppet masquerade performances and values of, xv–xvi; interpretations of masquerades and tension between individual and, 181. *See also* Kirango; specific ethnic groups

Coulibaly, Assista, 39, 154

Coulibaly, Biton, 203n.20

Coulibaly, Boli, 43

Coulibaly, Budagari, 26, 27, 144–45, 192n.2

Coulibaly, Morbidane, 48, 50

Coulibaly, Moussa Nakamissa, 194n.29

Coulibaly, Nanyan, 39, 96, 114

Coumare, Bina Fatouma, 34–35

Creation myth (Mande), 20, 135

Cultural performance, puppet masquerades as, ix

Dajè, the Roan Antelope (masquerade character), 9, 54, 76, 102–103, 121, 124, 125, 167, 199n.13

Dalilu. See Power objects

Dance and dancers, in youth association puppet masquerade: as element of performance, 89–97; gender and, 117, 202n.11; performative relationships between audience and, 126, 128; evaluation of performances by, 128–29. *See also Bònjalan;* Circle dances

Dasiri Sogo, the Dasiri Antelope (masquerade character), 55

Dawòorò drum rhythm, 99

d'Azevedo, Warren, 200n.21

Delafosse, Maurice, 42, 197n.2

Dettwyler, Katherine, 173

Di (tastiness), 102, 121

Diakakan (dialect), 198n.4

Diakhite, Namaja, 39

Diakhite, Sebu, 50

Diarra, Da Monzon (1808–1827), 28, 135, 198n.5

Diarra, Kirango ben, 42

Diarra, Marou, 34

Diarra, Mei, 39, 96, 114, 168, 176

Diarra, Ngolo (1766–1787), 31, 42

Diarra, Numu Jon, 34, 35, 194n.21, 194n.24, 194n.25

Diarra, Ousmane, 48, 140

Diarra, Youssouf, 35, 36, 194n.21

Dieterlen, Germaine, 20, 148

Diop, Abadoulaye-Bara, 200n.3

Divorce, changes in family law following independence in Mali, 178

Djamarabougou theatre, 48

Djennekan (dialect), 198n.4

Do bò (puppet theatre in Segou region): use of term, 25–26, 192n.3; as distinct from Sogo bò, 46

Dònkan (ceremony), 5–6, 142

Drumming and drummers, in youth association puppet masquerade: in 1979 Bamana Tonko festival, 4, 6; as element of performance, 89–97; performative relationships between audience and, 126, 128

Duga, the Vulture (masquerade character), 166

Dugu-duman-yiri-bi-wooyo, The Good Village's Tree Cheers (masquerade character), 73, 168–69

Duguma Sa, the Ground Snake (masquerade character), 80

Dugutigi (leader of village), 157, 200n.2, 202n.17

Economics: and decline of youth association puppet masquerade, 41; and changes in labor patterns in Kirango, 43; women and revolving savings and credit associations, 178. *See also* Labor

Entertainment, local definition of Segou puppet theatre as, 21–22, 187

Ethnicity: in residential quarters of Kirango, xii–xiii; impact of colonialism on group identity in Mali, 131; precolonial history of Segou region and, 133–38; and historicity and style in masquerade performances, 138–48; definitions of, 197n.1. *See also* Bamana; Boso; Maraka; Sòmonò

Ethnography and ethnographers: early accounts of Segou puppet masquerade, 19–20; masquerades representing, 74, 75

Fadama (hunter/hero), 192n.2

Fadenya (sibling relationship): as theme in Sogo bò performances, 156–57, 163–70; Mande concept of and social identity of puppet masquerade actors, 188

Falakani (generic bush animal puppet), 44, 46, 194n.30

Famori (heroic epic), 204n.25

Fane, Adama, 32

Fane, Mamary, 50, 55

Fane, Moussa, 32

Fane, Saliya, 32, 55

Fane, Siriman (of Koke), 31–33, 35, 50, 52, 54, 75, 98–99, 193n.17, 194n.24

Farming communities: and history of Segou puppet masquerade, 26; and masquerades representing hunting, 145; and youth associations, 160; division of labor between sexes in, 172–73; married women and kinship patterns of, 204n.27

Films, of youth association masquerades, 194n.27, 196n.3

Finisogo (cloth masquerade), 63–64

Fishing villages: and history of Segou puppet masquerade, 26, 27–29, 46; and ethnic identities of Boso and Sòmonò, 136, 199n.10, 200n.2, 200n.19; ethnicity and style of masquerade performances, 140–41, 141–42; water animal masquerades in, 144

Folktales: and gender in Kuranko, 174–75; and animal characters of Sogo bò, 179–85. *See also* Myths
Frank, Barbara, 138
Fulani state (Masina), 132
Furusa Tilè, Divorce Today (masquerade character), 178

Gallais, Jean, 137
Gardi, Bernhard, 193n.12
Gender: women's roles in youth association puppet masquerade, 37–39; process of becoming a performer in youth association puppet masquerade, 117–18; and social relationships in youth association puppet masquerade, 149–56, 170–79; and clowns in masquerade performances, 197n.9
Genies, as characters in youth association puppet masquerade, 82. *See also* specific characters
Genre, Segou puppet masquerade as regional, xii
Gòn, the Baboon (masquerade character), 4, 8, 12, 59, 64, 66, 122, 126, 162
Government. *See* Mali
Griots: role of in Bamana society, 92, 201n.5; performances of Mande epics by, 93; as professional artists, 150; as sorcerers, 201n.7
Grosz-Ngati, Maria, 107, 150, 154, 178, 192n.4, 196n.5, 197n.8, 202n.18, 204n.27
Guinea, oral histories of puppetry tradition in, 29

Hardin, Kris, 102, 197n.7
Henry, Abbè Joseph, 59, 90, 104
Historicity, in masquerade performances, 138–48
Hoffman, Barbara, 92, 105, 151, 186, 201n.7
Hòròn (free person): precolonial history and group identity, 134; and social relationships in Sogo bò, 149–56; translation of term, 200n.2; Wolof caste system compared to, 200–201n.3; and view of nyamakala as sorcerers, 201n.7. *See also* Age
Hunting and hunters: mimesis and characterizations of in masked dancing, 90; timing of Sogo bò and, 109; commonly held beliefs of farmers and fishermen and masquerades representing, 145; fadenya and youth association puppet masquerade, 164–67; Boso youth association performances and, 192n.2, 195n.5; older men and funeral celebrations for, 202n.12; and formation of precolonial class of warriors, 203n.23

Islam: and history of Segou puppet masquerade, 28; calendar and annual cycle in Kirango, 108; prayer times and village festivals, 109; group identity of Kirango Bamana, 134; Sòmonò as early practitioners of, 136; Maraka and, 137; elder men and public entertainments, 155; and age at circumcision, 201n.8, 201n.9

Jackson, Michael, 115–16, 117, 156, 170, 174, 178–79, 186
Jado Nama, the Hyena (masquerade character), 10, 95–96, 183, 185
Jako (embellishment of sculptural form), 102, 121
Jara men's association, 60, 68
Jarawara, the Wildcat (masquerade character), 3, 11, 55–56, 57

Jayan (sculptural form), 102, 121
Jelikan (griot language), 92
Jinè (Genie), as characters in youth association puppet masquerade, 82
Jinè-Faro, the Female Water Genie (masquerade character), 83, 89, 176
Jinè-jan, the Tall Genie (masquerade character), 84
Jobali, the Boso Woman (masquerade character), 14–15, 122
Johnson, John, 93
Jòn (descendants of slaves), 134, 150, 201n.3
Jo society (Bougouni), 69

Kaeppler, Adrienne, 101
Kalakadane, an Antelope (masquerade character), 78, 180
Kalaka Sogo masquerade, 46, 63
Kamalen (young man), 152–53, 201n.8, 201n.10, 202n.19
Kamalen Sogo, the Young Man's Antelope (new masquerade character), 48, 71, 73
Kamalen ton. See Youth associations; Youth association puppet masquerade
Kane, Bafing, 32, 33–34, 35, 68
Karankaw, People of Karan (masquerade character), 194n.33
Kasfir, Sidney, 138
Kawule (season): annual cycle in Kirango, 108; youth association festivals during, 109; as customary timing for masquerades, 111–12
K'a ye (category of masquerade character), 70–71, 86–87
Keita, Modibo, 200n.20
Kèlèko nyènajè (warrior dance), 42
Kendall, Martha, 151, 157, 159, 201n.3
Kinship: concepts of badenya and fadenya, 156–57; marriage and status of women, 172, 204n.26, 204n.27; breast-feeding and patterns of, 173; English terms for relations among Bamana, 193n.19
Kirango (Mali): description of community, xii–xiii; and history of Segou puppet masquerade, 25; introduction of carved wooden masks and puppets into theatrical repertoire in, 30; history of youth association puppet masquerade in, 41–57, 203n.20; youth association festivals and annual cycle, 107–13; precolonial history of, 134, 202n.17; ethnic identities and masquerade styles in, 139–40; population of, 191n.1; distribution of age-sets in, 202n.19
Kirina Kònò, a bird (masquerade character), 192–93n.8
Kita (Bamako region), voiced masquerades in, 195n.8
Kòmò men's association: reenactment of processional in 1979 Bamana Tonko festival, 12, 13, 14, 68, 145–46; masquerades of compared to youth association masquerades, 23, 105–106; sculptural form of masks and masquerades, 59, 60, 104–105; and drum rhythms in youth association masquerade, 99–100; power objects and, 192n.5, 192n.6; and view of blacksmiths as sorcerers, 201n.7. *See also* Men's initiation associations
Konate, Tenbaba, 194n.21
Kone, Beni, 194n.21

Kono (Mande-speaking people of Sierra Leone), 102
Kònò masquerades, 23, 62, 82
Kònònin, the Bird (masquerade character), 124
Kònòsogonin, the Ostrich (masquerade character), 180
Koon, a Roan Antelope (masquerade character), 79, 140, 199n.13
Kòrèdugaw (clowns), and youth association puppet masquerades, 90–91, 162, 197n.9
Kòrè men's association, 69, 104, 192n.5
Kòrò (senior men), 201n.10
Kotèba youth theatre (Beledougou), 22–23, 27, 195n.5
Koulikoro (Mali), 34–35
Kule (carvers of domestic wares), 200n.2
Kumare, Manyan, 32, 52, 54, 193n.20
Kumare, Seri, 51
Kuranko (Sierra Leone), 115–16, 117, 118, 174–75
Kuruntigi, the Boso Boatman (masquerade character), 74

Labor: seasonal migrations of and decline of youth association puppet theatre, 41, 196–97n.5, 202n.18; colonialism and changes in patterns of in Kirango, 43; standard work week of government agencies, 196n.4
Labouret, Henri, 19
Lem, F. H., 70, 98, 193n.11
Lewis, John, 134, 159, 202n.18
Ligers, Ziedonis, 19–20, 146, 193n.12, 200n.19
Lunar phases, timing of youth association theatre performances, 112

Maani (people as masquerade characters), 74–75, 82
McNaughton, Patrick, 22, 61, 90, 101, 102, 105, 183, 192n.5, 195n.1, 196n.12, 204n.29
Madame Sarata (masquerade character), 16, 17, 50
Maisa (masquerade character), 99
Mali: celebration of independence from French colonial rule in puppet masquerade, 15, 46, 48, 51–52; history of Segou puppet theatre in, 24–29; government-sponsored festivals and dissemination of puppet masquerade, 39–40, 194n.26; history of masking in south central, 60–61; impact of colonialism on group identity in, 131; precolonial history of, 132–33, 199n.12; masquerade performances and national identity, 147; dissolution of federation with Senegal, 156; hunters and mythology of south central, 166; changes in marriage and family law following independence, 178; drought and poverty in present day, 181; history of nomenclature for Bamana and Bambara, 197–98n.2
Mali, the Hippo (masquerade character), 79
Mali Bonyè, Celebrate Mali (masquerade character), 87
Mali Kònò, the Bird of Mali (masquerade character), 1, 15–16, 100, 128, 191n.2
Malinké state (Mali), 132
Malo (social constraint), 149–56
Mande: interpretations of puppet masquerade and creation myth of, 20; expressive forms and evaluation of arts, 101–103, 106; Boso and creation myth of, 135; speech acts and social life of

communities, 186; artistic forms and performance in context of communities, 186–89; approach to history, 200n.21; and Wolof system of castes, 200–201n.3; griots as sorcerers, 201n.7
Manden Mori (heroic poem), 164
Manifestations du Dò de Jarabugu (film), 194n.27
Manyan masquerade, 23–24, 192n.7
Mara, Cheik Omar, 27, 48
Maraka: precolonial history and ethnic identity of, 132, 137–38, 199n.11; historicity, ethnicity, and style in masquerade performances, 138–48
Marriage: women and kinship patterns, 172, 204n.26, 204n.27; patterns of among villages, 202n.13; *furu ton* association and, 202n.15
Masks, sculptural forms of in Sogo bò, 58–61. *See also* Puppets; Rod puppets; specific characters
Mauss, Marcel, 115
Mead, Margaret, 115
Meaning, production of in performance of puppet masquerade, 161–63
Media, electronic, and dissemination of puppet masquerade, 39–40
Men's initiation associations: and local definition of youth association masquerades, 22–24, 187; and masquerades performed in youth association festivals, 87; production and transfer of knowledge in Bamana society, 192n.4; power objects and rites of, 192n.5; demise of and expansion of youth association festivals, 196n.1. *See also* Kòmò men's association
Mèrèn (female masquerade character), 63, 70, 98–99, 175
Mimesis: in masquerade dancing of south central Mali, 89–90; gender and dance styles, 118. *See also* Hunting and hunters
Minan, the Bushbuck (masquerade character), 46
Misi, the Cow (masquerade character), 3, 46, 93–94, 103, 120
Misicè, the Bull (masquerade character), 11
Misimuso, the Cow (masquerade character), 11
Monteil, Charles, 28, 198n.7
Morality: Segou puppet masquerades as defined by participants, xvi; imagining of moral universe through animal characters in puppet masquerades, 179–85
Museums: National Museum of Mali and youth association masquerade performances, 40, 196n.3; ethnicity and artistic style in holdings of Segou puppets and masks, 138–39
Muso (adult woman), 153, 170–79
Musokòrò (elder woman), 153, 154
Myths: on origins of puppet masquerade, 26–27; and hunters in south central Mali, 166; on family names of Boso, 198n.6. *See also* Creation myth

Nama, the Hyena (masquerade character), 44, 46, 122, 127, 183, 185
Nama masquerades, 23, 59–60
National Museum of Mali, 40, 196n.3
New year: description of 1979 puppet masquerade in Kirango, 1–17; and annual cycle in Kirango, 108
Nganaw (heroines), 171

Ngongo, the Land Turtle (masquerade character), 171–72

Nienou (Shianro village), 34, 193–94n.21

Niger River: early journal accounts of puppet masquerades, 18–19; fishing villages and development of Segou puppet masquerade, 25, 26–29; ethnic identity and dialects of Boso, 198n.4

Njona, the Wildcat (masquerade character), 11, 37

Nkolokun (masquerade character), 144

Npogotigi (girls), 153

Npogotigi kuntigi (leader of women's section), 158

Ntilen, the Giraffe (masquerade character), x, 11, 51, 80, 93, 99, 122

Ntomo, boy's initiation association (masquerade character), 11, 12, 62, 88, 192n.5

Numu (blacksmith), role in Bamana society, 201n.5

Nyama (energy or life force), 101, 196n.12

Nyamakala (blacksmiths and bards): precolonial history and group identity, 134; and social relationships in Sogo bò, 150, 151; translation of term, 200n.2; as sorcerers, 201n.7. *See also* Blacksmiths

Nyènajè (subset of play), 21

Nyi (goodness), 102, 121

Nyò-susumusow, Women Pounding Millet (masquerade character), 67

Occupations, and ethnicity in Kirango, xii–xiii. *See also* Blacksmiths; Fishing villages; Farming communities; Griots; Kule; Numu

Orthography, of Bamana words, xxi

Pageard, Robert, 20–21, 70, 97, 192n.3

Pâques, Viviana, 191–92n.1, 200n.2

Pari, an Antelope (masquerade character), 178

People, as characters in youth association puppet masquerade, 82, 85. *See also* specific character

Performance, of puppet masquerades: author's participation in, xiii–xiv; scholarly influences on analysis of, xiv; description of 1979 Bamana Tonko festival, 1–17; local taxonomies of, 62–68; dancing, drumming, and singing in youth association, 89–97; evaluation of arts across traditions, 104–106; process of becoming a performer in, 113–20; timing and production of youth association events, 120–30; historicity, ethnicity, and style in, 138–48; production of meaning in, 161–63

Performative behavior, artistic experience in Mali and definition of, xv

Play, definition of Segou puppet masquerade performances by participants, xiv–xv, 22, 187

Polygamy, relationships among women, 176–77

Power objects: and local definition of puppet masquerades, 22–24; Kòmò masks as, 68; men's association rites and, 192n.5; blacksmiths and access to carving of theatrical sculptures, 194n.24; and reenactment of hunting scenes in Kirango Boso performances, 195n.5

Production, and timing of youth association masquerade events, 120–30

Puppet masquerades, of Segou region: as specialized form of performance, ix; as regional genre, xii; description of 1979 spring festival in Kirango, 1–17; history of in early published accounts, 18–21; history of from late nineteenth century to present, 24–29; historicity, ethnicity, and style in performances of, 138–48; voiced masquerades in Bamako region, 195n.8. *See also* Sogo bò; Youth association puppet masquerade

Puppets: construction of masquerade armatures, 2–3; sculptural forms of in Sogo bò, 58–61. *See also* Rod puppets; specific characters

Radio: announcements of puppet masquerades on Radio Mali, 2, 23; and public awareness of puppet masquerade, 40

Religion, interpretation of puppet masquerade as process of secularization of traditional, 21. *See also* Islam

Rivalry, exploration of in Sogo bò performances, 163–70

Roberts, Richard, 137, 198n.8

Rod puppets: description of Malian, ix, xi; as characteristic of youth association puppet masquerade, 57, 59. *See also* Masks; Puppets; specific characters

Royce, Anya, 197n.1

Saalen, the Nile Perch (masquerade character), 81, 140

Saga, the Sheep (masquerade character), 54, 103

Samiyè da (beginning of rainy season), 110

Sama, the Elephant (masquerade character), 46, 69, 103

Sanfè Sa, the Tree Snake (masquerade character), 46, 63, 65

San yèlèma (new year): description of 1979 Tonko festival in Kirango, 1–17; and annual cycle in Kirango, 108, 110; inclusion of grass masquerades in festival of, 195n.2

Savings and credit associations, women and, 178

Schechner, Richard, xv, 113–14

Sculpture: articulated masks or puppets and Malian, xi–xii; Shianro blacksmiths and carving of wooden masks and puppets, 30–35; forms of puppets, masks, and masquerades in Sogo bò, 58–61; local taxonomies of Sogo bò, 62–68; forms of characters in Sogo bò, 68–88. *See also* Art

Secrecy, in context of youth association puppet masquerade, 193n.10

Segou: history of puppet masquerade from late nineteenth century to present in, 24–29; precolonial history of, 132–38, 199n.11; definition of Sogo bò as play and entertainment, 187. *See also* Puppet masquerades

Self, process of becoming a performer in Sogo bò, 116

Senegal: cultural performances compared to Segou puppet masquerade, xiv; dissolution of federation with Mali, 156

Sexuality, youth association masquerades and female, 175–76

Shape-shifting dances, mimesis in, 90

Shianro region: history of puppet masquerade and fishing communities of, 26, 28–29, 199n.9; blacksmiths and carving of wooden masks and puppets, 30

Sierra Leone, bodily practice in Kuranko initiation, 115–16

Sigi, the Buffalo (masquerade character), 10–11, 50, 56, 103, 124, 165–66, 181–83

Sigimuso, the female Buffalo (masquerade character), 81

Simultaneity, as dimension of theatrical experience, xv

Sinè, the Gazelle (masquerade character), 11, 64, 103

Singers. *See* Song and singers

Slavery: and precolonial history of Mali, 132; outlawing of by French colonial law, 198–99n.8; Mande concepts of hòròn and jòn, 201n.3

Social relationships: age, gender, and status in Sogo bò, 149–56; relations between men and Sogo bò, 156–61; and production of meaning in Sogo bò performances, 161–63; relations between men and women and Sogo bò, 170–79

Soden Mali la, Malian Horsemen (masquerade character), 147

Sogo: use of Bamana term, 62; list of youth association masquerade characters, 77

Sogoba (big animal), 65

Sogo bò (puppet theatre): use of term in Segou region, 25–26; age, gender, and status and social relationships in, 149–56; social relationships between men and, 156–61; production of meaning in performance of, 161–63; exploration of unity and rivalry in performances of, 163–70; social relationships between men and women and, 170–79; and imagining of moral universe through animals, 179–85; in context of Mande communities, 186–89. *See also* Puppet masquerade; Youth association puppet masquerade

Sogoden (children of the animal), 68

Sogodenw (performers in puppet theatre), 68

Sogokunw (carved masks and puppet heads), 65

Sogoni Kelen, an Antelope (masquerade character), 52, 54, 124

Sogo nyenaje (animal masquerade entertainment), 25

Sogow (film), 194n.27

Soleillet, Paul, 18–19, 26, 61, 109, 193n.9

Sòmonò: and ethnicity in Kirango, xii–xiii, 199n.16; and youth associations in Kirango, xiii; and history of Segou puppet masquerade, 25, 27, 28; precolonial history and ethnic identity of, 132, 136; historicity, ethnicity, and style in masquerade performances, 138–48; ethnicity and dialect of, 198n.4; fishing and ethnic identity of, 199n.10, 200n.2

Song and singers, youth association puppet masquerade: women's roles in, 37–39, 170, 199–200n.17, 202n.11; as element of performance, 89–97; performative relationships between audience and, 126, 128; evaluation of performances by, 128; in Boso and Sòmonò masquerade performances, 201n.6

Songhay state (Gao), 132

Soninke state (Ghana), 132, 198n.5

Son-min-te-maa-na, The Character a Person Doesn't Have (masquerade character), 170

Sonsan, the Hare (masquerade character), 103, 179–80

Sorcerers: nyamakala and griots as, 201n.7; use of term *mògò dankalen*, 204n.29

Sorko, ethnic identity of, 198n.4

Sotigi, the Horseman (masquerade character), 67, 86

Speech acts: and puppet masquerade in Kirango, 162; and social life in Mande communities, 186

Spring festival. *See San yèlèma*

State, origin of puppet masquerade and formation of precolonial Segou, 27, 28

Su fè sogow (evening masquerades), 63

Sumusonin, the Little Sorceress (masquerade character), 10, 125, 178–79

Super Biton (orchestra), 48, 50

Suruku Malobali, the Shameless Hyena (masquerade character), 8–9, 48, 49, 64, 124, 183–85

Suruku Nama, the Hyena (masquerade character), 8, 51, 125, 183, 185

Taasi Dòoni, Reflect a Little (masquerade character), 16, 48, 50, 73, 89, 177, 204n.28

Tall, El Hadj Oumar, 28, 42

Tall, Tijani, 136

Tarawele, Buwakoro, 51

Tarikh es–Soudan (seventeenth-century chronicle), 199n.12

Television, dissemination of puppet masquerade, 40

Theatre, contemporary puppet masquerades and history of Malian, xv

Thiero, Maimuna, 140

Tile fè sogow (daytime masquerades), 63

Time and timing: concepts of and masquerade performances, xv; and definition of Sogo bò theatre, 107–13; and production of youth association masquerade events, 120–30

Toboji Centa (culture hero), 26–27

Tògòma (people of different generations sharing a first name), 102

Toguna and Cèko (film), 194n.27

Tommoura, Kare, 198n.7

Tonjòn (descendants of precolonial military class), 134, 202n.17

Tonko: description of 1979 festival in Kirango, 1–17; as category of relative age, 25–26; and definition of youth association puppet masquerade, 161

Ton sogow (association-owned masquerades), 48

Tontigi (leader of ton), 157, 160–61, 202n.17

Toucoulour state (Segou), 132, 136

Traore, Moussa, 193n.18, 194n.26, 200n.20

Traore, Sungolo, 51

Traore, Vadama, 144–45, 192n.2

Travélé, Moussa, 19

Tubabu, the European (masquerade character), 36

Unity, exploration of in Sogo bò performances, 163–70

Wagadu Sa, the Snake of Wagadu (masquerade character), 142, 143

Waraba, the Lion (masquerade character), 13–14, 103, 167

Waraba Caco, the Striped Wildcat (masquerade character), 16, 64, 120, 125

Warrior tradition: origins of youth association puppet masquerade, 42, 203n.20; hunters and formation of precolonial class of, 203n.23. *See also Tònjòn*

West Africa, youth associations throughout, 159

Wòkulò, the Bush Genie (masquerade character), 66, 84
Wolof, system of castes, 200–201n.3
Woloma (women's ritual), 117–18
Women. *See* Gender; Marriage; Mèrèn; Songs and singers; Yayoroba
Wright, Bonnie L., 200n.3

Yan Ka Di, This Place Is Good (masquerade character), 70–71, 72, 147
Yayoroba, the Beautiful Woman (masquerade character), 1, 12–13, 55, 70, 89, 98–99, 174
Yiri kun (carved masks and puppet heads), 62
Youth association puppet masquerade: local definitions of, 21–24; blacksmiths and development of, 29–35; young men as catalysts in development of, 35–37; roles of women in, 37–39; electronic media, government festivals, and dissemination of, 39–40, 194n.26, 194n.27, 196n.3; demise of local theatres, 40–41; history of Kirango's Bamana theatre, 41–57; sculptural forms of puppets, masks, and masquerades in, 58–61; local taxonomies of sculptures and their performances, 62–68; sculptural forms of characters in, 68–88; dancing, drumming, and singing in, 89–97; incorporation and movement of forms into, 97–101; compared to Kòmò masquerades, 105–106; process of becoming a performer in, 113–20; timing and production of performance events, 120–30; secrecy in context of, 193n.10; performance exchange with French puppeteers, 196n.3; age-set of junior elders and organization of, 203n.21. *See also* Puppet masquerade; Sogo bò
Youth associations, membership of in Kirango, xiii. *See also* Sogo bò; Youth association puppet masquerade

Zahan, Dominique, 95, 104, 183, 192n.4, 197n.9

Mary Jo Arnoldi is curator in the Department of
Anthropology of the National Museum of Natural
History at the Smithsonian Institution.